WHATEVER HAPPENED TO
GOOD, OLD-FASHIONED CHILDHOOD?

It seems more endangered than the rain forests—an old-fashioned childhood, one in which play is deliciously unorganized; children are left alone to make their own fun; parents talk with and shape their children instead of analyzing and scheduling them; children are members of the family, not prized possessions.

I want to raise children who are children, first of all, who are delightfully different from adults, who believe in fairy tales and magic, and who see the world in that crazily skewed way that kids do. I realize that I risk being thought indulgent and nostalgic, and I'm willing to take that gamble. Our parents, or I suppose I should say my parents and other parents I knew, were child-centered enough to give us paradise, but not so child-centered as to spoil us with its fruit. I see no reason why we can't hold on to many of the time-tested ways. In fact, I *know* we can—as long as we have faith in ourselves and trust our instincts. We may have to dig deep to remember the old songs and sayings. And if our parents raised us wrong, then we must do better. But we don't have to second-guess every gut feeling we have. . . .

—from *Parents Who Think Too Much*

PARENTS WHO THINK TOO MUCH

WHY WE DO IT
HOW TO STOP

Anne Cassidy

A Dell Trade Paperback

A DELL TRADE PAPERBACK

Published by
Dell Publishing
a division of
Bantam Doubleday Dell Publishing Group, Inc.
1540 Broadway
New York, New York 10036

Library of Congress Cataloging in Publication Data
Cassidy, Anne
Parents who think too much: why we do it,
how to stop / Anne Cassidy.
p.   cm.
Includes bibliographical references.
ISBN 0-440-50812-6
1. Parenting.   2. Child rearing.   3. Parent and child.
I. Title.
HQ755.8.C395   1998
649'.1—dc21   97-50127
                                                        CIP

Printed in the United States of America

Published simultaneously in Canada

July 1998

10   9   8   7   6   5   4   3   2   1

BVG

For my mother,
Suzanne Concannon Cassidy

Acknowledgments

Parents Who Think Too Much is about families, so it is my family I acknowledge first. I couldn't have written a book about parents who think too much had I not been raised by parents who thought just the right amount. So above all, I thank my mother and father, Suzanne and Frank Cassidy. They brought up four children with wisdom, love, and humor, and all they used was Dr. Spock! I thank my father for his ready kindness and his unwavering optimism. Most of all, I thank him for always believing in me. To my mother, fellow writer and kindred spirit, who read each chapter the minute it rolled off the fax machine, I owe more than I can ever repay or describe. Her sensitive criticism of my early childrearing "style" helped me think less and feel more; many of the thoughts in this book are ones we've talked about for years. Her love of ideas and her writerly encouragement are constant inspirations.

My husband, Tom Capehart, has been the calm heart at the center of the storm that is writing a book, keeping me steady with his insight and devotion. He always seemed to know when to take the girls out to the park or the hardware store or halfway across the country in a small station wagon so I could get some writing done. I thank him for this, for reading and talking about every chapter and for cheering me on again and again.

Without my daughters, Suzanne, Claire, and Celia, there would be no book. They have given me a glimpse of the depth and kindness of a child's heart, and I hope they won't mind that I've shared some of their stories. So here's to Celia, who learned to say "book" before many other words; to Claire, who when I was hurrying to meet my deadline admonished me, "Mommy, we want you to be done, but don't go too fast, we want your book to be good"; and to Suzanne, who one day early in the project gave me a written pep talk, which said, "Have faith in yourself," "Enjoy it," and "Share it with all family members." Well, here it is!

My sister, Ellen, and my brothers, Phillip and Drew, prove that the bonds we form in childhood can sustain us all our life long. I thank them for always being there for me.

Much gratitude goes to my agent and friend, Lisa Bankoff, of International Creative Management. From the moment I uttered the words "parents who think too much," she has been an unflagging champion of this book. She "got it," when there wasn't much yet to get and found this book a loving home at Dell. No writer could hope for a more enthusiastic editor than Mary Ellen O'Neill. She has been with me, and for this book, every step of the way. I greatly appreciate her warmth, insight, and encouragement.

I owe a debt beyond measure to all the parents who helped me by sharing their thoughts, stories, and confessions. A few went far beyond the call of duty. Chris Anderson spoke to me on numerous occasions and always seemed to know what kind of anecdote I needed. Heather Babiarz hosted a discussion group for me one hot summer day. Tiff Wimberly kept me posted on television specials, Web sites, and possible interviewees. My book group friends became a special cheerleading squad. My thanks go to Kathy Boesch, Sue Brickman, Linda Falkerson, Donna Konigsberg, Maureen Lynch, Eileen O'Neill,

Diana Scott, Toosie Smith, Susan Tullington, and Marianne Vakiener. And then there are my friends of the heart: Nancy Emison, indexer extraordinaire; Deborah Costlow, legal adviser; and Kay Rolland, "foreign correspondent."

My deepest appreciation goes to the many fine magazine editors with whom I've had the privilege to work. My career as a writer would also not be possible unless hundreds of parenting experts had taken the time to talk with me through the years. I thank them all—editors and experts. In spite of the general comments I make in this book, I have the utmost respect for their integrity and accomplishments.

Finally, where would any working mother be without someone to watch over her children when she can't? I was lucky enough to find Eva Kenderesy about the same time I began work on this book. She has helped give our children an old-fashioned childhood when we haven't been there to do it.

Contents

Prologue

For the last 12 years, I've written over a hundred magazine articles for parents. I am part of a vast network that carries information and opinions from psychologists and other experts to millions of people like you. The topics range from thumb-sucking to self-motivation, but the underlying message is always the same: go easy on your child and hard on yourselves. If your youngster acts up, he's just expressing "developmentally appropriate behavior." To deal with it, you must learn techniques to sidestep right and wrong. Forget parental outrage; it is hopelessly out of date.

Like many modern mothers and fathers, I have thought a lot about the kind of parent I want to be. Not for me a blind acceptance of yesterday's wisdom, of telling children to behave "because I said so." I've tried to rear our three daughters in a more enlightened way. I've read widely about children and childhood, weighed decisions carefully, pondered the nuances of each child's behavior, all in hopes of creating bright, well-adjusted kids.

This has not been a very good idea. Our oldest daughter's first year was punctuated with mini-crises arising from milestones I feared were being missed. Our baby was two and a half months old and she still wasn't taking a swipe at her mobile. What was the matter? Nothing, as I discovered a few weeks later when she did reach this milestone.

It was the beginning of a pattern I've followed throughout our children's early years. Something I might have read, or heard, or noticed on a poster in the doctor's office makes its way into my brain and sets up shop there.

What's happening to me is happening everywhere. The information revolution that is reshaping our world is changing American childrearing from an intuitive, intimate act to a highly analyzed, expert-driven procedure. It has helped create hordes of parents like me, who shop for car seats with a consumer's guide in hand, check out preschools as if they were scouting colleges, enroll in parent education classes, haunt the childrearing sections of bookstores—all of us frighteningly determined to be the most perfect parents we can be.

When our second child was on the way I spent so much time preparing our oldest for a sibling that I nearly suffocated her with my good intentions. Had we put the crib up too early? Was she feeling displaced? Well-meaning friends dutifully brought a gift for her when they visited the baby so the oldest wouldn't feel left out.

By the time our secondborn was toddling, these childrearing methods had begun to bear fruit. After giving our kids plenty of choices, after validating their feelings repeatedly and at great peril to my own, we now had two children over whom I had no control. Everyday excursions were a nightmare. I was exhausted trying to give each my undivided attention.

I looked for answers and found only more questions. Parents around us were experiencing similar doubts. "I don't know what to do," my neighbor complained. "In my parenting class they said you're not supposed to make a big deal about little decisions, so I've given our kids lots of choices. I even let our daughter go outside in the winter without a coat. I figured she'd come inside when she started shivering. But now she doesn't listen to me." Other friends wondered why they were constantly exhausted, why they had no time for themselves.

I thought about our friends, I thought about us. And then I realized—it's the thinking that's the problem. We've thought too much. We've pondered every step so much that the juice, the joy, and worst of all, our confidence, are gone. We've abandoned precedent for book learning, instinct for technique. We know so many childrearing methods that we are virtually paralyzed with choice. We now turn to psychologists for basic operating instructions: whether a two-year-old should try to boss us around; whether our kids should watch a celebrity trial on television. (The answers are yes and no.) We waffle, coddle, and analyze. We imagine young egos as so delicate that any cross word or action will stunt them. In the process, we lose sight of how fundamentally endearing children can be.

There are many reasons why we have become parents who think too much. We've had fewer children later in life so we've had more time to ponder. We've grown up as research on infant and child development has come of age, so there's been no shortage of material to think about. As a generation we've prided ourselves on self-improvement and we bring the same zeal to child improvement. We're less likely to live close to our families, and so are more likely to seek out expert solutions.

If you've read parenting books, you've probably noticed that many of them begin with a caveat, something to the effect of: "You, the parent, are the true expert. *You* know your children best." But a few pages later the caveats are forgotten and the authors are telling you how to raise your child, as if *they* know best. This book contains the same caveat: You know your child best. You are the true expert. But I mean it. If you want someone to tell you how to raise your child, this book is not for you.

On the other hand, if you wonder why you lack confidence in yourself as a parent, why our society has become so child-centered that some parents are—and most ought to be—on the verge of rebellion, then read on. Think of this as a consciousness-raising book, something that will, I hope, embolden you to reduce the size of your parenting library, drop out of a parenting class, adjust your priorities so that your entire household does not buzz around your six-year old's soccer schedule. My mission is not to push one method of childrearing over any other because, indeed, there are no right "methods" except your own. Instead, I hope this book encourages you to find your own parental voice and style.

The stakes are high because the way children have been raised for centuries is on trial. There have always been disagreements between generations about how best to rear children and experts willing to step in and make up the difference. But never before have experts held such sway among educated, thinking parents. (For in my experience it is the brightest among us who think the most, who entangle themselves the most thoroughly in the knots of childrearing advice.) For modern parents, there is information run amuck, consumerism that preys on our fears, and children wise enough to seize the moment when we abdicate it. We have lost the counterweight that each generation has held against the experts of their time—a counterweight composed of confidence in self and system and the simple, uncompromising belief that kids usually turn out okay.

Though we invest of ourselves greatly to establish a bond with our children, we mistrust the bonds formed years ago with our own parents. A common complaint is that we were brought up in repressed homes; our feelings were squelched and our emotions were routinely denied. So we will give our children the "validation" we so sorely lacked. If there is any collective wisdom within us, an unconscious memory of how the human species has been brought up before us, it has been drowned out by the cacophony of new voices that seek to convince us there is a better way.

I wish there were one easy answer to this dilemma, one step we could take that would make it all easier, one piece of yarn that when pulled would unravel the whole skein. But there are many strands to this story.

What I do know is this: Something is terribly wrong. I see it at the bus stop, in the grocery store checkout lines, and in the pediatrician's waiting rooms. I glimpse it daily through the tinted windows of the minivans that fill our roads. I hear it in the conversations of other parents who, like me, are trying to do their best but who are often befuddled by the hype of so many childrearing gurus. Saddest of all, I see it in the children treated like grown-ups since infancy. They don't know how to play on their own, they never met an adult conversation they wouldn't interrupt, and they seem weary of life—even though their own lives have scarcely begun.

Our homes, our weekends, our calendars—almost everything we do is geared to children. "Soccer moms" were declared a major force in the 1996 presidential election, the Walt Disney company is taking over the entertainment industry, and license plates proudly proclaim, "Kids First." After eight years of feeling the pull and tug of child-centeredness in my own life and years more of observing it all around me, I wanted to find out why it exists. My answer is this book.

Our lives are child-centered because we think too much. We believe everything hinges on whether we breast- or bottle-feed, whether we enroll our five-year-old in kindergarten or hold him out a year. Thinking too much has dealt discipline a severe blow and replaced it with feel-good approaches to what is the most difficult but important job we do as parents. Thinking too much encourages us to pay so much attention to our children when they're young that they grow up addicted to the spotlight. Thinking too much has made us easy prey for advertisers and manufacturers, who have eagerly pounced on what must be the most enticing new market since China was opened to the West—indulged youngsters and their ever-consuming parents. Thinking too much has given us a world so fixated on minute safety concerns that we overprotect our children; a world so busy that we don't have time to get to know our children on their terms, or ours; a world so competitive that we start pushing our children in preschool and never stop.

If all this meticulous thought and concern paid off later on, if our tactics were producing a generation of fine young people, then we might have some justification for our approach. But by most measures, the children now entering adolescence have some real problems. Children in this country face the highest rates of murder and suicide of any of the world's 26 wealthiest nations. Adolescent marijuana use here has doubled since 1992. Honesty is in short enough supply that college students at one university were told that if they pledge not to cheat they will get discounts at local shops. When asked what comes to mind about today's children, over half of the Americans surveyed by the opinion research firm Public Agenda said they thought of them as lacking in discipline, rude, or spoiled. The assessment of teenagers is even more negative: Two-thirds of the respondents said that the words "irresponsible" and "wild" come to their minds when they think about teens. Only 37 percent believe that today's children will make this a better country when they grow up.

Of course, these problems have a plethora of deep-seated and complicated causes. Many see them as a result of parents who think too little rather than too much. I don't propose that thinking too much is the only problem families face. But it's a problem I see every day, a problem I battle; in fact, it's a problem I helped create. So it's a problem I want to help solve. And I want to solve it now, when my children are still young.

To me, this overreliance on experts is the canary in the coal mine, warning us of trouble. Many of us have heard that once we learn a technique or understand a "stage," our children will practically raise themselves. But when kids hit school age, the issues they face are more complex. The cookbook approaches that may have worked a little for parents of toddlers make no sense at all with older kids. We find ourselves bereft of theories, with no support other than our own good sense, which has been whittled away for years. Meanwhile, we don't know our children half as well as we would have had we listened to ourselves instead of others. Modern parents hit their kids' adolescence like tall oak trees weakened by decades of root rot. One strong wind can topple them.

We may correct the faults of our parents, may encourage our kids to speak out rather than hold in, may know more about child development than our parents ever could have imagined (if, indeed, they had ever heard of child development), but we are making our own mistakes. Years from now our kids may bemoan the fact that we expected them to vent their emotions so often they never developed a private life. They may resent the fact that we tiptoed around them as if they might break and gave them few limits or guidelines. Despite our manuals, our parenting classes, and our earnest conversations, our children will not escape imperfection. There is no secret formula for childrearing. And searching for one can only make us crazy. A pediatrician once said to me that the parents she sees think that if they do everything right, then childrearing will not be hard. But it is hard, and the information and advice just make it harder.

Why have we become parents who think too much? What can we do about it? How much "book learning" does it take to raise children well? I will try to answer those questions—not scientifically because I am not a research scientist, not authoritatively because I am not an expert, but personally, through my own experiences and those of other parents.

Before we begin, let me say that I have a few assumptions about you, the reader. You've probably collected a few parenting books and are well-versed in today's politically correct parenting terminology. You know that "time out" is in, that the "difficult child" is now the "spirited child," and that one never "punishes" but "disciplines," instead. You're well-educated, have a career (even if you're taking time off to raise a child), and approach parenthood with great zeal and attentiveness.

But lately, a tone of exasperation is creeping into your voice. You've lost your sense of humor. You're tired of the strategies, of watching what you say when other parents are around. When you talk to your child, you find yourself bouncing like a Ping-Pong ball between "I can hear that you must be angry" and "Go to your room this instant." You're tired of measuring your words and calibrating your child's stage of development and state of mind. Come to think of it, you're just plain tired. You've set yourself some pretty high expectations, and you often have trouble meeting them.

Sometimes you have a fantasy; it comes painfully close to one of those '50s sitcoms. You come in from work and retreat into that paneled library and have a "talk" with your child. He listens to you respectfully and actually complies with what you say.

But of course, you don't have a paneled library, your child is only four, and he never listens to what you say. Besides, you're embarrassed admitting this at all.

You are not alone. There are other smart, thinking parents who have this fantasy, too. They are not knee-jerk reactionaries, either, but they've decided there's something to be said for the old-fashioned ways. They've decided they don't have to reinvent every wheel. Sometimes our first thought *is* our best thought.

We may not be able to reverse the social structures that have made us parents who think too much. But we can think a little bit more, enough to think our way out of them. We can understand how, when, where, why, and by whom our childrearing decisions are influenced. We can sift through the advice and decide what to use and what to discard.

I don't expect you to change your ways in a day or even a month—lots of other books suggest that and it is an impossible task. But if we can understand where thinking too much has gotten us, individually and collectively, we'll have the motivation to clear our minds of the clutter that comes from the books, articles, and classes. And then we can get down to the business at hand, the care and guidance of the little people entrusted to our care. There *is* a way out. It starts here.

1

Raising Children by the Book ...
When You'd Rather Raise Them by Heart

"Where is human nature so weak as in the bookstore?"
—Henry Ward Beecher

I bought my first parenting book before I was a parent. The book was *What to Expect When You're Expecting*, and I picked it up because of the serene pregnant woman on the pastel cover. I was hoping to become a serene pregnant woman soon, and the book told me what would happen to my body, month by month. I can still feel my hand reaching toward the shelf, a little hesitantly, because I was superstitious. Surely I was tempting fate to buy a book about pregnancy before I was even pregnant. When I look back on that moment, the hesitation takes on another meaning. It says, You were right to waver because books about parenthood ought to be handled with care.

Unfortunately, my ambivalence lasted about five seconds. I bought that book and many more. Through three pregnancies and our children's early years, books were the answer. They told us when to call the doctor, what stroller to buy, and how to calm a crying baby. Eventually, the information and advice they contained made me analyze almost every decision I made about our kids, ignore my instincts, and continually question myself.

They were addictive, too. Each one left me needing another fix. And each one slightly refashioned me as a parent until there was little left of my original dreams, plans, and intentions. I didn't mean for it to happen, but it happened anyway. I had begun to raise our children by the book.

My friend Sue has probably read more parenting books than I have. Often after reading one, she tries out a new philosophy on her children. Her son caught on to her transformations when he was five. "Did you read a new book, Mommy?" he asked when she tried an upbeat conversational style to encourage obedience.

Sue introduced me to a book group. The first volume we discussed was *How to Talk so Kids Will Listen and Listen so Kids Will Talk,* by Adele Faber and Elaine Mazlish. It said that we shouldn't say things like, "If you jump on the couch again you'll be punished." Instead we should say, "Couches are not for jumping." We agreed that this new way of talking to kids was eminently sensible. But it often didn't work. You had this feeling that thousands of other parents were saying, "Couches aren't for jumping" at the exact same moment you were—and thousands of kids were jumping anyway.

I won't say I have no use for parenting books. When we're new on the job they tell us how to bathe a baby, and when we're strung out on the job they assure us that other parents feel the same way we do. Sometimes they even help solve our problems. Thousands of families are sleeping better tonight because Dr. Richard Ferber showed them the way to let their babies cry themselves to sleep.

But we pay a price for our habit. One book may roll off our back, and the next might, too. But by the time we read the fifth or the seventh or the twelfth, the messages begin to stick. Read enough books and you'll want to read more. Read enough books and you'll *have* to read more because you'll think you can't bring up kids without them. Books have become our constant companions, their language our new mother tongue. Their words buzz in our heads, like the pop song we heard in the elevator and can't get out of our mind.

I should admit that for a dozen years I've been a sort of professional parenting book reader. As a writer for family and women's magazines, it's part of my job to read childrearing manuals and interview the authors. So while I was reading books for myself and fretting, I was also getting an earful from the experts I interviewed and fretting some more. Often it was hard to separate the two, since I usually wrote about things that our children were going through at the time. My husband, Tom, has gotten used to my mood swings. One day our toddler is fine; the next, I'm worried that she's not bonding to a transitional object to help her separate from us during the second year of life.

But even I, parenting book maven that I am, cannot claim to have read anywhere near the more than 2,000 books in print on childrearing topics. I try, but no sooner do I finish reading one than a new one pops up in its place. I get dizzy every time I make one of my weekly trips to the library or bookstore. Maybe it's from looking sideways at the book titles or maybe it's from realizing my children are needy in ways I have only begun to imagine. From *The Magic Years* to *The Magical Child.* From Dr. Spock to Dr. Brazelton. From *Good Behavior* to *A Good Enough Parent.* From *Dare to Discipline* to *Children: The Challenge.* There were five times as many parenting books published in 1997 as in 1975, when the word "parenting" was not yet a classification and books about childrearing were listed under "Children—management." Now an infinite variety of books tempts us with information and the hopeful, misleading message: We can help you make sense of your child even if no one else can.

You don't have to read books to raise your kids "by the book." Books are at the heart of parenting classes that operate out of church basements and school cafeterias across the land. The lofty theories expounded by experts seep from books into magazines, Web sites, and from there, it seems, into the very air we breathe. There's a synergy to it all. Magazine articles rely on commentary from experts who are also the authors of parenting books. Classes elevate book techniques to near cult status.

This advice is not foisted upon us; we eagerly seek it out.

Nearly half (46 percent) of 1,000 parents surveyed recently say they pay serious attention to news reports and newspaper articles about early childhood development issues. Thirty six percent regularly look for information in magazines and 39 percent say they regularly pick up literature in their pediatrician's office.[1]

There are about 100 parenting magazines being published today and scads of newsletters. There's plenty of advice available in newspapers, on television and radio, too. Our daily paper, the *Washington Post,* has several articles on kids every week and a regular parenting column on Wednesdays. Family issues have long been staples of the television talk-show circuit, and they've recently become favorites of prime-time news shows. A cursory review of these shows for one week this year found segments on child prodigies, children out of control, and parents who lost custody of their kids. Turn on the morning or evening news and you're as likely to hear about teaching kids values or the popularity of Beanie Babies as you are the deficit or unemployment. Our need for information and advice has not been lost on the advertising community. Baby food and disposable diapers pitch themselves by "ages and stages." Advertorial "magazines" combine articles on teething with formula advertisements.

What you don't get from the media, you hear from your child's school or doctor. Our children's elementary school offers classes for parents several times a year and sends home advice on how to motivate kids in its weekly newsletter. Pediatricians give child development information and discipline advice with each well-child checkup. They can also refer us to child psychologists, an increasingly more common need as parents grow more bewildered and less in control.

And then there's the telephone. Whereas in the past the parenting advice you'd get over it would most likely be from your mother, now you can dial 900 numbers for tips on everything from bed-wetting to weaning, at the rate of 95¢ a minute. If you're worried you might harm your child, you can get free advice by calling a hot line staffed by trained volunteers. In our area there's now a "warm line," which offers parenting advice of a less urgent nature.

Hospitals offer instruction on how to give birth to a baby; how to diaper, feed, and bathe one; and how to prepare a sibling for one. In a move that seems almost self-parodying, one hospital near us offers an "entire evening of informative, straightforward" discussion "for couples *considering* parenthood." (That's their emphasis, not mine.) No longer is the decision a private one; now it's a discussion topic to share with possible parent wanna-bes. With this kind of introduction to parenthood, it's no wonder we sign up for baby exercise and "toddler taming" classes.

And for some parents even this is not enough. They move on to the "harder stuff," parent conferences or expos or the weekend seminar I was invited to recently—"Parenting 2000." Parents pay $500 for this weekend to "discover ways of sustaining a child's happiness and aliveness while preparing him for the coming millennium."

The Internet has become a major source of parenting information and advice. If it is the future, which many think it is, then tomorrow's knowledge will be more specific, personal, and interactive. It may be less accurate, too, since the fact-checking methods that protect parents from bogus claims in books and magazines aren't in place on the information highway. Still, I know parents who've learned about chromosomal abnormalities or found help with breast-feeding problems through the Internet. One of the hottest new Web addresses for parents is the "Preventive Ounce," an interactive site which gives you a profile of your child's temperament and suggestions on how to deal with it.

When I found this site I was reminded of something my friend Mary Scott once said to me. "I go through phases of getting the neurotic parent books out of the library and reading them. I always hope to God one of them is going to say, 'This is exactly how you deal with Kate Scott.' " Kate Scott is her oldest daughter, age nine. Who hasn't harbored this secret desire when opening up a book, that it will tell us exactly what to do with our own particular child? The closer we can come to satisfying that need, the more hooked we'll become.

The Advice Industry

The point is, whether you ask for the advice or not, whether it's useful or not, it's there. It's part of the way we raise kids today. We now seek expert assistance for activities once considered as natural as breathing or eating. Even if you only flip through a parenting magazine a few minutes a month you've become part of an advice industry that is changing one of the basic elements of life—the way we bring up our young.

Let me zero in on magazines for a moment. I've written enough articles—and I'm sure you've read enough—to know the formula by heart. They begin with a problem; let's say a child who lies. After an anecdote in the beginning about a bicycle accident that never was or some other fib, there are explanations of what lying is, why kids lie, how kids lie for different reasons at different ages, all with a liberal sprinkling of quotations from experts. Next come the solutions, the tidy steps we can take to assure that our child doesn't lie again. Yet most problems are not tidy. Lying, for instance, raises profound moral questions which cannot be easily dealt with by strangers in a couple thousand words.

Read enough of these articles and you begin to think there are lots of neat, pat ways to deal with bedtime, tantrums, homework, you name it. You begin to think there are one-size-fits-all answers to every childrearing query. When the one-size-fits-all answer doesn't fit you and your child, which it often doesn't, it's easy to worry, "What's wrong with me?"

Of course, I'm familiar with the other side of the story, too. I know how the magazines take great pains to promote the soundest studies and the most recent research. Every factual article I've written had to be backed up with studies or quotations. You can't imagine the relief with which I've written the words, "research shows" or "experts report." I've gone to great lengths to find a new study, track down its author, and elicit a comment for an article. Time and time again, well-meaning experts have patiently explained their theories and plans to me. I've listened, asked follow-up questions, and tried to square their answers with the reality of my own family. Never mind that many of the suggestions didn't work with my kids or any kids I knew. I reported them faithfully.

I would be remiss if I gave you the impression that all published childcare literature is the same. Some of it is information, plain and simple: sunburn prevention, vaccination schedules, swingset safety. Some of it is new research: the latest theories on infant colic or SIDS or reading. When it comes to advice on behavior, you might occasionally chance upon what I would call old-fashioned suggestions, that parents be authority figures and children learn to obey them. But most advice tells us that our chief task is understanding our children rather than guiding them, that instead of issuing straightforward commands to our kids, we solicit their opinions and ask them how they feel.

Likewise, when I say "experts," realize that I am lumping together psychologists, psychiatrists, pediatricians, teachers, parent educators, and others—and that there's a vast difference between them. Often I've interviewed academic researchers who have studied a particular subject for years and know as much as there is to know about children's sleep or infant temperament. They back what they say with carefully accumulated data. They are good scientists and they care about children and families. Other times I've talked with child or family therapists whose strength lies in their ability to diagnose and help their patients. They seem to carry the weight of the world on their shoulders, or at least the confessions of troubled families and the turmoil of small souls. Still other experts are successful because they have come up with a way to package a problem and sell solutions. Perhaps they have even created an advice-giving persona, inspiring us with a sense of trust in their grandfatherly or grandmotherly wisdom. Some, the superstars, have done all of the above.

The part of me that is accustomed to researching articles wants you to know that I am lumping these experts together for a reason. And the reason is that regardless of their quality or specialty, regardless of the fact that they have helped particular parents with particular problems, they have the same *cumulative* effect on parents. They take away our confidence and our common sense. The advice industry has not set out to hobble us. But just because the assault isn't planned and unified doesn't mean it isn't there. Even a book that gives no advice at all can break our stride and make us think too much. Here's an example of what I mean:

Shortly after the birth of our third daughter, I found myself reading *The Diary of a Baby,* by Daniel Stern, a book that paints an evocative portrait of what a newborn sees, hears, and feels. I was mesmerized by Stern's description (based on infant research) of how a baby can stare and be stared at. Perhaps at no time other than the first few months of a new romance can two people hold each other so long in a gaze. An infant is so sensitive to the subtleties of this eye contact that he can sense when a parent is distracted and then avert his eyes. This was a fascinating book. It wasn't trying to tell me what to do. It was giving me not so much information as impressions, and giving them in such a lyrical, urgent way that I felt as if I had crawled into my baby's skin.

But even a book like this one—a quiet, poetic volume that wasn't pushing me to be one kind of parent or another—threw me slightly off course. I found myself trying to look at our baby a little more than usual after reading it and feeling guilty when I had to turn away. "Look at what you're missing," I'd tell myself, "the perfect opportunity to stare longingly into your infant's eyes." Thoughts like these add up. They drain parenting of its energy and freshness and originality. They put us on the defensive. They make bringing up a child more difficult than it needs to be.

Instead of learning yet another technique or theory, I'm ready to ask myself some basic questions: How much do I need to know about child development to raise our children well? Does an increase in knowledge mean more enlightened parenting? How much advice can I absorb before I begin to question every instinct I have? These are questions you need to answer for yourself. I hope this book helps you begin.

The Cradle of Our Obsession

Our generation may have made parenting manuals all the rage, but we did not invent them. Even the Bible contains child-rearing tips. They are, as you might expect, more along the lines of James Dobson than Nancy Samalin. "Hear, my son, your father's instruction, and reject not your mother's teaching" exhorts the first chapter of Proverbs. Since those words were written, there have been midwives' manuals, doctors' pamphlets, psychologists' case books, and everything in between. But the sheer preponderance of modern information—its psychological urgency, sophisticated tone, and cloak of scientific validity (which may or may not be deserved)—make it impossible to resist. That's why for me, and for many people, books have become an indispensable accompaniment to modern parenthood.

It makes sense. We are, after all, the first generation to be thoroughly identified with a book our parents read, Dr. Spock's *Baby and Child Care.* We put books that tell us how to heal our inner child or become a better lover on the best-seller lists. It only makes sense that we have made books a staple of parenthood, too.

It is through books that most of us first get hooked on information. Reading is the stone tossed into the pond which ripples out in a hundred concentric circles. Books are the cradle of our obsession. In one of the few studies done on how women develop an image of themselves as mothers, books came out way ahead of friends, classes, doctors, mothers, and husbands as a source of information on pregnancy and childrearing. In fact, books were the most frequently cited information source for 87 percent of pregnant women and 91 percent of new mothers.[2]

There are many explanations for why we have been so captivated by the books and other sources of information; I'll discuss them further in the next chapter. But for now, consider that many of us live nowhere near our parents when we start our own families, and even if we do, we don't want their advice. "My mother was a good mom. She did the best she could under the circumstances," one woman confessed to me. "But I want to go beyond her. I want to give our children intellectual stimulation, that sort of thing." We want to be good at what we do, and parenting is no exception. We don't want yesterday's solutions, but today's. Never mind that the ink is barely dry on the just-published studies, we want only the best—which means only the latest—information for our child.

Many parents begin reading before they even conceive a child. Sometimes they read so they *can* conceive a child. "Using the method in *Your Fertility Signals,* my husband and I succeeded in getting pregnant in the second month of trying," raved one woman in an Internet news group. Other readers, more interested in looking ahead to what will happen once they become parents, plunge into books such as *When Partners Become Parents: The Big Life Change for Couples,* by Philip and Carolyn Cowan.

But the real incentive for a trip to the bookstore comes once the pregnancy test is positive. Based on the success of books such as Eisenberg, Murkoff, and Hathaway's *What to Expect When You're Expecting,* with millions of copies sold (it's successful enough to have a parody, *Expect the Unexpected When You're Expecting*), publishers quickly realized the potential market of pregnant women and their concerned mates. There are now specific books on working, eating, and making love during gestation. Expectant parents can decide whether they want to know what's happening to their baby week by week or month by month. If they want to know what baby looks like growing in the womb, they can peruse the latest edition of Lennart Nilsson's *A Child Is Born.* (No, gestation hasn't changed, but intrauterine photography methods certainly have.)

Although most women choose one of the many comprehensive pregnancy guides, such as *What to Expect* or *Sheila Kitzinger's Complete Book on Pregnancy,* some mothers seek out alternative fare. Emily Agnew, of Rochester, New York, found the best books were the ones she borrowed from her midwife's shelf, books like *Spiritual Midwifery,* which contains birth stories from women on the Farm, a Tennessee commune.

There's a whole slew of books written especially for dads-to-be, too, including one called *When Men Are Pregnant—Needs and Concerns of Expectant Fathers,* by Jerrold Lee Shapiro. These books are tapping into the politically correct fathering movement, characterized by dads who say "we are pregnant" and talk knowingly of trimesters and labor stages. I should add that, despite valiant attempts to draw dads into book-reading and book-buying, most parenting books, indeed most books in general, are still purchased by women.

I suppose you could make the case that pregnancy books do more good than harm. They disseminate important information about which drugs are safe to take; they help women decipher the maze of tests now available, the alphabet soup of AFP and CVS, to say nothing of amnios. In a time when parents must make more complicated decisions during pregnancy, books can help them make sense of their choices. They also teach today's older, more sophisticated mothers-to-be what's happening to their bodies so they don't have to suffer unnecessary cesareans, and so they, rather than their doctors or midwives, are truly in charge.

But this control is illusory because pregnancy is when many parents get hooked on books. The sense of ourselves as parents that takes shape during these highly charged nine months stays with us forever. So the information a pregnant mother consumes is as important to her psyche as the food she consumes is important to her growing baby. And some of us put on way too much psychological weight:

"By the ninth week, I knew what to expect in the ninth month. I knew what I should take to the hospital by the tenth [week]. . . . By about month four, the pregnancy archive had lost its allure. I moved on, to childrearing. . . . I pondered the authorities on when to wean five months before the start of breast-feeding. Soon it became clear that this, too, was getting out of hand. I was into the toddler years and in danger of moving on to deal with my difficult adolescent," wrote Ruth Marcus in *The Washington Post*.[3]

Compare this with our own mothers' pregnancies. "I don't think my mother read a thing," says Colleen Sullivan, a neighbor of mine. "She went to the doctor, and he said, 'You're pregnant. Don't gain more than 25 pounds.' But I read everything. How could I not?"

It makes sense that pregnancy is when parents get hooked on information. They have the time (or at least more of it than they'll have after the baby is born), and they certainly have the interest. Reading about pregnancy can help fill the weeks between one checkup and the next. There's nothing like a parenting book to keep you company through a sleepless night.

The books raise as many questions as they answer, though. If this is the month you should begin to feel those first faint flutterings of life, and you don't (or, which is more probable, you do, but you think it's something you ate), then you're in for a long month indeed. So even though the books seem to assuage parental fears, they actually play on them. They gird us for parenthood as if for battle.

Emily Agnew was still in her first trimester when the pregnancy nutrition books she was reading made her so anxious about her diet that she began to get headaches. "One book said I should be taking in this many milligrams of calcium and another said I should be taking in another amount. So at a certain point I just threw out my books and stopped reading about nutrition." As soon as she went with her instincts about what she should eat, she did just fine. "One day after I'd gotten rid of the books, I picked up a magazine and came across a pregnancy diet. It told you exactly what you should be eating for each meal, and I was eating a diet almost exactly the same as the one in the magazine." Agnew hastens to add that she normally eats two pounds of kale a week and so may not be the best example here. But all the better to illustrate the knots into which books can tie us: If pregnancy books can make a woman who eats two pounds of kale a week worry about her diet, then what can they do to the rest of us!

During my first pregnancy I almost lived for the moment when I'd graduate from one month to the next in *What to Expect When You're Expecting*. Occasionally, I'd steal a glance ahead. Sometimes I'd skip all the way to the end: "Labor and Delivery." It was this book and our thoroughly modern childbirth class that sent me trudging out, eight months and counting, to buy tennis balls, sour lollipops, ice packs, and other items deemed necessary for natural childbirth—items, I might add, that never made it out of the suitcase.

Meanwhile, I was hooked. Along with the layette, changing table, basinette, and teddy bear wallpaper border, I had gotten a little library all ready for when we brought the baby home. I had files of clipped articles in my arsenal—helpful stories about colds and croup and crawling. I was embarking on modern parenthood borne along on a veritable tide of advice. Thus does the information addiction precede the child.

Some people handle books better than I have. Sue Brickman, who lives in Reston, Virginia, does not think books have made much difference in how she and her husband are raising their two children because she naturally gravitates to books that support her own theories. Books have given her some helpful strategies—she now gives one-word commands instead of long lectures—but they have not led her astray or dented her confidence as a parent.

But for every Sue there is an Eleanore Keenan. When Eleanore became a mother, she subscribed to four parenting magazines. She's felt inadequate and guilty ever since. She's a good example of how easily advice can turn to blame. Eleanore can't imagine not taking advantage of parenting information because the stakes are so high if she doesn't. "It's not like reading up on which new washing machine to buy. I could be messing up my kids if I don't find out what the experts say," says Eleanore, who lives in Salem, Connecticut. Even though Eleanore has had a second child and doesn't have much time to read, she is, in a strange sort of way, still attracted to the advice. She keeps a file of parenting articles by her bed and then feels guilty when she reads a Ken Follett novel instead.

What I Learned From Penelope Leach

Most of us read up to the last minute. We may even take a parenting book or two to the hospital with us. And then . . . nature calls a halt to our book reading. It's called the newborn period.

Unless your baby actually sleeps the 16 to 18 hours a day the books say newborns do, you have to wing those first few weeks based on what you've already learned. When we brought our firstborn home, I found she'd been given some extra immunity from the advice industry—she had colic. For the first three months we had no time to read anything.

But when her crying stopped, my reading began. Our bible in the beginning was *Your Baby and Child,* by Penelope Leach. Our friends Kip and Kim Draper recommended it to us. "Be sure to get *Your Baby and Child,*" they said. "She tells you that whenever your baby cries, he's trying to tell you something." This sounded like a nice, intellectual way to look at baby's upsets, and Kip and Kim had a five-month-old son, which made them experts in our eyes. So I wasted no time in buying a copy of *Your Baby and Child.* I liked the book. Penelope Leach was British, and she was not Spock, which was good, since we wanted to be different from our own parents. *Your Baby and Child* had probably sold well over a million copies by that time, so we weren't the only ones smitten.

Months passed, and instead of learning slowly on the job, I crammed facts about infant development into my head. I would have gotten over the early feelings of ineptitude on my own, given time. But because I turned to the books in the beginning, I got hooked on their tempting promises and soothing assurances. It took me a while to notice their underlying message. When I began to write this chapter, I took *Your Baby and Child* from the bookshelf where it sat almost untouched for the last few years. I was shocked to discover passages like these:

"*Your Baby and Child* is written from your baby or child's point of view because, however fashions in childrearing may shift and alter, that viewpoint is both the most important and the most neglected," Leach begins. "If you make happiness for him [your baby], he will make happiness for you. If he is un-happy, you will find yourselves unhappy as well."[4]

Later in the book Leach deconstructs spoiling: "Whatever you may overhear people saying when your child throws a tan-trum in the supermarket; however guilty you may feel about that pile of birthday presents, your child is not spoiled if you enjoy him or her and he or she enjoys life."[5] And she has this to say about discipline: "If he will insist on throwing his toys around in a rage, one of them will eventually get broken. . . . A gradual and gentle exposing of the child to the results of his own ill-advised actions is the only ultimate sanction you need."[6]

These thoughts seem more startling now than they did in those early sleep-starved months when I took them so much to heart. Now I'm amazed at how clearly they express the errors of a generation, that a child's happiness is the pinnacle from which all else flows, and that you should give in to him often.

In the beginning of the book, Leach thanks her own family for helping her: "Because I have the good fortune to be part of a close extended family, my own education in parenthood began with my own mother and sisters. In part it is this knowl-edge, taken in while I was too young to be conscious of learn-ing, which I am trying to share."[7] It's a lovely but ironic tribute, considering the extent to which Leach's book and others have supplanted the simple sharing of experience in so many mod-ern families.

I realize now that reading Leach in those formative early months made me overly child-centered. I felt guilty if we weren't constantly holding and playing with our little girl. When she grew older and began to challenge our authority, we didn't know what to do. So we turned to more books. Though Leach eschews "by the book" childrearing in favor of what she calls a "by the baby" approach, have no doubt that "by the book" is how you'll end up.

By the Book

"By the book" is certainly how I ended up. But "by the book" is not how I want to stay. So I've embarked upon a campaign to get rid of the artificial voices in my head and make room for my own. One of the first steps I've taken is to categorize the books, to realize there's a difference between books that inform, which tell us *how* children behave, and books that advise, which tell us how to *make* them behave. Although some are a deft combination of the two, most fall more into one camp than the other.

The First Twelve Months of Life and *The Second Twelve Months of Life,* by Frank and Teresa Caplan of The Princeton Center for Infancy and Early Childhood, are examples of the first type. They provide facts on when babies roll over, crawl, walk, and speak. These books present the information, then let us decide what to do with it. Kathy Minton, of New York City, decided that's what she really wants from a book—basic developmental information. Her son, James, is only a year old, but she realized early on that she doesn't want other people making decisions that she and her husband, Bob, would rather make on their own.

Advice manuals, on the other hand, give us specific techniques with which to understand and discipline our children. *Parenting Young Children,* by Dinkmeyer, McKay, and Dinkmeyer, is a good example of a techniques book. In fact, it's the manual for the STEP (Systematic Training for Effective Parenting) classes that so many parents have taken. Diane Lin, who lives in California, says this book was "invaluable" when her six-year-old son was a toddler.

Obviously, books that give us "just the facts, ma'am" will sway us less than those which lure us with strategies. But it's not quite as simple as that. The books we choose depend upon the kind of people we are. To communicate the breadth of our habit, to give you a sense of just how far-gone many of us are, I've come up with a technique borrowed from self-help books, and I use it now with tongue most definitely in cheek. Admittedly, the profiles you are about to read are caricatures. I've drawn them this way to make a point. Most of us don't fit squarely in one or the other. I see a little bit of myself in all of them. But once I began to understand what it was about the books that drew me to them, I could begin to put them behind me. I became a critic rather than a devotee. I think it's a nice way to turn the tables.

The Take-Charge Parent You're used to being in charge at the office, and now you want to be in charge of your child's development. You want to make sure it's "optimal." So you peruse the Gesell Institute books *(Your One-Year-Old, Your Two-Year-Old)* with their clever diagrams that show youngsters moving through periods of equilibrium and disequilibrium every six months. Or you subscribe to "Growing Child/Growing Parent," a monthly child development newsletter that tells you what your child is doing, thinking, and feeling from birth to six years. You find plenty to read about in the mainstream parenting magazines, too.

You also appreciate volumes designed to prevent your child from getting a problem he doesn't have, but might succumb to in the future, such as *The Optimistic Child,* by Martin Seligman. This book seeks to "innoculate" children against depression. Of course, in your efforts to stay on top of your child's growth and development, you're the one being controlled.

The Reference Reader You see parenting books and magazines as a reference, rather than a bible, and so you may have escaped the worst ravages of thinking too much. You've never felt the need for a parenting class and you only consult books when you're figuring out if your baby has croup or just a bad cough, or when trying to entice your toddler to eat something besides macaroni and cheese. You want reassurance and comfort rather than the latest take on Piagetian theory. If you get a magazine, it's probably the free one that comes along with your diaper service.

For you, the primers are just fine: *Your Baby and Child, What to Expect in Baby's First Year, Dr. Sylvia Rimm's Smart Parenting,* or T. Berry Brazelton's *Touchpoints.* These are *The Joy of Cooking* of parenting manuals. If they're all you crave, consider yourself lucky. You may worry you're not well-informed enough to be a good parent, but you are. Don't let parental peer pressure convince you otherwise.

The Technician You know where you're headed and have no doubts about your ability to raise your child. However, you're always open to new and better ways to do it. You enjoy books with specific techniques for specific problems, rather than tomes which bore you with explanations of why kids behave as they do.

You seek out books such as *One, Two, Three Magic,* by Thomas Phelan, with its simple recipe for child compliance, or *Good Behavior* by Garber, Garber, and Spizman, a cornucopia of childhood mischief and calm, can-do remedies listed in numbered paragraphs. You also appreciate books by famous authors with numbered agendas, such as *The 7 Habits of Highly Effective Families,* by Stephen Covey, and *The Seven Spiritual Laws for Parents,* by Deepak Chopra. You become a walking encyclopedia of strategies for problems your children have—bed-wetting and daydreaming—and maybe even problems they don't have.

The Hypochondriac If your child looks a little pale, you drag out your dog-eared copy of *The Portable Pediatrician for Parents,* by Laura Nathanson, or *Your Child's Health,* by Barton Schmitt (a personal favorite). When you're really concerned, you seek help in *The Columbia University College of Physicians and Surgeons Complete Medical Guide,* which planted so many fears in one parent's mind that she was driven to the closest medical library for information to assuage them.

You fret about behavioral and psychological problems, too. If your child seems a little jumpy you pick up *Driven to Distraction: Recognizing and Coping with Attention Deficit Disorder from Childhood through Adulthood,* by Edward Hallowell and John Ratey. You also make frequent trips to the pediatrician, armed with a list of questions inspired by the various books you've been taking too much to heart. The books upset you, yet you worry you're not reading enough of them. Truth is, were you reading more, the whole family would be at the Mayo Clinic.

The Intellectual You have a great respect for education, which may explain why you take parenting classes, subscribe to three magazines, and read thoughtful and intelligent books about childhood, such as *The Emotional Life of the Toddler,* by Alicia

Lieberman, and *Your Child's Growing Mind,* by Jane Healy. Because you like to take a proactive approach to childrearing, you find books such as *Raising Your Child to Be Gifted,* by James Reed Campbell, to be essential.

But you don't stop there. You picked up a basic college primer on child development, and it has led you to original works by Piaget, Vygotsky, Maslow, Erikson, and others. Even if you do nothing with this information it affects you anyway. It lingers in the crevices of your consciousness and makes you feel guilty every time you do *not* use it. What thoughtful parent doesn't want a window into his child's mind? But therein lies the rub. As an intellectual parent you may forget that you're not going for a Ph.D. in psychology, you're raising a little person.

The Playful Parent Forget all this heavy stuff. You're up for the "fun" books, those that titillate you with the costumes you can make, the cookies you can bake, the vacations you can take. There are scads of volumes like this, little how-to books such as *Cabin Fever,* which includes activities to do inside on rainy days, and the many guides (both official and un-) to Walt Disney World. (That we *need* a guide to Walt Disney World is a point I'll take up later.) You're a charter subscriber to the magazine *Family Fun.* For substance, you seek out *Playful Parenting,* by Denise Chapman Weston and Mark S. Weston, with its telling subtitle "Turning the Dilemma of Discipline Into Fun and Games." Scary thought, indeed.

All of these titles describe a world of excitement for which a child is the only price of admission. If your family is not having fun right now, or if you have a low guilt threshold, these books will upset you as much as those filled with daunting developmental milestones.

The New Dad You are a father in love with your baby and eager to participate wholeheartedly in raising him. You turn to books such as *Father's Almanac,* by S. Adams Sullivan (which says on the cover that it has "over 300,000 in print"—just so you'll know that, yes, other fathers are reading, too) or *Fathers and Babies* and *Fathers and Toddlers,* both by the two-woman team of Jean Marzollo and Irene Trivas.

From *The Measure of a Man: Becoming the Father You Wish Your Father Had Been,* by Jerrold Lee Shapiro, to *Coaching for Fatherhood* by Lewis Epstein, for the father who started off wrong and wants to do better, you absorb the stories and the exhortations. You think of yourself as a pathfinder, and therefore must always be on your guard lest you do something that marks you as an old-style dad. This takes a lot of thinking and a fair amount of reading, too.

The Back-to-Basics Parent You've had it with asking your child how he feels and have come to believe in a sort of childrearing affirmative action.

You find confirmation in John Rosemond, a highly opinionated back-to-basics proponent, who has been raising the blood pressure and/or consciousnesses of readers in books such as *Parent Power* and *A Family of Value,* and in his syndicated parenting column. You may also turn to James Dobson's *Dare to Discipline,* a classic critique of permissive childrearing, newly revised.

Depending upon your religious persuasion, you may convert to Christian parenting books, such as *How to Really Love Your Child,* by Ron Campbell. In other words, you're getting tougher. But in these times, you need an expert to tell you how!

The Natural You are a psychologically aware parent. You breast-feed, carry your baby in a sling, and sleep with her, too.

You tried the mainstream stuff and it did not move you. So you read *The Family Bed,* by Tine Thevenin, and *The Baby Book* and others by William and Martha Sears, parents of eight, who describe disciplinary encounters as "loving guidance." *The Continuum Concept,* by Jean Liedloff, is your bible. *Mothering Magazine* is also on your list. As a thinking and feeling parent, you want to give your child something richer and deeper than the usual mass-market stuff. You see yourself not as a parent who thinks too much but as a parent who feels just the right amount.

The Doubter You're an experienced parent and may have a couple of children who each spent several years in the terrible two's. You've begun to think the parenting books you've read had something to do with that, and so, you've begun to be wary about parenting information. You may have noticed, for instance, that books travel in packs. A few years ago, self-esteem was hot, but now those tomes have the worn-out sound of last year's hit song.

You're glad that morals are in—that you can find such fine books as *Raising Good Children,* by Thomas Lickona. But you think to yourself, if we are so concerned about the model we're providing our children, then what about providing them a model of parental self-sufficiency, too? So for that reason you've let your parenting magazine subscriptions lapse, and you've started reading novels again.

Because you've become somewhat disenchanted with the experts, you're attracted to titles such as *Parenting by Heart,* by Ron Taffel (with Melinda Blau). It's one of many books which encourage us to trust our intuition even as they dismantle it. "From having parents who may have rarely reflected on their childrearing, we have in one generation become parents who question ourselves endlessly," Taffel says. He's certainly right on that one. But wait. Even though "connecting [with kids] is not such a mysterious and complex business," Taffel spends the rest of his book telling you how to do it. "Trust yourself" books are proof that parents are becoming wary of expert opinion— but *you* should be wary of these books because they're still in the advice business!

Doubts to Share

I'm sure there are other types of parents who think too much, but I'm going to stop with "the doubter." I have some doubts of my own to share—not just about parenting books but about the entire advice industry. I hope my doubts will increase your doubts to the point where you believe in yourself again.

Whether they say it directly or merely hint at it, magazines, classes, and books teach us that our first thought is seldom our best thought. For example, the book *How to Talk so Kids Will Listen and Listen so Kids Will Talk* is filled with cartoons that make it clear that the old ways are much less useful than the new skills the book will teach us. These cartoons are often exaggerations of heartless parenting. In one of them a mother shopping in a supermarket tells her son, "If I catch you running again, you'll get a smack!" In the next panel, the mother has turned the child over her knee and, spouting the words "You asked for it," is spanking her son. In the new and improved version, the mother calmly tells her son, "Billy, no running. Here are your choices: You can walk or you can sit in the cart. You decide." The next panel shows mother calmly putting Billy in the cart. The message I receive from the cartoon is that if you follow your instincts, you will hurt your child. No wonder we're unsure of ourselves.

Books also make us hesitate by telling us that if we choose the wrong words to talk to our child we'll inadvertently crush his ego: "It is better to say '*As soon* as you do your job *then* I'll be able to do mine,' rather than '*If* you don't do what you're supposed to, *then* I won't help you.' '*If*' implies a threat whereas 'as soon as' suggests cooperation," is a bit of advice you'll find in *The Preschool Years,* by Ellen Galinsky and Judy David.

Keep in mind that a book or article is as much about what's left out as what's kept in. We often get our facts from a two-page magazine article that barely has enough room to explain a problem, let alone propose any meaty solutions to it. The magazine editors I know work wonders with the space they're allotted. They manage to distill complicated ideas into 1,500 snappy words. But you just can't explain attachment theory in 1,500 words. It's a shame that we dispense with our own ideas based on the overview we glean from the shiny pages of a magazine.

What's lost in the translation is the subtle context that would put the advice in its place. What's lost are the qualifications and the "maybe nots." If we knew these, we'd be less tempted to take the words to heart. But let's face it. We could read an entire book on attachment theory, yet most of us don't. What stops us is our own lack of time and the mistaken notion that we already know what we need to know because we read the magazine article.

Like any other stories these days, parenting stories—or trends in parenting advice—don't have a very long shelf life. "It's not 'In God we trust.' It's 'In what do we trust?' " laments my friend Chris Anderson, the mother of two daughters. "Over and over again we've had the rug pulled out from under us. We're trying to do the best for our kids and we're reading all these books and six months later we find out that the guy didn't know what he was talking about."

One moment the hot item is how girls' self-esteem plummets in adolescence; another it's the titillating bombshell that babies can "count." The keepers and the throwaways, the calming and panic-provoking alike pelt us continually. Right behind the big splashy studies, like commentators after a news conference, is an expert's take on how to incorporate the new findings into our repertoire of parenting techniques. If babies can count, then we must integrate more math into their daily lives. If girls' self-esteem plummets in adolescence then we must innoculate them with confidence when they enter middle school.

Sometimes, wrong ideas get loose and cause considerable mischief before they finally fade away. A few years ago parents heard that in order to bond with their infants, they must spend quality time together, skin-to-skin if possible, immediately after birth. Although the research on which this suggestion was based was conducted on animals and had limited application for humans, it took years to debunk the notion that unless your baby is put immediately into your arms, you're doomed to an unbonded future.

When we base our childrearing decisions on the theory "du jour," we are prey to a constantly shifting view of what it means to be a parent, or for that matter, what it means to be a child. The books encourage us to try on new fashions of childrearing as if we were trying on a new pair of jeans. We lose the time, space, and quiet to ponder what we think our children need. Each article, even the teaser copy on the jacket of a new advice manual, drags us off in its own direction. For instance, a book might tell us we need to encourage our kids rather than praise them. The differences between the two are so subtle that we need a book to figure them out. Yet while we concentrate on a "tree" like this, we lose sight of the "forest"—which, among other things, may consist of teaching kids to praise others.

When we see childrearing as a subject we must study rather than part of life, as inexorable as the change of seasons, we don't realize that we already have what it takes to bring up the next generation. We have ourselves.

Guilt, Fear, and Addiction

Our parents brought us up in a time of economic prosperity; we are rearing our children in a time of psychological plenty, when every child's birthright is total and complete understanding. Since giving this to them is an impossible task, we are left with a nagging sense of incompletion. Meanwhile, we disparage the qualities we do bring to our children—our wisdom, intelligence, sense of humor, perspective. "In general, every time I read something I *did* do, I discounted it as 'everybody does that'; if I read about something I *didn't* do, I felt guilty and labeled myself a bad mother," said one parent.

As children blossom into well-respected (but often disrespectful) youngsters, our fear takes another turn. Now we're not as afraid of hurting our children's feelings as we are afraid of our children, period. We tiptoe around them, unable to give a command or make a decision. "I see parents visiting our preschool with their three-year-olds," says Diana, a teacher I know. "The parents are asking their kids, 'Do you like this school? Do you want to come here?' I mean, why don't they make that decision for their child? Their child can't make it for them! But it's like the parents are saying, 'I can't figure it out on my own.' "

Perhaps we can't figure it out because we've become so used to being told what to do—first by the experts and then by our children—that we no longer know what's important. Recently I huddled for a quarter of an hour with three other adults in a parenting class. Our "assignment": to devise new bedtime strategies for our kids. As we struggled to come up with fresh solutions to this perennial problem, a problem that wouldn't plague us in such epidemic proportions if we had more control over our children, I almost laughed out loud. Here we were, intelligent people who could have been doing any number of worthwhile projects—curing the common cold, volunteering in a homeless shelter, playing Monopoly with our eight-year-old—but instead we were coming up with convoluted new ways to put recalcitrant children to bed.

The advice industry feeds on itself; it's addictive. The more we know, the more we want to know—and the less we think we do know. Only 38 percent of the parents surveyed in the poll I mentioned earlier felt totally sure their child's emotional development was healthy. "Parents thirst for more information on how to promote their young children's healthy development," concluded the organization that commissioned the poll. Their summary was headlined, "Parents of Babies and Toddlers Face 'Information Deficit' on Healthy Child Development."[8]

Guilt is the legacy of our addiction. It's what remains after we cede our job to the experts. Some books attack the guilt head-on. *If Only I Were a Better Mother,* by Melissa Gayle West, bears the long-winded subtitle: "Using the Anger, Fear, Despair, and Guilt That Every Mother Feels at Some Time as a Pathway to Emotional Balance and Spiritual Growth." Others encourage the guilt to grow. How does *Loving Your Child Is Not Enough,* by Nancy Samalin, make you feel?

The ideas found in some modern books may be derived from family therapy techniques, in which the whole family is treated, not just the child. But I believe they have more to do with the kind of parents we are—committed to human growth (our own as well as our children's) and unable to separate ourselves from our kids. Needless to say, they don't do much for our self-confidence.

The advice industry enthralls us, however, because it offers shortcuts. We are, for better or worse, one of the busier generations of adults ever to bring up our young. Much of our busyness is self-imposed; that is, it is not the same kind of busyness that an eighteenth-century farmhand or nineteenth-century factory worker experienced. It is busyness dictated by the kind of lives we think we're supposed to provide for ourselves and our children. Pinched for time, we need ways to sidestep the old-fashioned, labor-intensive methods of getting things done. And the classes and books lead us to believe we can skip over the apprentice stage of parenthood. "It's easier to pick up a magazine for three or five bucks than to formulate what's wrong with my relationship with my child," says Chris Anderson. It's easy to forget that raising kids requires a good deal of hard-won wisdom, and the only way we acquire it is by making the tough decisions on our own, one by one.

Professional Parenthood?

In the 1940s, Evelyn Millis Duvall, director of the Association for Family Living, said that parenthood was "the last stand of the amateur."[9] This dismayed her; she thought social workers had a duty to teach women and men how to be mothers and fathers. By the 1950s, family experts had "reached a consensus about the condition most likely to produce healthy, well-adjusted, cooperative, achievement-oriented, and upwardly mobile offspring: parents who had absorbed the ideology of mental health," said Christopher Lasch.[10]

Forty years later, the advice industry has convinced some mothers and fathers that professional parenthood is the only way to go. Jim and Tiff Wimberly and their three young children live on a mountaintop in central Arkansas, a place that seems beyond expert intrusion into private life. Jim and Tiff are close to their own parents. They trust their common sense, and they're not letting their children run all over them. And yet, Tiff considers parenthood a profession. "My parenting magazines are my trade journals," she says, and she subscribes to several. She also reads books and peruses the Web. "If it's out there and it's something I want to know, I'm going to find it and read it. I do a lot of homework, or what I call homework, when it comes to parenting. I did it prior to becoming pregnant. I read about what I could do to have the best pregnancy possible. Then during the pregnancy I read to find out what I could do to continue having a great pregnancy and what I could do to be a good parent. I read *What to Expect When You're Expecting, What to Expect the First Year,* and *What to Expect the Toddler*

Years. I'm going to be lost if they don't put out a book soon called, *What to Expect from Four to Six*."

Tiff seems quite certain about the path she has chosen. But other parents said that even when they strive to be professional—reading books and attending classes—something interferes. One mother I know had me laughing out loud when she told me her experience with logical consequences, a disciplinary method built on the premise that instead of punishing a child with a penalty, you devise a consequence that flows from the misbehavior. Heather Babiarz learned about logical consequences in a parenting class at her children's school and was eager to use this strategy with her younger daughter, Tasha, who had trouble remembering to put the top back on the toothpaste tube. Heather was tired of nagging, but she was stumped. What kind of logical consequence could she inflict for leaving the top off the toothpaste tube? Make her four-year-old endure dried-out toothpaste? Tasha didn't mind. Forbid her to brush her teeth? Of course, that was no good. So one morning, faced with another caked tube, Heather fumed and she sputtered, and finally she said, "Okay, Tasha, you're going to . . . you're going to have a *consequence* for this." Tasha looked up, all smiles, and asked, "What's a consequence, Mommy?"

When you think about it, our experience with parenting books has a catch-22 quality to it: Books tease us with promises of how well they'll help us handle our kids even as they set us up for failure. Sometimes we fail because we can't do what the books tell us to. After all, children are children, and real-life scenarios are never as clear-cut as the ones on the printed page. Other times we fail because we actually do what the books tell us to and thereby lose control of our children.

To use another literary analogy, the books are full of doublethink, the ability to hold two contradictory ideas in our heads at the same time. One way the advice industry encourages doublethink is by recasting problems as psychological diagnoses. Defiance is renamed the "search for autonomy." A four-year-old who refuses to share is "asserting her boundaries." Hear enough of this and you will hold two contradictory ideas in your head at the same time: the problem you originally had and the mistaken notion that it is no longer a problem.

I guess a lot of it comes down to what we think good parents ought to be. Well-informed or clearheaded? We attend so carefully to the "letter" of childrearing that we lose the "spirit" of it. We're less nimble, less able to improvise, laugh, and roll with the punches, which could be our greatest assets as parents. The harder we try, the harder raising children becomes. A by-the-book attitude can make us lose sight of the kind of family we want to create; it can even blind us to the dearness of our own children. How will we find the answers unless we follow our own dreams—not someone else's? If there is any endeavor in which I want to be an amateur, it's raising my own kids.

"Eleanore Liberation Day" and Other Ways Out

Now that I've challenged the advice industry, I feel as if I have to offer you something in exchange. But what? I'm certainly not going to ply you with childrearing instructions. Instead, let me swing a yellow caution light before your eyes and suggest that you be more careful about the advice you take in, that you realize the power it can have over you.

Some parents I know have taken decisive steps in this direction. Donna Konigsberg, childrearing class veteran, decided to bypass the classes and seek advice from her friends if she needed it. Eleanore Keenan canceled three of her four magazine subscriptions. The day she did it, she dubbed "Eleanore Liberation Day."

Some parents told me that they had to touch bottom before they started to trust themselves. When Chris Anderson's youngest daughter, Rebecca, was born, her oldest, Liz, was three years old and didn't take kindly to the new arrival. "I'd read all the books about how to help your firstborn child deal with jealousy and self-esteem when a younger brother or sister is born. I took Liz to a sibling preparation class. I'd done everything the articles said to do, and it was the biggest mistake of my life. Because I was taking this child who already felt she was

queen bee and giving her permission to go on with her tantrums about the baby,'' Chris said.

What helped Chris change was her own sure knowledge that
things had gone too far. "One day Liz did something to Rebecca; I don't even remember what it was now. And I said: 'Liz,
this baby is staying with us. She is your sister. I love her very
much and so does your dad. We are not getting rid of her. You
have to get used to having her around the house.' "

"It was like a revelation to her," Chris continues. "You could
almost see the lightbulb going off in her head. And the tantrums pretty much stopped. I know she's had jealous feelings
since then. What sister or brother hasn't? But I finally set the
boundaries. I finally said, regardless of what you're feeling,
whatever you want to do is *not* okay."

Chris had tried understanding her older daughter's problem, she had given her plenty of chances to vent her feelings,
which is what the books say to do when Number Two arrives.
But what solved her problem was when she finally decided to
take action. You could say Chris was just falling back into old
patterns and stereotypes when she took charge as she did. But
she was doing the most natural thing in the world—setting a
limit, a very welcome limit, apparently, for her young child.

Sometimes I seek relief from thinking too much by talking to
parents who don't take the books to heart. Maggie Mulqueen,
who lives outside Boston, is a psychologist and therefore accustomed to the lingo of the parenting books. But she's also a
mother of three young sons and therefore a realist. "I find most
of the advice books so simplistic," she says. "I want to say, 'Oh,
yeah, why don't you come to my house at five o'clock at night
and try some of these things.' "

Another friend, Anne Wolf, from Oak Park, Illinois, who has
a nine-year-old son and a three-year-old daughter, said, "I just
started to read this book about how to raise a healthy son, not a
macho man. And it was so goofy. Who does these things?" She
laughed at herself for having picked the book up in the first
place, and I teased her for doing it, too. Anne is from a family of
nine children and once edited a magazine about social justice.

Her husband, Jim Ahrens, is a smart, kind man who jokes about golf as a "male bonding" sport. I couldn't imagine any parents less likely to raise a "macho man." Apparently, Anne came to the same conclusion. "I decided that that book just was not us. I guess we have confidence in our own abilities as parents."

My conversations with Anne and Maggie were largely possible because they are old friends. They are exceptions to the rule that the advice industry makes it difficult for us to speak honestly with each other (a point I'll talk about more in the next chapter). On the whole I've found that the more we turn to the books or magazines the less likely we'll feel a need to seek out each other. All the more reason to put childrearing information in its place. One way I've done that is by categorizing the books, as I did above. This helps me think critically about them, and when I think critically, I'm making sure that the advice jibes with my own internal sense of right and wrong. It keeps me intellectually honest.

I have some other tricks which help me size up a book before I invest too much of myself in it. Maybe you've thought of these, too. For instance, I always read the author's biography before anything else. I appreciate authors who don't have an axe to grind or a program to promote. I look for a little humility, for Ph.D.'s that aren't emblazoned on the cover, for a solid but modest résumé. I scan to see if the author has written any other books. If she has, these give me advance notice about her opinions. I want to know whether she's a fundamentalist Christian or a liberal activist; a social scientist describing her research or a psychologist who relies on her client roster for stories and anecdotes. Most importantly, I want to feel, after browsing through the book for a few minutes, that I like the author and that her book is worth my time and effort.

Lately, I've noticed that many books are written "by parents for parents." *Teaching Your Children Values,* by Linda and Richard Eyre, is an example of this type. (It helps when the parents have eight children, as the Eyres do.) A rebellion against "expert" advice is healthy, but even "just another parent" can become a tyrant if he sits on your shoulder and continually whispers in your ear.

Before I buy a book, I also read the table of contents. If it doesn't hold my interest, I don't buy it. If I do choose a book, I let it sit on my shelf a while. Now that we raise our kids by the book, or by the article, it's frightening to think that the information comes to us unbuffered by time and perspective. We may read about a study in a newspaper the day after it's been released in an academic journal. It hasn't been around long enough to be truly tested. It's like buying a new-model car the first year it's out.

When I finally read the book, I do so with a critical eye. I keep in mind that it mirrors the political and social context of the times in which it was written; in other words, I notice how trendy it is. I make sure it's something I can live with because once I read it, it could be part of me forever. This was especially true for me in early parenthood, as illustrated by Leach's *Your Baby and Child*. It is early on that we can get hooked. The first books leave the deepest impressions.

This book is not entitled *Parents Who Read Too Much* because it's not the reading that's the problem. It's what we read, and what we do after we read, that leads us astray. You've probably read books that have given you the right thoughts at the right time, and you will never forget them. Like anything else, some childcare manuals are solid, heartfelt, and engagingly written; others are not even worth the paper they're printed on. Despite everything else I've said, I remain a book lover at heart. I persist in believing that books can change us deeply and for the better.

In fact, books may be where we find some of our first and fondest models of parenthood. Increasingly, the books that mean the most to me as a parent are not the advice manuals, but the classics. I've always had a soft spot for the Micawbers of Dickens's *David Copperfield,* perhaps because something in their this-time-our-ship-will-come-in optimism reminds me of my own parents. Your favorites may be the novels of Louisa May Alcott or Anne Tyler, Oscar Hijuelos or John Updike.

If there is any way in which books can improve us as parents it is when they improve us as people. So instead of *40 Ways to Raise a Nonracist Child,* I read *To Kill a Mockingbird.* Instead of *Your Five-Year-Old: Sunny and Serene,* I read *An American Childhood,* by Annie Dillard. It is a book that makes me remember what it was like to be a child, to dip my toes into the bathwater and feel the tingle up my spine, to hear the silence of a house as if it were a giant clock, ticking. I've taken special pleasure in rereading books I loved before I had children. Their truths sound even more deeply now that I'm a parent.

In the course of writing this book, I've read many fine books which analyze modern childrearing practices rather than pitch modern childrearing principles. *The Tentative Pregnancy,* by Barbara Katz Rothman, takes a look at how amniocentesis and other tests have changed our concept of gestation. *Greater Expectations: Overcoming the Culture of Indulgence in America's Homes and Schools,* by William Damon, analyzes the failure of self-esteem programs and other modern childrearing tactics without ever becoming strident. *The Disappearance of Childhood,* by Neil Postman, *Perfect Parents,* by Christina Hardyment, *Children Without Childhood,* by Marie Winn, and *Haven in a Heartless World: The Family Besieged,* by Christopher Lasch, put our childrearing practices into historical perspective. *The Moral Intelligence of Children,* by Robert Coles, is one of the more recent of many fine works by this author. David Elkind has written a number of books that critically examine the status quo, books like *The Hurried Child,* which helped put the skids on the superbaby movement. In a more recent work, *Ties That Stress: The New Family Imbalance,* Elkind analyzes the emphasis on technique that is such a dominant part of childrearing today. These books get to the heart of the matter; they lead us to our own best thoughts, rather than away from them.

How did parents raise their kids a generation or two ago, when books were few but mothers-in-law closer at hand? In some ways it was much harder, of course. Go back 50 years and you'd have no polio vaccine. Go back 50 more and there would be few child-labor laws. I don't want to romanticize the past, but I do want to point out some very important facts about it: Parents were less confused. They knew their place. They did not agonize over whether their kids should take karate or gymnastics. They did not add "okay" to the end of every command.

Some would criticize parents of the past for their willingness to do things the way they'd always been done. They would claim that our predecessors didn't know enough about child development, that they repressed feelings, disciplined excessively, and brought up their children to fear, rather than challenge, authority. But the truth of the matter is, most of us are happy, productive, civilized human beings, and we got that way being raised more or less as our parents and grandparents were.

It has taken reams of studies, tons of books, and a cultural revolution to bring us to the point we are now. Throughout recorded time, in times when parents believed that babies were blank slates and in times when parents believed that babies were noble savages, mothers and fathers have still, for the most part, trusted the basic principles with which they were raised enough to pass them along to their own offspring. Immigrants landing on new shores bundled up not only precious family heirlooms but also enduring family traditions. We, the current generation of parents, have broken the chain. For us, there has been a "better" way. Why us and why now? That's what the next chapter will show.

2

Our Children, Our Selves
Why Childrearing Is Now Called Parenting

"Children begin by loving their parents; as they grow older they judge them; sometimes they forgive them."
—*Oscar Wilde*

A few years ago I had an epiphany in the parenting aisle of my local library. I'd come to research a magazine story, but, as usual, I was sidetracked. I was noticing the book titles—*The Shock of Motherhood, Coaching for Fatherhood, Change Your Child's Behavior by Changing Yours, Growing Up Again: Parenting Ourselves, Parenting Our Children.* These books are not as much about kids as they are about us, I thought. From the '60s toothpaste commercials, "Look, Ma, no cavities!" we've evolved to "Look, World, no periodontal disease! And have you noticed we're parents now?" We are parents who think too much, and it's not just our kids we think about. It's our performance.

When you think about yourself thinking, you're engaged in what scientists call metacognition. When you think about yourself parenting, you're engaged in what I call "metaparenting." This hip, new, self-conscious style of raising kids is designed to deal critically with the way we were brought up. You could even say it's designed more for that than for anything else. Once you become aware of metaparenting (meta-metaparenting?), you'll notice it everywhere.

In a book called *Man Enough,* psychiatrist Frank Pittman says: "The guys who fear becoming fathers don't understand that fathering is not something perfect men do, but something that perfects the man. The end product of child raising is not the child but the parent."

In a childrearing class, mothers and fathers fill out a questionnaire to see how spirited their kids are, then answer the same questions about themselves. Before the class is over, some members refer to themselves as "former spirited children" and the room buzzes with confessions. I think for a minute that I have wandered into a meeting of recovering alcoholics.

In a magazine article reaching hundreds of thousands of parents, esteemed pediatrician T. Berry Brazelton writes: "It's certainly true that whenever we meet an impasse—a parenting or behavior problem that's particularly difficult or to which we overreact—one of our own 'nursery ghosts' is apt to turn up from deep in our unconscious." He goes on to say that we must deal with our "nursery ghosts" before we can fix what is wrong with our child.

Of course we love our children and want to do all we can for them. But we seem to have twin goals in mind. Let our child express her feelings and we'll better vent our own. Discover what bothers our child and we will learn what hurts us. Now that we are parents we will undo the sins of our fathers and mothers. We won't be inflexible and unyielding; we'll be frank and friendly. We will "grow" with our kids. It's parenthood as transactional analysis. No wonder childrearing is now called "parenting." The term is not only gender-neutral and otherwise politically correct, but it also puts the emphasis on *parents* rather than children. The difference is more than just semantic.

Some of this self-absorption flows from our penchant for self-improvement. We've made household words of "I'm okay, you're okay." We've discovered that we're addicted to love; we have a problem with our mothers; and men are from Mars and women from Venus. And we have found in parenthood the perfect continuation of our quest for the well-tuned personality. Whether it's deciding to have natural childbirth or an epidural, one child or two, every decision we make is a very big deal. We have read *Passages* and no longer view adulthood as one vast wilderness but as a series of stages, sort of like childhood. We expect to keep changing all the time. Our children's childhood is the perfect vehicle for our ongoing transformation. We can raise ourselves while raising our children.

Of course, being responsible for young lives does touch us deeply, does—if we're not sleepwalking through it—transform us utterly. But now, instead of keeping those feelings to ourselves, in effect plowing them under so they can enrich our daily lives, we air them in magazine essays, books, classes, and even advertisements.

"The toughest job in the world isn't being President. It's being a parent," reads the public service announcement from the Coalition for America's Children. Above the words is a picture of President Bill Clinton with his wife and daughter. They are striding across a field together in the sunshine. From all accounts, the Clintons are good parents. They have succeeded at this difficult task. They are also good icons for our generation of parents. Education is very important to them. Bill Clinton has made national standards and other educational initiatives a focal point of his second administration. Hillary Rodham Clinton has long been interested in the emotional and intellectual development of children. I don't know if the Clintons are parents who think too much. But they certainly talk the talk. So their conspicuous placement in this advertisement seems quite appropriate. They could be any of us who bear the weight of childrearing on our shoulders.

Is it really news to us that parenting is difficult, albeit in a different way than running a country, teaching a student, cleaning a carpet, or preparing a legal brief? Did we think raising kids would be easy? Do we emphasize the difficulty of the task because we feel our predecessors shortchanged it? Or do we simply want everyone to notice we have taken this hazardous voyage, this journey of parenthood? Are we trying, with our children, to prove we've come of age? What else accounts for the incessant notice we give this timeless process of bearing and rearing children, which used to be regarded as a simple fact of nature and is now exalted as a brave undertaking? The answer I usually hear is, "It's harder to raise kids these days."

The pressures on parents may be greater than in some periods of our history, and raising kids seems more complicated (though the superabundance of information may be responsible for much of the complication). But we certainly cannot corner the market on difficulty. It's only been within the last couple of centuries that children in this country had more than a 50-50 chance of living past their fifth birthdays. No, I think there's something more than the difficulty of the job to explain why we think so much about raising our kids. But what is it? Why out of generations of mothers and fathers before us have we been given this dubious distinction?

I think it's from a rare combustion of supply and demand. We talked about the supply in the last chapter. It's the books, articles, classes, the seminars, and the newsletters. What's driving all this advice are reams of studies on infants and children conducted by psychologists, psychiatrists, pediatricians, educators, sociologists, and other experts. Their findings, often valid but seldom time-tested, have become the raw material from which thousands of books and articles are spun. This is the "supply." And in modern parents it has met its "demand," its perfect audience. We are journal-keeping, quiz-taking parents, constantly tinkering with our technique, forever revising our opinion of ourselves. We ponder decisions, and then we ponder ourselves pondering them.

This chapter is about the demand, which means it's about us. Why are we so receptive to this advice? Why do we continue to seek and create it? Good consumers all, we know there wouldn't be a supply if there wasn't a demand. So why the demand? Are there clues in the past, in the generations upon generations of parents who've preceded us, that reveal how we've arrived at this point?

Spare Spartans, Progressive Puritans, and Other Ancestors

Throughout recorded history, parents have wondered how best to rear their children and lamented their problems with the next generation. "Our earth is degenerate in these latter days. Bribery and corruption are common. Children no longer obey their parents," wrote a scribe in Mesopotamia about 4,000 years ago. But even in the ancient world, some people had clearer ideas about children than others. In ancient Greece, Spartans were known for the care they took in training their youngest citizens. Raised by nurses away from their parents for the first seven years of life, Spartan boys and girls were fed little, taught to wrestle, throw the discus, and endure flogging without a whimper. Other Greeks both admired and ridiculed the Spartans' get-tough childrearing methods. No one could dispute that they produced the kind of adults valued in Spartan society—warriors and mothers of warriors. Still, they weren't exactly an advertisement for thoughtful childrearing.[1]

One reason that relatively little mind was paid to young children in ancient times and for centuries to come was that parents couldn't count on their youngsters' survival. Infanticide was common well into the sixteenth century. If babies weren't killed or abandoned, then disease or accident often claimed their lives. Even in the eighteenth century nearly 50 percent of children died before they were five, most before their first birthdays.[2] Parents were not indifferent to their offspring, but they kept some psychological distance, some referring to newborns as "it" or "the little stranger," reluctant even to invest the child with a name.[3]

Understandably, then, some of the earliest childcare advice books concentrated on how to take good physical care of children. In one of the more famous, *An Essay on the Nursing and Management of Children* (published in London in 1748), William Cadogan speaks out against lancing the gums of teething infants and swaddling babies. (This is not swaddling as we know it, but the tight binding of babies with layers of cloth, a practice which immobilized infants and slowed their heartbeats.) Cadogan was a pediatrician when pediatrics was in its infancy, and his book undoubtedly helped parents take better care of their children. But it also gives us a hint of the expert-dominated approach that bedevils us still: "It is with great Pleasure I see at last the Preservation of Children become the Care of Men of Sense," he writes in the opening pages. "In my opinion this Business has been too long fatally left to the management of Women."[4]

But Cadogan and others like him were careful to stop at physical advice and leave children's emotional and mental development to others. Usually the "others" were parents, teachers, and the church. But some philosophers got into the act, too. Two of the most renowned were John Locke and Jean-Jacques Rousseau.

Locke theorized that children arrive as blank slates on which experiences create a personality. In *Some Thoughts Concerning Education* (published in 1693), he told parents they must squelch their instinctive love for their children in the interest of instilling proper character. He believed in toughening children by putting them to sleep on hard beds, feeding them dry bread, dousing them in cold water, and dressing them in light clothes. A firm believer in education, Locke nonetheless held that young children were to be instilled with "fear and awe." Although some criticized his advice because it was unrealistic, noting that he was a bachelor with no children of his own, educated mothers read his works and tried to follow them. There were 26 editions of his book before 1800.[5]

Less than a century later, Jean-Jacques Rousseau, who abandoned his five illegitimate children in foundling homes, countered with his own view of childhood—that children are "noble savages," wise and capable from the beginning. In 1762, he published *Emile,* the story of an imaginary boy and his unfettered childhood. Rousseau believed that from ages two to 12 children should be free to play as they wished; no lessons for them—other than the ones they took from nature.[6]

Although the history of childrearing is complex and driven by many forces, in a very general way our attitudes toward children swing back and forth between the philosophies of Locke and Rousseau. The romantic sees children as Rousseau did: born with everything they need to grow up fine and strong and good as long as parents give them enough berth. The pragmatist sees them as Locke did: born neither good nor evil but in great need of civilization. Locke's modern heirs range from behaviorists, who believe a child can be programmed like Pavlov's dogs, to modern conservatives such as James Dobson, who urge parents to mold the growing child. Rousseau's descendents are the permissive parenting gurus of the '60s, such as A. S. Neill, who said, "I believe that to impose anything by authority is wrong,"[7] and whose progressive school, Summerhill, seems tailor-made for latter-day Emiles. Even today's behavioral geneticists, who think family experiences make little difference in how children grow up because heredity is the key to behavior, can prompt parents to act Rousseauian. If what we do makes so little difference, then why do much at all?

Locke and Rousseau, of course, were Europeans. When parents crossed the Atlantic and began to raise their children in the New World, they took some of their traditions and books with them. But they also developed their own way of doing things. In some cases, they came here precisely so they *could* do things their own way.

The Puritans began as zealous reformers of the Church of England. They were critical of the world in which they lived, and so were among the first parents who felt they could not rely on their neighbors or existing institutions to help them socialize their children. Though in many ways Puritan parents differed greatly from us—their chief goal, for instance, was helping their children achieve eternal salvation—in other ways they seem modern. Because Puritans were on the outside looking in, they felt more strongly than most parents of their time that the future rested in their offspring. Puritans believed that learning begins long before the school years and were the first to publish books specifically for young people. In a world where mothers routinely sent their babies out to be nursed by others, Puritan mothers were urged to nurse their own.[8] We share the

Puritans' strong interest in childrearing. We, too, feel it is our duty to save our children from ruin. We may not define "ruin" as they did, but we often think as cataclysmically as they. We are as afraid of squelching our children's "spirit" as the Puritans were of damning their children's souls.

Of course, we part company from Puritans in many ways, especially discipline. "Spare the rod and spoil the child," was a common saying in the seventeenth century, and authoritarian advice continued through the eighteenth and well into the nineteenth centuries.[9]

On the other hand, our early American forebears seemed more child-centered than Europeans from the start. For one reason, they were forging a new country and needed every hand they could get,[10] even if it was a very little hand. For another, American parents were already passing along a sense of can-do optimism to their children. So much so that foreigners found American youngsters a little hard to take. A nineteenth-century Englishman said, "There are no children in our sense of the term in America—only little men and women. . . . The merest boy will give his opinion upon the subject of conversation among his seniors; and he expects to be listened to, and is." This new type of child was being raised by a new type of parent: A German visitor of the same era said American parents seem to "live altogether for their children."[11]

It's a small leap from "living for children" to reading about them. So it shouldn't be surprising that Americans soon had a number of childrearing books from which to choose. With the rise of industrialism, fathers were out of the house most of the day, and mothers were eager to raise children in a new way. "Never before in history had there been children so worried over and thought about as those little Americans born in the second quarter of the nineteenth century," says historian Mary Cable.[12] I bet today's kids could give them a run for their money, though.

The Civil War, the settling of the West, and the influx of immigrants with their own childrearing practices all served to stir things up later on in the century. The old authoritarianism and moral certainty was wearing thin. The Bible quotation of the day was no longer "Spare the rod and spoil the child" but "Provoke not your children to wrath." To show how attitudes changed, an 1848 book called *Christian Nurture,* which proposed that children pass through developmental stages and parents must be wise and self-controlled, was considered so permissive that its author, Horace Bushnell, a Congregationalist minister, withdrew it from circulation. Twenty years later, the book was reissued and became a best-seller.

"There had clearly been a revolution in child management, even though it took time for its impact to spread from the comparatively few parents who read books and magazines and were not afraid of new ideas," Mary Cable writes. "Some advice was reiterated for decades before it became common procedure."[13] Advice today needs only be heard once to reverberate through our homes and heads. Even though nineteenth-century parents had more—and more permissive—advice than their predecessors had, it was a trickle compared to the flood we have today.

By the end of the last century, women freed from some of the manual labor of the home filled their idle moments by coming together to discuss domestic and childcare issues. There were even National Congresses of Mothers, during which the few childrearing experts of the day shared their findings, and mothers were exhorted to be scientific observers of their children's behavior. These turn-of-the-century mothers thought they could elevate their position in the family by making childrearing more complicated. "If it [childcare] was to absorb the whole woman, it would have to be redefined, amplified, and enriched," say Barbara Ehrenreich and Deirdre English.[14] The solution: reinterpret motherhood as a profession. A writer in *Cosmopolitan* magazine at the time urged that motherhood be open only to those who could demonstrate "fitness." And National Congress of Mothers President Mrs. Theodore Birney addressed the second annual mothers' convention with these words: "It seems to me that we should all perceive what intelligent parenthood means for the race, and that to attain it is as well worth our effort and attention as the study of Greek, Latin, higher mathematics, medicine, law, or any other profession."[15]

In her words you can hear the noble intentions of today's eager readers and parenting course attendees. These are our forerunners; call them "great-grandparents who thought too much." It's comforting to know we have some historical company in our search for perfect childrearing. But it's sobering to note how quickly their good intentions were subsumed into the cult of the expert. "The birth of the 'professional mother' was shadowed, from the start, by the simultaneous birth of another kind of professional—one who would make it his specialty to tell the mothers what to do," say Ehrenreich and English.[16]

The Century of the Expert

When it began, the twentieth century was dubbed the "Century of the Child." It might have been better named the "Century of the Expert." In the early 1900s, the leading authority on children was pediatrician L. Emmett Holt. His *Care and Feeding of Children* went through dozens of editions. Originally designed as a training manual for nurses—Holt was head of the New York Babies' Hospital—his book and suggestions were models of scientific precision.[17] Babies were to be bathed and fed on a strict schedule. Infants who didn't like it could cry. Crying, after all, is baby's exercise, Holt said.[18] Keep in mind that this was the book that shaped our grandparents and great-grandparents. Even if their parents didn't read many childcare books, they probably heard of the Holt method from their doctors or neighbors.

While mothers may have trusted themselves before Holt, it's easy to see why the mothers after him did not. His methods were counterintuitive to an extreme.[19] And there were other experts who came between parents and their instincts. Granville Stanley Hall, a theology student turned psychologist, urged mothers to keep "life books" for each child, recording "all incidents, traits of character, etc., with frequent photographs, parental anxieties, plans, hopes, etc." Hall also conducted his own experiments as he helped create the new field of child study.[20] To him goes a good share of the credit for turning parenthood from an art into a science. It didn't take long for other experts to follow.

The child development research infrastructure in this country was put into place in the 1920s by John D. Rockefeller. Through the Laura Spelman Rockefeller Memorial Foundation, which Rockefeller set up to honor his late wife, research stations sprouted across the country. They promoted scientific solutions to the problems of raising kids. Home economists became trained "parent educators." Luckily, the economic crash of 1929 interrupted this standardization of childrearing. But it left behind a network for diffusing expert advice on childrearing and, more importantly, the attitude that raising kids is not something you can do by the seat of your pants. Parents need help in this daunting endeavor.[21]

And they would get it from behavioral psychology. John B. Watson, a psychologist who cut his experimental teeth on monkeys and pigeons before turning his attention to human babies, believed that parents could produce model children simply by giving them the right stimulus. His 1920s book, *The Psychological Care of Infant and Child,* preached strict discipline, feeding, and toileting. Affection was anathema to Watson. He advised mothers never to hug and kiss their children but, "If you must, kiss them once on the forehead when they say good night. Shake hands with them in the morning."[22]

In 1946, *Baby and Child Care,* by Benjamin Spock, burst upon the scene. "Trust yourself, you know more than you think you do," Spock wrote. *Baby and Child Care* would become the bestselling book in American history, next to the Bible. It's easy to see how refreshing Spock must have seemed to parents after decades of scientific precision and detachment. How freeing it must have been for the pendulum to swing away from Locke's blank slate back toward Rousseau's noble savage. As Spock himself admitted, though, his words often had the opposite effect of what he intended. They depleted parents' confidence instead of building it. In his first edition, Spock urged an end to strict scheduling and other forms of authoritative guidance, and entreated parents to go easier on themselves and their children.

But by his second edition, published in 1957, he worried that parents were now being intimidated both by experts *and* by their own children. "Don't be afraid to love him [your child] and respond to his needs," Spock wrote in his first edition. "Don't be afraid to respond to other desires of his as long as they seem sensible to you and as long as you don't become a slave to him," he wrote in his second edition. Also in that edition he mentions parents' "hesitancy," which he thought was "the commonest problem in childrearing in America today." Resurrecting the old ways is "nothing to be ashamed of," Spock said. "This is the way Nature expects human beings to learn childcare—from their own childhood."[23]

It's an ironic retrenchment, considering the extent to which parents began to rely on experts instead of raising their children the way they'd been raised. Perhaps Spock's call for independence of mind could not withstand the hordes of advice-givers which his popularity had made possible. Each one of these other experts was ready to lend parents another idea, another voice. And, with the rise of infant research and changing social theories on the family, parents felt they needed additional help.

Dr. Spock's Babies

And so, with Spock, we come full circle. We are the children he told parents how to raise. Spock said parents know more than they think they know. Now we know more than we need to know. And the advice manuals that once seemed tangential have become an integral part of the process.

It's easy to say that we're parents who think too much because we were raised permissively as Spock babies. We grew up expecting our own lives to be easy and our children's even easier. But Spock was much a reflection of the baby boom years as he was their creator. Our parents must have been ready to believe him. Maybe it's because they were filled with postwar expansiveness and not in the mood to schedule and ration their children. They had scheduled and rationed themselves during the war years, and now they wanted a break from it. This was a whole new world they were creating, and Spock had the advice to match it. They could afford to make their lives more child-centered. Women were staying home and having babies. (During the 1950s, the rate of population growth in the U.S. approached that of India.[24]) And families were scattering, so parents couldn't turn to their parents for help. "The postwar American families wanted space for stretching out, space for their children (and from them), space from their parents and in-laws," says historian Todd Gitlin.[25]

We can't blame Spock, but we can look to the personality of the baby boom generation for clues to why we are the kind of parents we are. I realize, of course, that some of you are too young to be baby boomers. You may even be children of baby boomers. But I do think that baby boom principles set the thinking-too-much trend in motion, and younger mothers and fathers are following our tortured lead.

Those of us born from 1946 to 1964 are, after all, the pig-in-the-python, raised on educational entitlement, demographic entitlement, and, for many, just plain old entitlement. It took many of us years to find ourselves, longer still to get a job, marry, and have children. In some ways we still think of ourselves as children. A '60s rock and folk radio show in Washington, D.C., bills itself "Songs for Aging Children." We're called "baby boomers," a childhood nickname that has followed us into middle age.

There have always been so many of us, and we came of age with television. Accustomed to the spotlight, we've always had the feeling that the whole world is watching to see how we turn out. Not only that, but we were raised in an era which elevated domesticity to high art. "The 1950s stand out as the golden age of the American family, a reference point against which recent changes in family life can be measured,"[26] say social historians Steven Mintz and Susan Kellogg.

Postwar parents told their children that life would be rich and rewarding. "We encouraged them to express themselves and to fulfill themselves, believing that somehow, sheer abundance would support them," laments author Susan Littwin, the parent of grown children. Instead, she says, "They came of age in the eighties only to find that scarcity was back."[27]

Eventually, of course, baby boomers swallowed hard and went back to business school or law school or endured whatever purgatory was necessary to get a real job. We "made a commitment" to a partner and made up for lost time—not as our parents did, by producing a bumper crop of kids—but in our own way. Childrearing is more heralded, scrutinized, and analyzed than it ever has been. And much of that is due to the kind of parents we are and to our place in history.

"The fact is, that the pattern of family life characteristic of the fifties differed dramatically from any that has been observed earlier in our history or since," say Mintz and Kellogg. The birth rate was uncharacteristically high and the divorce rate uncharacteristically low.[28] Jobs were plentiful, the economy was booming. Mothers stayed home to care for their large broods. And kids grew up believing that postwar bliss was the norm. But there was a flip side to the domestic harmony: depressed mothers who were blamed for their children's problems.

When I think about the high expectations and low self-confidence parents have now, a combination that drives us to seek advice, I wonder if we didn't pick it up not only from our position in history but also from our own parents. They were told to trust their instincts, but often made to worry that their instincts were wrong. Ehrenreich and English point out that " 'instinct' proved to be a harsher taskmaster for women than discipline and study had ever been. If anything should go awry in the mother-child relationship or in the child's development the finger of blame would no longer point at the mother's faulty technique, but at her defective instincts. . . . As she played out her subconscious urges through the act of mothering, a woman wrote on the baby's psyche, as it were, with invisible ink. In time the ink would become legible to the expert, who would read it—and judge."[29]

As the first boomers turn 50, many still wrestle with "unresolved" feelings about their own parents. Many still don't feel settled, despite families and mortgages. Maybe it's because we've always fancied ourselves as innocents among the jaded. We still don't trust anyone over 30. We identify with our kids and want to be their equals. We encourage their friends to call us by our first names. We enjoy a brisk game of laser tag.

We emphasize not only equality and justice, but also inclusiveness. We want to know how a psychologist from Yale or the Yequana Indians in the Amazon jungle raise their children. Every viewpoint is sacred to us, it seems, except the one with which we were raised. And we're reluctant to foist our own philosophies, which we often call "baggage," on our children. When I asked one Massachusetts mother how she stayed true to her own dreams for her children, she said, "I want my daughters to find their *own* dreams. Why should they follow mine?"

Postponed Parenthood

Regardless of whether you believe the boomer zeitgeist has made us think too much, certain facts are indisputable. We have, as a generation, postponed parenthood. Between 1980 and 1994, the number of babies born to women in their 30s almost doubled, and the number of babies born to women in their 40s did double. One in five mothers over 40 delivered her *first* child in 1994, according to the National Center for Health Statistics. In certain pockets of the country, like the suburbs of major cities, first-time parents in their 30s or 40s are the norm.

In many ways being older has made us better parents. "There's a certain wisdom to being over 40 that's really wonderful to me as a parent," Mary Scott said to me one day. Because we wait to start our families, we've had time to start a career, see the world, or do a little of both. We bring perspective and maturity to the job.

Ours has not been just any young adulthood, either. We came of age with the birth control pill and legalized abortion, and because we've had this one choice—to have or not to have a child—we've had a hundred thousand more. So many possibilities have shimmered before us that when we did say yes to children, after many years of saying no, we felt we owed something to this choice. We needed to confirm and guarantee it.

Postponed parenthood has made us worrisome parents, though. Older pregnant women often focus as much on what can go wrong as on what will go right, since the chances of miscarriage and fetal abnormalities increase with age. When I ask my friend Rita, pregnant for the first time at 40, how things are going, she always replies, "I can't believe it, everything is fine." But just to be safe, she drinks a lot of raspberry leaf tea because she's heard it tones the uterus.

Older parents are more aware of their own mortality. Dreams of seeing our children marry or of holding our own grandchildren are well-padded with "maybes" and "if onlys." Time has sped up for us and we have a different sense of the importance of things. As I was writing this book, a 63-year-old woman, who lied about her age to become part of a donor-egg program, gave birth to a child, setting off a debate about the ethics and gender inequities of late parenthood. For the time being, it seems, older mothers and fathers are with us to stay.

As older parents we've had fewer children (a point I'll talk about more in the next chapter) and more time to become "set in our ways," a phrase I grew up hearing used to describe maiden aunts, but which fits many elegant condo-dwellers with short tempers and oriental rugs. We have gotten used to our lives being more or less under our control, and when children come along, we see no reason to start living otherwise.

It's easy to see how this desire for control can make us turn to books and classes. They dangle before us the promise of what our friend John Keenan, the father of two young sons and husband to Eleanore, calls "optimal childrearing"—the way we would raise kids if we had a "support staff" to help us, a sort of "childrearing enterprise." We were graced with easy childhoods; now we'd like perfect parenthoods, too.

The Loneliness of the Long-Distance Parent

But no matter how much we perfect our own parenting, we do it more in isolation than most parents who've come before us. In *The Future of Motherhood*, sociologist Jessie Bernard analyzes childrearing in many other cultures and concludes that the isolation of the American mother is unique. I think our loneliness accounts for some of our frantic search for advice. We are a mobile society. Many of us live in suburbs where we never walk and barely know our neighbors. The easy ways of finding answers to childrearing questions have evaporated. And so the hard ones have come to take their place.

We are more likely to be divorced, more likely to worry about job security, and then there is the general stress of making it in a world that requires more and more money to pay for the basic necessities (and one in which the basic necessities are forever expanding). The world we are living in seems to reinvent itself every few years, and we turn to experts to make sense of it.

Seventy-five percent of mothers work outside the home, and almost all fathers do. Many children are in daycare, which is, by necessity, more organized than a family home. We participate less in the daily grind of childrearing, but that doesn't mean we think less about it. In fact, it sometimes seems as if we're trying to make up for our absence by thinking about our children all the time.

Working affects us in other ways, too. We live in a world where the two-week vacation seems quaint, and people take their relaxation on the run in three- or four-day increments. Fast foods are dietary staples.

Accustomed to solving problems in an office setting, we attack childrearing in much the same way—with reports and deadlines and projected goals. (And in fact, a parent seeking outside advice on how to raise children is not unlike a C.E.O. who brings in outside consultants to reorganize his ailing corporation.) It's easy to say that working parents read childrearing books to make up for the hands-on learning they miss by not being home with their children full time. But I think there's a deeper explanation, a confidence shortfall, an intuition deficit.

We have few opportunities to obtain information naturally from each other, to seek what Susan Ginsberg, who publishes the "Work and Family Life" newsletter for working parents, calls "parkbench reassurance." Our need to recapture some of this closeness, the "kaffee klatch" connectiveness our mothers or grandmothers had, drives us to books and magazine articles, which, with their reader panels and suggestion pages, try to recapture a sense of belonging. This longing also propels us into news groups on the Internet. We want reassurance that we aren't the only ones whose six-year-old can't tie his shoes.

Chris Anderson, whose two daughters are nine and twelve, says it's lack of time that keeps us apart from each other and devoted to the books. "You can read a book or a magazine article quickly, but if you don't have time you can't do the work of chatting with people."

When we do gather to discuss childrearing, it's often in an organized class or support group, where we don't bat around ideas as much as rationalize and intellectualize. Phrases like "logical consequences" trip lightly off our tongues. We're far more likely to ask, "What have you read about nightmares?" than "What do you do when your child has one?"

Every parenting class I've attended has this in common: Parents want to meet each other, they want to connect. And more than a few parents have told me that it's finding others in their predicament—or worse—that makes the classes addictive. But what we find in them is only the thin veneer of camaraderie. The confessions of the parenting class are like the intimacies of the shared plane seat. We spill our souls because we know we'll never see these people again. What we don't have is what we sorely need: parents with whom we can share deeply the joys and questions of raising little people. Perhaps because we're so reluctant to seek advice from our families, good friends are especially important to us. And yet they seem ever more difficult to maintain. In addition to the time dearth that threatens so many parents' sanity, there is also the working versus non-working chasm that divides us. It's not always easy to stay close to pre-baby friends, especially if you take different approaches to parenthood.

I had a conversation recently with a mother of one of our children's friends. We were talking about our kids' bouts with a nasty stomach virus. "It really is so hard on the little guys," she said. And I agreed with her. Of course it is hard to see our children sick, even when we know they will get better soon. I did not say, "And God! Can you believe the laundry? I did five loads before noon." This comment was on the tip of my tongue, but I didn't say it. I didn't feel I knew this woman well enough. What would she think of me—that I cared more about my time than my children? Parents talk to each other now in sound bites that seem lifted from the pages of parenting magazines. Our performance anxiety drives us away from each other, and we are not only reluctant to share our frustrations but even our joys. Perhaps because we don't know each other as well as we'd like, we hesitate to simply marvel together over the random and wonderful ways our children touch us.

As I wrote this book, I was able to talk with parents on a deeper level than the usual chats in the preschool parking lot. One mother told me she was still surprised by the times she felt pride in her children. "My daughter started swim team this year. She's on the underdog team, but she doesn't care. She's not one of the fast swimmers. But she wanted to do the intramural trials with the fast people. When we were at the swim meet, I had butterflies in my stomach. But the pressure didn't faze her at all. She got in the lane and did her thing. I was so proud."

Chris Anderson told me how amused and touched she was when her daughter Liz, then in third grade, said to her, " 'Mom, I'm so glad you're not one of the beautiful moms.' I said, 'What's a beautiful mom?' She said, 'You know, one of those moms whose hair is all perfect and makeup all perfect. I don't like them. I like moms like you.' That was the best compliment."

But I heard these stories, and many more, because I solicited them. It's harder to come across them in the course of daily life. "One of the things I'm always struck with as a parent and as a professional is, 'Who can you really tell about your parenting?' " says psychologist Maggie Mulqueen. "It's a very hard thing to be honest about." When she went to a parenting workshop once, for instance, she found that "I was revealing six levels down from what anybody else in the group was, so I just shut down." To work her way around this, she started her own support group, which she calls Just Son(s). She and other mothers of boys can talk about the unique pleasures of sons, such as knowing the name of every truck in existence. "There's been a level of honesty with the women in this group that I don't have with people I know much better," she says.

Lifelong Learners

Another reason we think so much is our respect for education. For many of us, a college degree was the way from the middle class to the professional class. Though we consider ourselves iconoclasts, we have always sought gurus and mentors. We respect learning, we crave credentials. So when it came time for us to raise our well-considered children, we wouldn't think of doing it without consulting people with letters after their names. Judy Tyrer, a parent I met through an Internet news group about parenting books, says she read more when her two children were younger because "I was new to the job and that's how I approach everything in life. I read all I can about it, talk to professionals and friends, and then figure it out for myself. I guess I don't view parenting as any different."

Our love affair with education explains why the women in the study I mentioned in Chapter One turned more to books for information on pregnancy, labor, and motherhood, than they turned to their friends, mothers, husbands, or doctors. When we need answers about our children we dip into the well of psychological research and scientifically calibrated timetables. Unlike raising our children on instinct, rearing them on science requires continual retooling. The truths of psychology are not eternal. They change according to fashion. Educating ourselves as parents, then, becomes a lifelong occupation.

My friend Rita has not yet had her first child and she's already a graduate of several parenting classes. First, she and her husband, Mike, took childbirth classes. From those they graduated to a childcare class. Then, six weeks *before* her baby was due, Rita attended a breast-feeding class. I was curious how this could possibly work. Breast-feeding without a baby? Rita said that the lactation consultant (that term alone speaks worlds about what has happened to childrearing) used videos and dolls to give mothers-to-be an idea of what will happen when they nurse their real babies.

"It always seemed to me that the baby knew just what to do. Infants have an instinct to suck, you know," I reassured Rita. She laughed. On one level, she knows this is all crazy. "Oh, that's just the opposite of what the lactation consultant told us. She said babies don't always know what to do, so we have to show them." Of course, if babies knew what to do, then we wouldn't need lactation consultants.

When our need to know bumps up against the trickier problems of later childhood, then we really seek out expert advice. I'm thinking about a woman who seldom read a parenting book and was content to raise her children much as she was raised. Then her son entered school, had trouble concentrating, and began exhibiting other signs of attention deficit disorder. Everywhere she turned for help, though, someone had a different theory about what her son needed. Their difference of opinion drove her to books. Now she's reading up on ADD and ADHD, so she can come to her own conclusions about what her son needs and become her own expert, so to speak.

She is part of a nationwide trend toward self-help that prompts the pharmaceutical industry to advertise prescription drugs directly to patients and that prompts one million visits a day to the popular Medline Web site. We think our doctors aren't looking after us, and so we must look after ourselves. Do parents feel similarly bewildered? Saturated in expert advice but without the family physician or even meddling relatives to keep us grounded, we are often the only advocates our child has. Parents have to understand more now because there is more to understand. Even if all we understand is what to avoid. And this brings me back to metaparenting and the big-dealness of raising children today. Every decision is laden with significance. With all the research out there telling us how to grow good children, there's no excuse for us not to. So of course, we worry about our performance.

Meeting of the Minds

Twice this year, I invited grandmothers and mothers together to talk about how raising children has changed in a generation.

"It seems that our children were calmer and easier to control than the children I see now," said Wanna Hinchee, who raised her four daughters in the 1960s. "Maybe there's something in the food today. I don't believe our four two-year-olds ever had the kind of tantrums that I have seen in some of my two-year-old grandchildren."

"I must have been spanked," said Wanna's youngest daughter, Donna Konigsberg, the mother of three. "But I don't remember it. I remember a look, and my father can still give it. If you got that look across the dinner table, you stopped whatever you were doing. That look had to have been backed up by something, though."

"It hurts when somebody you love looks disgustedly at you," Wanna replied.

But Donna is still perplexed. "You never raised your voice with us, Mom."

"Oh, sure, I did," Wanna disagreed.

The comments ranged from the difference between washing diapers and using disposables to today's highly competitive sports programs for kids. More fascinating than the remarks was the difference in demeanor: The older women were calmer and more sure of themselves than the younger ones. Maybe this is because they're removed from the daily grind; their children are grown. But I doubt we will be this placid when our children are adults. I can see us now, shoving articles in front of their faces. "It says here that you're supposed to hold babies more than you're doing," we'll insist.

The more we turn childrearing into a course of study, the less likely we'll act on any instinctive notions we might have imbibed from our own upbringing. The techniques we learn are like the rooms in a brand-new but not particularly well-built house. They are clean, they are big, they have lots of light. When you walk into one you know you'll get a fresh start there.

Compare the new house with the house of advice we inherit from our parents and grandparents, the little things and big things that went into making us who we are. These rooms have been lived in for years. There are cobwebs in the closets and mildew in the basement and a thousand mingled smells in the kitchen. But the walls are solid, the foundation is strong, and there are treasures in the attic.

Some of us have no house to go back to. There are bad parents in every generation. But it seems strange that there were so many bad ones in our parents' generation. Might it be those high expectations again, rearing their ugly heads? Many people I've talked with say they read books because their parents provided no "model" for them to emulate. Experts I interview tell me that parents should avoid behaving as their parents did because to do so means they are on automatic pilot. But it's advice like this that's driving us crazy. At some point, it seems, we have to ask ourselves whether we like ourselves enough, approve of our basic principles and values, to replicate them in our children.

Talk to yesterday's parents, our parents, and what comes through is the relative ease of their childrearing. Of course they had problems, but they didn't make as much fuss about the normal ups and downs as we do. They read Spock, and maybe an occasional magazine article, but that was all. They didn't take classes, but they did talk more to their families and neighbors. Sometimes I imagine what it was like when our mothers and fathers met and married and started their lives together. My mother tells me it was something that happened quite naturally with her and her friends. Many of them left their parents' houses for that first small apartment they rented with their husbands. They may have finished college, though many did not. Some worked for a year or two before they married, but most had no long-term career goals in mind. Without the pill the babies came quickly. Yes, there was an inevitability about this, and inevitability can be stultifying. But I wish I had some of their nonchalance.

You might say it was easier because they didn't understand

the full impact of what they were doing, or because the world was a simpler place. You'd be right both times. But maybe it's okay to understand a little less, if we think a little more clearly.

I read a story recently in a newsletter for parents. It's about why it's silly for us to do things the way we were brought up to do them. I'd read this story before, though I couldn't remember where. Maybe it's the parenting equivalent of an urban legend. Anyway, it goes something like this: A young mother prepares a ham. Without thinking, she cuts it in half. That is the way it has always been done in her family. One day she wonders about this practice. So she asks her mother, "Why do we always cut the ham in half?" And her mother says, "I don't know. We've always done it that way. Ask your grandmother." So the young woman asks her grandmother, "Why do we always cut the ham in half?" And her grandmother says, "I don't know. We've always done it that way. Ask your great-grandmother." So the young woman asks her great-grandmother (conveniently, this is a long-lived family), "Why do we always cut the ham in half?" The old woman chuckles, glad that someone has finally asked her: "That's because when my mother first married, her oven wasn't big enough to hold a whole ham, so she cut it in half to fit it in," she says. The moral of the story, of course, is that we have outgrown the old ways. We have a large oven that can hold a whole ham. We have a modern child who requires Other People's Ideas to be properly raised.

Of course, we cannot remain mired in the past. There is always room for improvement. But childrearing is not a science, it is an art. And in art, we use the part of us that is closest to the bone, the creative part that was laid down years ago when we were young. If you think enough about why we think too much you may decide it's because we've thrown out much of who we are and replaced it with the ideas of strangers. I hope this reflects more on what we're turning toward, on the allure of scientific explanations, than what we're turning from, our own past and heritage. But I do think that as long as we're growing along with our children, we might want to consider why we've rejected the practices buried deep within us.

"In most societies in world history, the meaning of one's life has derived to a large degree from one's relationship to the lives of one's parents and one's children," says sociologist Robert Bellah. "Tocqueville said that Americans would come to forget their ancestors and their descendants, and for many that would seem to be the case."[30]

Realize, though, that we pass judgment on our upbringing based on today's expectations. Conditions that may have been fine when we were living through them don't seem as healthy when viewed under the close scrutiny of a heavily psychologized world view. Those of us who have "forgiven" our parents feel they did the best they could given their "ignorance." If we haven't forgiven them, we are cut off from our own past. A generation from now our children may put our efforts under the same intense scrutiny, only with a different microscope.

Conscientious parents always try to fill in the gaps in their own upbringing. But we've taken that impulse many steps further. Pushed by the advice industry, we're now encouraged to throw out the baby with the bathwater, to discard the ideas that are longest held and most dear. The irony is that we who so value our own growth as human beings are losing out on the best chance we might have for a deeply felt life. Being truly open to our children is being able to see them—and ourselves—without the blinders of other people's assumptions. But this can only happen when we're raising our children sincerely. What the books and classes urge us to become, what history and demographics have poised us to be, is parents programmed by others. But if we really want to be the *best* parents we can be, then we have to be the kind of parents *only* we can be.

One of the turning points of childrearing for me was working in the cooperative nursery school our daughters attended. As I would help children glue cotton balls on Popsicle sticks or paint egg cartons, I would notice each child's little clipped nails or double-knotted shoelaces. Some children were more tidy than others, of course. There was always the one with sagging socks and paint on her sleeves. But noticing these details made me think of the parents clipping the nails and tying the shoes, pulling up the socks and scrubbing the paint out of the sleeves, and I began to see that each of these children was loved as much as our children were. They were just as precious to their parents as our girls are to us. It's not that I didn't know this before, but once I knew it down deep, I felt even more respect for individual parental effort—and even greater sadness at how much we devalue it.

More than anything else, our need for advice may be telling us how much we've lost our way. What can be more fundamental than teaching children how to live? Have we forgotten how, forgotten why? "As we get more and more advice we seem less and less sure of what we ought to do for our children," said historian John Sommerville. "One of the most surprising things about us to anyone visiting from the past would be how unsure we are about what to pass on to our children."[31]

Some say that our childrearing, like our faith, has lost its center, the sense of moral purpose that used to infuse it. Perhaps our uncertainty as parents, our need for help, is proof we're living through a great tectonic shift. The old truths, the ones that bound us together, have fallen apart. And no new ones are in sight. In the meantime, though, we have children to raise. How will we do it? How much thinking, how much feeling, how much laughing and crying does it take to do it right? No one can know. But we can realize how much overthinking affects choices we make about our children's lives. I hope the next few chapters help you get started.

3

Attention Excess Disorder

The Malady of the Decade, and What It Means for You

"As our baby grows more into her own life,
so I recover mine,
but it is an ambiguous blessing."
—*Louise Erdrich*

It took a case of laryngitis to diagnose our kids with the condition I've named attention excess disorder. The laryngitis was mine. The attention excess disorder was theirs. This is not attention deficit disorder, mind you. Our children have no trouble paying attention. And they certainly have no trouble getting it. But they do have trouble relinquishing it. With all due respect to youngsters who suffer from attention deficit disorder, I think attention excess disorder is more of a problem for kids, parents, and society.

Our children's attention excess disorder (AED) was present for years, but it took me a while to put my finger on it. AED is more subtle—and more prevalent—than spoiling. Kids who have AED don't necessarily talk back, demand expensive presents, or pitch fits when they don't get their way. But they do require large doses of parental attentiveness. "Look at me, Mommy." "Can you play Candyland, Daddy?" "I want more juice." It's not one request but scores a day. Children have always sought their parents' attention. But never before have they snagged so much of it.

We are parents who think too much. And because we think too much, we offer choices, stimulate cognitive growth, assess feelings, and encourage conversation. This requires that we pay plenty of attention to our children, that we build our lives around their needs. We do this in several ways. For example, we insinuate ourselves into their play. And because parental attentiveness is quite habit-forming, our kids quickly think we're supposed to be part of their games. So we become their hostages. We are afraid to leave them alone because we might hurt their feelings, stunt their development, or turn them against us. After five or six years of this, we feel we can no longer entertain our kids properly, so we sign them up for art lessons and martial arts classes, soccer, and ballet. Birthday parties are major events, held at indoor playgrounds or kiddie pizza parlors we reserve months in advance. In our area, parents worried that their child doesn't have enough friends can turn to an outfit called Playgroup Connections, which "finds playmates for you and your kids"—for $35 per child. We may be at the endpoint of a trend that's been developing for centuries. "For the past 400 years children have enjoyed or endured increasing adult attention," says historian John Sommerville. The title of his book, *The Rise and Fall of Childhood,* suggests this is not necessarily a positive development. Modern children are high-maintenance. They want you to know they are here.

Diagnosing AED

I began to isolate AED in our daughters the first day I couldn't speak. Suddenly I couldn't provide them with the constant verbal encouragement they had come to need. One of them sulked, the other screamed, the youngest held up her arms and cried. Each in her own way proved that without a steady stream of prattle about what a good job she's doing or what she'd like to do next, she's bereft.

We didn't mean for this to happen. My husband and I have

been careful not to shower our kids with every material advantage. But, like many parents we know, we have tried to give them every psychological advantage. Somewhere along the way I decided that mind reader and mother were interchangeable, and I tried to figure out what our daughters needed even before they did. You have to pay a lot of attention to kids to figure out what they're thinking, so they began to assume I would always be theirs for the taking. They didn't grow horns or donkey ears, but they did begin to interrupt adult conversations, ask a steady stream of questions, and interfere with anything else that came between them and my undivided attention. This is how I feel on bad days, of course. But even on good days, I know that our children, though kind and sweet, have quite a craving for parental feedback.

I can't tell you what a relief it was to diagnose AED. Even though our girls are not yet cured, at least we've defined what ails them. And they do have an advantage over many of their peers: With three children, we haven't as much attention to go around, so our daughters must content themselves with whatever we can give them. We still notice them mightily, but at least we don't continually solicit their opinions or end every day by getting down on the floor and playing with them, a practice recommended by some experts. Instead, we encourage them to help us out with dinner preparations. Suzanne sets the table, Claire chops the vegetables, I cook, and Celia, the youngest, unloads the dishwasher (which means stacking all the clean plates on the not-so-clean floor). I know that kitchen chores are an "adult-led" rather than "child-led" activity, but since we are hungry, and since our kids will eventually become adults whereas I will never again be a child, I think this makes more sense.

Of course, it's crucial to talk with children, to read to them and sing to them, to spend quiet moments and funny moments and sad moments together, to understand and guide them, to help them become the best people they can be. But AED works against this. Parents who give too much attention become drained and resentful; they lose themselves and their vision.

They are not guiding their children but responding to one need after another. They are so caught up in the minutiae of their children's lives that they can't see the grand plan.

Their children are whiny, passive, self-centered, and cheerless. They aren't ill-behaved monsters; they more closely resemble unhappy little adults. This makes sense, because AED blurs the line between child and parent to the point where children are less kid-like and parents less parent-like (a phenomenon I'll talk about more in Chapter Eight). Unaccustomed to quiet reflection, children with AED can't play by themselves and must constantly be entertained with TV, computer games, imported friends, or the ever-attendant adult. Imaginary companions must be an endangered species these days, since kids seldom have the solitude they need to befriend them. Kids lack the privacy they need to dream and be. They are denied the delicious pastime of being left alone while a parent does grown-up things nearby. Can't you remember that experience as one of the coziest and happiest of your childhood, the feeling of being both apart and together? Well, our kids don't have many chances to feel it.

If not checked in early childhood, AED worsens. I'm thinking of a six-year-old boy I know, a charming little guy I've watched grow up. But the last few times I've seen him he hasn't let his mother speak more than a few sentences before he interrupts her with some important need of his own. Though never an endearing habit, interrupting grown-ups is particularly unattractive in older children.

School-aged youngsters with AED find that even a world bent on pumping up their self-esteem at every turn will not give them as much attention as their parents do. Many grow angry when they realize that attentiveness must be earned; that it is not a birthright. According to one survey conducted a few years ago, parents and teachers reported that children were far more likely to destroy things belonging to others, do poorly on schoolwork, be whining, sullen, stubborn, and irritable than they used to be.[1] Older children with AED up the ante with which they attract their parents' notice. Seldom a year passes that our quiet suburb isn't plagued by mailbox bashing, petty theft, and other crimes committed by teenage vandals. Gang activity is now a problem even in upper middle-class neighborhoods. Social scientists have many theories on what ails our young people, but perhaps they ought to consider another— AED.

Of course, most experts think parents give their children too little attention, not too much. Their solution: Spend more quality time with your kids. If your child acts up, she probably just isn't getting enough "positive" attention and so has to get some "negative" attention instead. (Are you guilty yet?) When experts say attention they mean time and notice, special trips to the mall together, or cozy breakfasts for two. They don't mean the time and energy it takes to wean a child from your constant regard. No wonder AED is a virtual epidemic. Children may need more from us—more confidence and more vision—but in the anxious, affluent families I know, they don't need more attention.

Our "Problem That Has No Name"

Everywhere I go I hear parents talking about AED. They may not use the words or the acronym, but that's what they're talking about. A couple days ago I overheard a mother waiting to pick up her daughter at ballet. "You know, I just don't have time for anything anymore. I don't read, I don't knit. I just fall asleep at the end of the day." She said these words proudly, almost boastfully. Almost no one I know with young children can have an uninterrupted phone call. Weekends are devoted to kids' activities. Houses overflow with children's toys. Appointment books are filled with children's play dates.

A generation ago, Betty Friedan said that the "feminine mystique" was our mothers' "problem that has no name." I think our impulse to cater continually to our children is our "problem that has no name." It makes slaves of stay-at-home mothers and fathers and riddles working parents with guilt. Partly to resolve this guilt, but mostly because they feel it is in the best interest of their children, working parents choose daycare settings with good ratios and attentive caregivers who will ensure their child develops properly. When they take their children home at the end of the day, they spend every minute they can with them, often letting them stay up until the wee hours. These children seldom see adults do anything but feed, clean, and entertain them.

In the *Parents' Journal Guide to Raising Great Kids,* Bobbi Conner praises the creative way that a single working mother devised to spend more time with her two young children: She found a live-in college student who could do 15 hours of work around the house each week in exchange for free room and board. That way, the mother could give her kids "her undivided attention, reading books, playing, and chatting while her student-helper handled the household chores."

Some people argue that the problem with the two-career family is anything but an attention excess. They would say it's just the opposite: These kids suffer from an attention deficit. Not for a moment do I want to downplay the price of our work and our exhaustion. I know firsthand the toll it takes on families. And yet, AED is not just a function of time but of attitude. We don't have to spend lots of hours with children to give them AED. But if we spend most nonworking hours attending to them and if we feel guilty "wasting" our time together disciplining them, then it's likely they will develop the condition.

As prone to attention excess disorder as this makes children of dual-career couples, I've found that children of stay-at-home parents are even more prone to the malady. Women who leave paid employment for full-time mothering are full of energy and accustomed to the challenges of the work world. Highly motivated, conscientious, and eager to justify their decision to stay home, they make child-tending, which used to be done along with other household tasks, a job in itself. "Rachel has every moment of my attention. Sometimes I think she has too much of my attention, to the detriment of learning to entertain herself. But I'm here for her right now. The preschool years are very limited, and I can do housework another time," says Sue

Brickman, who stays home with her school-age son and pre-school-age daughter.

For some families, bucking the scheduled, harried world of two-career coupledom requires significant belt-tightening: They may live in small townhouses or apartments, forgo second cars, and other supposed suburban necessities. They're certainly devoted to their cause, and I applaud them for living out their convictions. But their sacrifice has intensified their attentiveness. They spend even more time nursing, enriching, and stimulating their children. They offer themselves to their children like a gift. It's the idea of professional parenthood, which I mentioned in Chapter One. And indeed, in almost every way except recompense, these parents are professionals. They read books and articles, belong to societies, keep up on the latest trends, and think of their work as a calling. I once heard a woman lament that she couldn't get a degree in parenting. It's probably just a matter of time.

The professional parents' heroes are people like Robert Reich, who cited a desire for more family time as a reason for resigning as secretary of labor, or Brenda Barnes, the former president and CEO of Pepsi-Cola North America. After 22 years working her way up the corporate ladder of PepsiCo, Barnes garnered much media attention when, after only 18 months at the helm of the company, she resigned to spend more time with her three children.

The All-Consuming Pregnancy

A child is born, and at the instant of his birth, he is, though himself, no more or less unique than any other human being born on this planet since the beginning of time. But there the similarities end. Because he is born in 1998 or 1999 means he has a far better chance of survival. He's no longer shipped off to live with a wet nurse and is less likely to be left to die because his parents cannot take care of him. Perhaps we parents have a worry gene, though, and deprived of that one overwhelming concern—whether our child will live or die—we now fret about whether we're holding him too much or too little or if we should diaper him with cloth or disposables. One thing we *should* worry about but *don't* is his likelihood of contracting AED.

Babies are not born with attention excess disorder. We give it to them. The seeds of AED are planted in our culture, in books and magazine articles, in our determination to do things differently from our own parents, in what we expect of ourselves. First of all, there is the big dealness of parenthood. Even if we'd done nothing else differently, our intense self-consciousness alone has radically changed what it means to rear a child.

And then there is the disappointment many of us feel about our own upbringing. We believe our parents overlooked our feelings; in particular, we were not allowed to be angry. We are eager to make up for this by letting our children express their emotions to the fullest. But we worry so much about the emotions they're expressing (Do they like us? Are we good enough parents?) that we are unable (once again and for different reasons) to carry out our first and perhaps best thoughts.

The same impulse that makes it difficult to discipline our children, the thought of wounding them beyond measure, pushes us to pay close attention to their emotional lives. We believe that children raised with loving, thinking, attentive parents will be golden girls and boys, fairly glimmering with the reflected radiance of our glow. Since nature abhors not only a vacuum but also a perfect child, it has a consequence for our action. Even if we do everything else right, our kids can still have AED. It's our very earnestness that has given it to them.

AED begins before the beginning. Even conception has become an event. I can't count the number of couples who've told us when they started "trying" to have a child. This puts friends in an awkward position. How do you greet them next time you meet? Do you ask for a progress report? Or pretend that you never heard such an intimate statement of intent? Older parents-to-be are more prone to fertility problems, which practically guarantee overattentiveness from the very beginning— that is, if the whole grueling process leads to a baby. On the other hand, fertile parents with reliable birth control can often decide when their child will be born. And this, too, requires more thinking. After all, family planning is just that, planning to have a family. And planning means paying attention.

Once a baby is on the way, there are countless opportunities to dote on it in utero. There are the plethora of pregnancy books, of course, and the childbirth classes. Now instead of going once a week you can indulge in a "Lamaze Weekend Getaway." Held at bed-and-breakfast inns or other relaxing spots, these gestational retreats combine the information of childbirth classes with gourmet dining. They give couples, in the words of one instructor, "the opportunity to focus on what is most poignant in their lives right now—which is having this baby. . . ."

Let us not overlook technology's contribution to AED. Parents-to-be can listen to the fetal heartbeat through Doppler stethoscope. If the heartbeat is inaudible when the doctor thinks it should be heard, the mother may be sent for a sonogram, "just to be sure." Sometimes this concern is warranted. Often it is not, and she and her husband will have worried in vain. They may as well get in the habit, I suppose. Many mothers have routine ultrasounds during their pregnancy, so that baby's first snapshot is often that distinctively blurry black-and-white one. Sometimes these early photos bring bad news. One woman, a newspaper reporter, was told her baby had a club foot. After consulting several experts and having the diagnosis reconfirmed, she and her husband began contacting specialists, organizations, and parents of children with club feet. After months of planning and adjusting to the fact that their baby would be born with this disability, he was born just fine—with no club foot.[2] Women have always worried about their babies while they were pregnant, but now we have the information to obsess beyond our wildest dreams.

Fetal well-being is monitored closely with tests ranging from maternal serum alpha fetoprotein testing (AFP) to amniocentesis. Because of these tests, women postpone announcing their pregnancy, agonize whether to keep or abort a "problem" fetus, and think of themselves as baby vessels rather than mothers-to-be, says Barbara Katz Rothman in her book *The Tentative Pregnancy*. Rothman points out that even when amnio news is good, the 80 to 90 percent of women who learn their baby's sex relate differently to their "fetal sons and daughters" than they would had the sex remained a mystery. Parents may name the child, buy a layette in appropriate colors, and decorate the nursery. With a name, a gender, a wardrobe, and a decor, the baby becomes a more knowable creature. I've seen Christmas cards signed in the name of an unborn child. This folderol may not change the way babies actually come into this world, but it certainly changes the way we think about them when they do. We're already worn out with worry and consideration.

Infant Stim

Once a child is born, AED begins in earnest. Not because we can expend too much attention on a newborn. It's difficult, if not impossible, for infants to develop AED in their first few months or so of life. I believe, as do many experts who have observed infant behavior, that nature gives parents a grace period. In the first few months of life, babies thrive if you feed them, change them, and hold them. For one brief, shining moment, what babies want is what babies need.

But what is happening to parents during these first few months of baby's life? What expectations are we developing? If we're reading, watching, or listening—if we're living without blinders on—then we're developing an attitude of hypervigilance about our child's emotional state and learning we must constantly squelch our needs for hers. The habits we learn in our early days of parenthood are deep ones, unlodged with great effort. When our literature, our technology, our very culture conspire to convince us that children require our constant care, it is difficult to believe anything else.

For instance, almost every decision we make about our infants is analyzed and counteranalyzed. Deciding whether to circumcise a boy baby, which was formerly determined by religious custom or force of habit, is now a highly charged, information-laden process that involves poring over books, getting several medical opinions, and perhaps even conducting an Internet search. Three times we deliberated about circumcision—I once stumbled upon a heated Web chat on the subject that had been going on for months—and each time we didn't need to because we had a girl! It's not that we should passively accept every practice and tradition without question, but we exhaust ourselves early on with our deliberations. Of course, it's hard not to. As book titles such as *Bottlefeeding Without Guilt* suggest, many of us believe that every childrearing decision we make is fraught with powerful and long-lasting implications. And this, again, makes us excessively attentive.

It's hard to nurture the kind of quiet communion that allows us to get to know our child when we begin our lives as parents believing that every minute must count, that we must stimulate our baby constantly. We're forever waving a black-and-white rattle in front of the poor thing or taking him to an exercise class, and then wondering why he falls apart at the end of the day. It takes us a while to figure out that we've overstimulated him, that he, like us, needs downtime. Over and over again mothers and fathers told me that it was when they slowed down and began to notice what their babies needed and give it to them— maybe it was a few minutes alone and quiet together at the end of the day—that they could begin to enjoy them.

Even something as simple as a baby monitor has made a difference in the way we rear children. I'm not talking about video monitors or the apnea monitor for babies deemed at risk for sudden infant death syndrome. I mean the plain old baby monitors that you get as a shower gift or as a hand-me-down from your friend. Here's an invention that suits our big houses and cellular phone mentalities. It's a convenience, but also a terror—as any parent who's ever listened to a newborn snorting through one can attest. You run to the room convinced that something is terribly wrong only to find your baby sleeping peacefully. A baby monitor means we know the instant baby wakes up from a nap. If we're not careful, we'll get him up before he's had a chance to lie there and play with his crib toys, which is good practice for him to learn to play—and be—on his own. Some parents with reluctant sleepers reverse their baby monitors. They put the "recording" part where they are and the "listening" part where baby is. That way, baby can hear their voices and drift off to sleep knowing they're nearby. Children, it's eight o'clock. Do you know where your parents are? Of course. They're only a monitor away. Talk about constant availability.

Think of how much the average middle-class child is videotaped. Palm-held video cameras let us record the infant's arrival (hopefully from a discreet viewpoint) and her every waking minute. Some enthusiastic parents even record the nonwaking minutes. I can still remember the pride with which we showed Suzanne's first video. In one of the more infamous scenes, she is waving her little arms and doing absolutely nothing else for five very long minutes while a National Public Radio announcer intones in the background, "Emperor Hirohito is dead" and gives a brief history of modern Japan. It was a perfect testimonial to parental excess. Even the grandparents snoozed on that one!

Perhaps to compete with video, baby books have also changed: "Mothers used to be able to get away with writing a few lines about baby's earliest months, pasting in a few snapshots, and letting it go at that. No more. Today's baby books range from fill-in-the-blanks simplicity to excruciatingly detailed accounts of everything from the 'state of the nation' at the time of baby's arrival to what provisions Mom and Dad have made for 'baby's nest egg.' One memory book asks parents to confront Junior with such questions as 'If I could change the world . . .' and write down his answer for posterity (or future political campaigns)."[3]

If They Call Us, We Will Come

Keep in mind that this early attention, the craziness of our first few months as parents, may *still* not be affecting baby. But it will soon. Because of psychological theories, especially the theory of attachment, which I'll discuss in a second, most books on infancy don't emphasize that by the second six months of life many babies cry out of frustration. They want to move around, but they can't yet. This is when many parents begin holding babies more than is good for them. Babies left to their own devices on the floor with a set of measuring spoons are far better off. You can find a brief discussion of this in *What to Expect the First Year* and a much more lengthy discussion in Burton White's *How to Raise a Happy, Unspoiled Baby.* (Some parents avoid Burton White because he has spoken out against spacing children less than three years apart and mothers of infants working outside the home. But on other topics and especially on the subject of AED, which he calls spoiling, he's well worth hearing out.)

I can hear the chorus of true disbelievers sputtering, in denial, "Of course babies cry for attention—and we ought to give it to them." But consider this: Babies are smart. They learn quickly that if they call us, we will come. But by the latter part of the first year, it's not good for them if we always come. Babies with an overdeveloped need for attention have less curiosity than they might have had they been allowed some frustration early on. It's a fact of human nature that children given everything when they want it will not learn how to get it by themselves. Of course we attend to babies' basic needs, and we spend time playing with them, too. But there comes a point—and most of us know when it is if we listen to our instincts—when they call us back because they want more attention than we think they need. We're afraid to acknowledge this, though, because we think it's anti-child to give babies less than our all.

Another place to spot early signs of AED is during what modern parents call the bedtime ritual. Children have always balked at ending their day's play, but never before have parents been so powerless in the face of their protests. At one point in my career, every other story I wrote seemed to be on children's sleep. The stories usually went something like this: Child won't sleep. Parents at wit's end. Here's what to do. It seemed to me then, and still does, that there's a story within a story here.

By the second six months of life, most babies are capable of sleeping through the night. But many of them do not, as the books and articles on kids' sleep make painfully clear. Putting babies to sleep at night is one of the first times in baby's young life when parents need to exert their authority. It's when we have to say, "Okay, Junior has had my attention all day. He's exhausted and I am, too. It's time for him to go to sleep." So there have emerged pediatric sleep specialists such as Dr. Richard Ferber, who gives parents the confidence to put their children to bed and let them cry for a while before checking on them. In his book *Solve Your Child's Sleep Problems,* Ferber explains how children's REM sleep differs from adults' and why it is that children who fall asleep with a bottle want you to feed them whenever they wake up during the night. He is careful to explain that his sleep strategies aren't for every child, but his practical suggestions and calming tone have enshrined him in the minds of exhausted parents everywhere. There's even a new verb in his honor: To "Ferberize" a baby means to put him to bed using this doctor's regimen. I don't want to downplay Ferber's contribution to pediatric sleep research, but I do want to point out that his method is a controlled version of letting babies cry themselves to sleep, something your mother or grandmother might have suggested you try. Your relatives, of course, lack the authority of a pediatric sleep specialist. It takes a credentialed expert to assure us that it's okay to do what we already know, deep down, is right.

As babies grow into toddlers, their bedtime rituals grow to gargantuan proportions: multiple readings of *Good Night Moon* or other current favorite, many cups of water, and saying goodnight to every stuffed animal in the room. Our children get so much of our attention right before bedtime that they are even more reluctant to leave us for sleep. It makes sense that mothers and fathers who pay nonstop attention to their kids during the day feel guilty if they don't do so at night. Some of them feel so strongly about nighttime nuturing that they turn their conjugal bed into a "family bed." By taking their children to sleep with them, there is literally never a minute when they aren't nearby. It sounds cozy on paper; so cozy, in fact, that one mother, upon reading a book called *The Family Bed,* decided to put the plan into action in her house—even though her child was eighteen months old at the time. The experiment was a disaster. The child was far too excited at the new arrangements to go to sleep. Finally, in desperation, the father moved into a separate bed so that at least one of the three would get some sleep. Co-sleeping lasted only a few weeks in this house.

AED Times Two

By the time a child is two, she has been stimulated and noticed right into a full-blown case of AED. She must be read to, sung to, and played with almost all the time. And then . . . she becomes a big sister. Parents read up on second-time parenthood with books such as *Your Second Child,* by Joan Solomon Weiss, looking, of course, for tips on how to give their undivided attention to *two* little people. They cart their firstborn to sibling preparation class and shower her with gifts. She gets a tour of the hospital, a T-shirt that reads "I'm the big sister," and lots of gifts. What might have been just a mild case of attention excess disorder before is now a roaring big out-of-control one.

For some parents, though, having the second child is a turning point. It's when the AED of the firstborn becomes painfully apparent. As you may remember from the first chapter, that's the way it was for Chris Anderson. "With the first child you can blow it and blow it and blow it and still delude yourself that you're not blowing it," she says. "You can say, 'Oh well, this child is so special.' You can rationalize ill-behaved children and put all your efforts into trying to fix your first child up. But when the second one comes around and you are frantically trying just to make it through the day, you don't have the luxury to do this anymore. You need the cooperation of the first child to make sure the family works. Then you look at this first child and think, 'You're a tyrant and I can't afford to continue making you one.' " Children with AED often seem like tyrants.

As for having more than two children, attention excess disorder has made that far less likely. It's difficult enough to give our undivided attention to two children; how will we do it with three or more? "The biggest issue with me is that I feel like I have to give my children tremendous amounts of time," says Monika Schiavo, a mother of a seven- and a four-year-old. "I look at people who don't feel that way and think they have a gift from God." But her belief in how much time each child requires has definitely influenced her family's size: "We're only going to have two kids because I can't handle more. I know I would go crazy with more because I want to do a certain kind of job with the two we have." It's an ironic side effect of modern parenting: by limiting our family to one or two children, we lose out on one of the best ways to become a confident parent—on-the-job training. If we had more children, we'd probably need fewer books. And if we read fewer books, we might have more kids. "A lot of the advice I've read is meant for families with one or two children," says Lucrecia Crimmins, a mother of three. Obviously the determinants of family size are many and various, but I'm convinced that AED is one of them.

As children get older and are in school all day, we cannot pay attention to them in the same ways that we did before. But we can bone up on their learning styles, volunteer in their schools, and "become their advocate"—that's a phrase I hear a lot these days.

It's no surprise that the parents who spend the most time on their children at home are the ones who spend the most time helping out at their schools. I know that in an era of downsizing, we need the help of concerned and dedicated parents for education to flourish. It's more a matter of what they're doing and how much. In the elementary school our children attend, some parent volunteers provide monthly art lessons to make up for a decline in arts funding in the district. They introduce kids to famous artists and their styles. But other parents work several hours weekly in the "publishing center," so that students can have their manuscripts typed and bound in "books." Now, I'm a writer and have a vested interest in publication, but it seems to me that grade-school kids don't need to be "published." It's proof, to me, of AED. And it's convinced children that writing a book is, as our second-grader sometimes reminds me as I write this one, "a cinch."

And what about the schools themselves? How can schools give kids the attention they're used to getting from their parents? How can they equal the adoring gaze of a mother or father, the mountains of books we read to and about them? How can anyone else ever compete with a professional parent who's bought into the idea of constant emotional availability?

Well, educators are trying. From grade school on, children are told that they are unique and special. They are pumped full of self-esteem. Frequent counselor visits to classrooms extend the therapeutic mentality from home to school. Taught from an early age to "sound out" words, students don't want to be confused with accurate spellings; they insist that their variations are just as valid. A study conducted a few years ago compared high-school students in Japan with those in the U.S. Although the U.S. teens scored lower than their Japanese counterparts in most subjects, they did score significantly higher in self-esteem.[4]

Many of the vans in our neighborhood boast stickers that read, "My child is an honor student at Anytown Elementary." Sixth-grade graduation is now a major event celebrated with numerous parties, plaques, and, at one school, a custom-designed video complete with the children's baby pictures. Some parents lament that cap and gown graduations from kindergarten begin a process that ends with $500 prom nights, complete with expensive gowns, limousines, and hotel rooms.

Even more telling is the burgeoning number of children in this country who are homeschooled, estimated at one-half to two-and-a-half million. (Reliable numbers are hard to come by.) Homeschoolers aren't all fundamentalist Christians. But they are True Believers in the parent-child bond. Surely there is something noble and very American about these can-do parents, who feel they can do a better job at home, freeing children of grades, peer pressure, and other hazards of standardized education. Parents who homeschool do so out of frustration with public education and a firm belief that there is a better way. But I think AED might be one reason why some mothers and fathers dedicate themselves not only to 18 or more years of childrearing but also to 12 years of teaching.

AED has infiltrated extracurricular activities, too. Scout troops have ratios of three or four children to each adult leader, and badges have become so much easier to snag that it seems to take longer for parents to sew them on than it does for children to earn them. A more telling example is a local soccer coach who recently filed suit in a county court alleging that league pressure to drop one of three eight-year-olds from his squad would cause that child "irreparable psychological harm." I wonder how our children will feel when they realize, years from now, that they've been cheated out of having almost any childhood experience by themselves?

What all these developments say to me is that once we start on the road to overattentiveness, it's difficult to turn back. Our institutions collaborate to keep the attention coming. And so do other well-read parents. I'm remembering a conversation I had recently with a friend, a bright woman who works part-time, has many volunteer projects, is smart, funny, and kind. We were talking about how we show our kids we love them when she made what I consider the quintessential AED statement: "I always let my son know that his needs are more important than mine." When we always put our child's needs ahead of our own and everyone else's, our child becomes the family focal point. Our marriage, our own adult lives, all pale in comparison. If we do grow frustrated with our child's behavior and think about changing it, we're likely to pick up a book. And the book, in all likelihood, will tell us that we'll ruin our child if we don't continue to attend to his every need. Because we care so much, it's hard to let this message roll off our backs. Let's look deeper and see how this attitude came to be so firmly embedded in our childrearing psyche.

Freud, Fraiberg, and Feelings

Since Sigmund Freud has been blamed (and credited) for so much this century, let's look first to him. The psychoanalytic view of human nature that he proposed drew attention to the importance of early experiences. Harsh toilet training, for instance, could mark a child for life, making him obstinate and compulsive. A child needs to have his infant needs gratified, so once Freudian ideas came in, scheduled feedings and early toileting were out. More importantly, the light Freud shone on unconscious drives still drives us to pay constant attention to our children's emotional needs. It is in large part from psychoanalytic ideas that permissive childrearing sprang. And it's permissive childrearing that has led us to attention excess disorder. Even though the tide is turning a little and rules and limits are coming back into fashion, our philosophy is still to pay inordinate attention to our children.

Spock introduced psychoanalytic concepts in his first edition of *Baby and Child Care,* published in 1946. Demand feeding, lenient toilet training, and attentiveness to the child's budding psyche—it's concepts like these that made Spock the first apostle of permissiveness—even though one admirer said his Freudian ideas were "camouflaged in such a palatable form that they slide like soda pop down the most distrustful gullet." Although Spock recanted some of his permissive advice in later editions of his book, as I mentioned in the previous chapter, the children who were raised by his first edition were already preteens, and a revolution had begun.[5] If you read Dr. Spock's book now, you won't find it particularly child-oriented. But it was quite a departure from the parent-centered model put forth by child-care experts such as John Watson.

Spock was only the beginning, of course. Selma Fraiberg popularized Freud for parents in her 1958 classic, *The Magic Years,* and many other authors followed suit. By the 1960s, permissiveness had led to a children's rights movement. A. S. Neill wrote, in *Summerhill,* "Self-regulation means the right of a baby to live freely, without outside authority in things psychic and somatic. It means that the baby feeds when it is hungry; that it becomes clean in habits only when it wants to; that it is never stormed at or spanked; that it is always loved and protected. . . . The child should not do anything until he comes to the opinion—his own opinion—that it should be done."[6]

The 1970s brought a new twist on permissiveness. If we *really* care about our children we will allow them, indeed encourage them, to express their feelings. *All* their feelings. In the book *Liberated Parents, Liberated Children,* by Adele Faber and Elaine Mazlish, the authors tell the story of their five-year association with psychologist Dr. Haim Ginott and how his theories changed their families forever. "From the outset, Dr. Ginott was intent upon communicating to us the importance of accepting children's feelings. In a variety of ways he would reiterate his convictions. All feelings are permitted, actions are limited. One must not deny a child's perceptions. Only after a child feels right, can he think right." After a few months in Ginott's class, Faber and Mazlish say, "My children's feelings had become as real to me as apples, pears, chairs, or any other physical objects. I could no more ignore what the children felt than I could ignore a barricade in the middle of the road."[7]

This obsession with feelings seemed to have no limits. By the 1980s, infant psychiatrists were telling us how to decode neonatal emotions and "woo" our babies. This notion even had other psychologists up in arms. "The danger is that the infant psychiatrists tend to pressure mothers to be constantly on the alert for any sign that they or their babies are deviating from the prescribed ideal," wrote psychiatrist Stella Chess in 1987.[8]

Among parents I know, children's feelings are paramount. Heaven help us if we gush, "*I'm* proud of you," rather than "*You* must be proud of *yourself.*" The former is forbidden because it focuses attention on us; the latter is approved because it focuses attention back on our kids and their feelings. "I do not praise in the way that many parents do, so that Dylan does not become accustomed to doing things to please me," says Diane Lin, the mother of a six-year-old. "I definitely believe that taking pride in one's accomplishments and having those accomplishments recognized in a 'non-gushy' way aids in the development of a child's self-esteem."

"Let your feelings out. Let them show," croons a character in the PBS children's show *The Puzzle Place.* And then there is the "empathy doll" I saw advertised at a child development conference. Turn the doll's head to change the doll's "feelings" from happiness to sadness to anger to fear. "The purpose of these unique toys is to support the healthy emotional development of small children," read the accompanying brochure.

This focus on feelings is so much a part of our daily habits that we don't even notice it anymore. Yet it affects the way we feed, dress, and talk with our children. We let them pick out their own clothes—even if they're inappropriate—and choose their own breakfast cereals—even if they're sugary. It has also made a tremendous difference in the way we toilet train kids. An activity that used to be completed by the second birthday is often not even begun by then. Listen to parents talk about toilet training their child, and you'll usually hear them say, "He isn't ready." They are so afraid of disrupting their child's developmental timetable and asserting their rights in the matter that they plead lack of readiness and put it off. I can understand postponing this job—I have a two-year-old in diapers right now. (My excuses are that I'm writing a book and it's not summer.) But I admit that *I'm* the one who's not "ready."

A few years ago, I wrote a story on when and how to toilet train a child. In the course of my research, I interviewed several experts, two of whom told me they thought the pendulum had swung too far. "What about parental readiness," they said, "doesn't that count? Parents need to put their own needs back into the picture, too." Delighted to find a fresh angle to a story that doesn't have a lot of angles, I gladly included the comments of these two well-respected doctors in my story. But when the published article appeared, their comments were gone. Articles are often trimmed to fit the space they're allotted, but I found it unsettling that this crucial advice was omitted from the final story. Was it because the editors lacked room for this digression? Or because they didn't want to put undue pressure on parents? After all, saying that toileting will work "when the child is ready," makes it sound incredibly easy, as if one day your three- (or four-) year-old will stroll out and say, "Mom, I've been meaning to tell you. I'm done with diapers. From now on, I'm wearing underpants and using the toilet." To me, the editorial change was further proof of how child-centered we've become, and how anything adult-centered is unwelcome. Like so much of the other advice foisted upon parents, toilet training instructions underline the pervasiveness of AED. We adjust to our children and their schedules, instead of the other way around.

During the same years when parents were being warned not to repress their children's feelings, they were also encouraged to play more with their kids. In the early 1950s, Martha Wolfenstein reviewed the "Infant Care" bulletins published by the U.S. Department of Labor Children's Bureau from 1914 to 1945. She found that parents in the early part of the century were told not to play with baby because they would overstimulate him and upset his regular routine. By mid-century parents were being told that for healthy development babies need to play and that parents should weave games and music into every activity they could. It was the beginning of a "fun morality," a trend that has only intensified, for as Wolfenstein notes: "Fun has become not only permissible, but required."[9]

Attached to Attachment

Let's look at another psychological theory that's furthered AED—the attachment research of John Bowlby and Mary Ainsworth. You may or may not have heard of attachment research, but even if you haven't you can be sure that it's having a tremendous influence on what you read in childrearing books and magazines. What these two psychologists, Bowlby and Ainsworth, introduced was nothing less than a revolution in the way of seeing the child. Bowlby said that infants need and seek affectionate relationships, and that children who are separated early in life from their parents, especially their mothers, experienced protest, despair, and detachment. In fact, it is upon this primary relationship, the attachment the child forms with his earliest and most precious caregiver, that he builds the rest of his emotional life, Bowlby believed.

Mary Ainsworth took Bowlby's research a step further by demonstrating that there are secure and insecure attachments, and that a certain type of mothering—warm, sensitive, responsive, and dependable—was a key ingredient in secure attachment. Ainsworth verified these discoveries with an experiment called the "Strange Situation," in which a child is observed in unfamiliar surroundings both with and without mom.[10]

While some aspects of attachment theory still provoke heated debate—especially contentious for working mothers is whether their absence affects their babies' attachment to them (although the most recent study gives a green light to working)—the basic premise is well-accepted now. Whereas 35 studies on attachment were published in 1975, 280 were published in 1994. And over 3,000 were published in the years between.[11] Article after article and book after book remind us that meeting our child's attachment needs makes a major difference in how the little tyke turns out.

"The baby is practicing loving for life. The more he can love, now, and feel himself loved back, the more generous with, and accepting of, all kinds of love he will be, right through his life. He will find it easy to respond to the emotional needs of your grandchildren when his turn comes for parenthood," says Penelope Leach in *Your Baby and Child*. So not only the future of our immediate family but the future of generations to come rests on how well-attached our baby becomes to us. A couple paragraphs later, Leach explains what this entails for parents. "If you try to override his [baby's] feelings, ignoring his cries, prying off his clinging arms, or shutting him in a playpen to stop him following, he will get more and more anxious. The more anxious he feels the more determinedly he will cling to you. If you try stealth, sneaking out of the room when he is busily occupied, he will occupy himself less and less because he will keep an ever-closer eye on your movements."[12]

I have tried to be sensitive to our children's attachment needs, but I've also made it a point to step quickly into the next room whenever one of them begins playing happily on her own or with a sister or friend. In fact, I've come to think that three of the most beautiful words in the English language are, "Let's pretend that . . ." When they are spoken by one child to another, it's almost certain that they'll have some lovely play together—and you can get something else done. But kids never have a chance to say these words unless we leave them alone, at least occasionally.

Attachment research shows that the first two years of life are crucial, but that part of the message is often downplayed. We think older children have as urgent a need for our attentiveness as little babies. We forget, I guess, that big kids can talk, that they already trust us, and therefore will not be crushed if we say, "Not now, in a minute." In other words, we hover long past the point when hovering is even remotely necessary.

Attachment research has helped make possible what is called attachment parenting. This is a sort of Rousseauian, back-to-basics childrearing method that endorses natural childbirth, breast-feeding, carrying or "wearing" baby in a sling, and sleeping together in a "family bed." These parents have become so leery of rush-'em-here, rush-'em-there childrearing that they propose a return to "traditional" methods.

For them, however, traditional doesn't mean replicating their own childhood. Instead, it means following the precepts set forth in books such as *The Continuum Concept* by Jean Liedloff, which describes childrearing methods in the South American jungle. Liedloff believes that the natives' habit of holding infants close to their bodies for the first several months of life (what she calls the "in-arms" phase), gives children a serenity and security that Westerners search for in vain the rest of their lives. Liedloff addresses fears that holding babies all the time will spoil them. She says that although native mothers hold their babies continually for the first six to eight months of life, they don't fawn over them. Quite the contrary. The children are always present but never the center of attention. When they begin to crawl they are left on their own. Parents are available but don't constantly supervise their young as we do. This part of Liedloff's book is often overlooked. But perhaps it's inevitable. Try as hard as we might, we are not a primitive society. Primitive peoples do not read books that tell them to join organizations such as the Liedloff Continuum Network. And they certainly do not consult a "baby wearing instructor," like one I recently read about in Gaithersburg, Maryland.

Attachment parenting and AED are not only hard on our instincts, but they can also be hard on our marriage. "I know people who are lavishing all this attention on their child because it's easier to say, 'The baby had me up all night,' than to say to your spouse, 'I'm avoiding you because I'm really mad at you and I can't talk about it right now,' " says Anna Noser, a decidedly anti-attachment parent from Nashville, Tennessee.

Like everything else, we've taken attachment too much to heart. It's now a major source of guilt and frustration for us. For isn't guilt the flip side of attention? Many of us give our children attention because we aren't with them as much as we'd like to be, or because we aren't working outside the home and want to prove that raising kids is a full-time job. In this post-Freudian, attachment-aware, feelings-drenched world, we often give children too much attention because we're just too guilty not to. If we could rein in our own guilt—the anxious feelings we have when we think about what we haven't accomplished with our child—our children's attention excess disorder would be on the run.

Lives Without Rough Edges

I'm having coffee with a friend and talking about the "guardian question." Three years ago, my friend and her husband bought a $100 quickie will at their daughter's school auction. But they've had trouble finalizing the will because they could not decide on a guardian for their two children. Like many modern couples, they live some distance from their families and though they have many close friends, would rather choose a relative as guardian.

No parents like to contemplate their own demise and the fate of their children should they not be around to raise them. These are not the only parents I know who have gone around and around about making a will and choosing a guardian. (Seventy percent of people under 40 do not have a will.) But as we sipped our large, low-fat lattes, my friend said that one way or the other, they were going to pick somebody soon and settle this issue. She said: "I finally realized that even if I got the right set of parents to be guardians I still couldn't prevent our children feeling loss or being in pain. My job is *not* to keep them from ever feeling pain but to say, 'This would be the best situation if this terrible thing were to happen.' "

As we talked it suddenly became clear to me that at the heart of AED is our quixotic attempt to create unruffled lives for our children, lives without rough edges. Sure, our overattentiveness stems from reading too many books and magazines. Guilt plays a part in it, too. But at the bottom of it all are our expectations for the little lives entrusted to our care. We are terrified of doing something wrong, of accidentally wounding our kids for life. Surely the apotheosis of AED is attempting to preserve our children's unsullied happiness even from beyond our (imagined) early graves. No parent knowingly creates hardship for her child. But doesn't maturity as a parent come when we realize we can't protect our children from everything?

The paradox, of course, is that all this notice does not lead to wisdom. It's paying attention to our kids on their terms, not ours. Just because we spend a lot of time with them doesn't mean we're doing what's best for them. If your children have AED, then you are their follower, not their leader. It's the same tendency that makes discipline so difficult for us.

What's becoming ever clearer to me is that child-knowledge, like self-knowledge, requires perspective. We must be apart enough to ponder who our children really are and what they really need. As it stands now, we have no time left to do the things we really need to do for our kids. And how will we feel when challenged by tough problems in their teenage years, by drugs and sex and the spectre of teen suicide? Can we give our children the kind of attention they really need, the tough kind, when we've spent their first few years tending to their every whim?

Parents in the throes of AED have trouble knowing where they leave off and their children begin. As I've said before, there's a reason why childrearing is now called "parenting," and it's not just our habit of turning nouns into verbs. In doting on our kids, we're also calling attention to ourselves as parents.

There is a certain "stage-motherish" quality about AED that makes me worry what we'll do when our kids are grown. Will we be like certain "band parents" I've heard about, people who stay "band parents" long after their children have left their tubas and gone off to college? Now there's a scary thought.

Overparenting is like trying to wrap your hands around the wind or stop the tides. Children grow up. We cannot hold on to them by paying too much attention to them because then we will not like the kind of adults they become. So we have no choice but to love them and, at least some of the time, leave them alone.

Ask yourself these questions: Did your holiday letter this year consist entirely of your child's wit and wisdom? Do you call yourself a "professional parent"? Does your child demand inordinate amounts of your attention and encouragement? Does he lack motivation, curiosity, the ability to see a job and tackle it? Does he expect you to entertain him? Is he a heavy juice drinker? (Pediatricians worry about children who drink more than twelve ounces of juice a day because studies show that these kids are likely to be shorter or fatter than those who drink less. I have a theory, based on personal experience, that soaring juice consumption has a lot to do with AED. Getting a glass of water is too easy; often, small kids can do it for themselves. Juice guarantees parental involvement.)

Answer these questions truthfully because the stakes are high. Even children who show no visible AED scars now may find themselves easily defeated and demoralized later on. They'll wonder what's wrong, but it may take them years to find out. Perhaps by then we will realize the problem—that they had no adversity to push against, that they lacked the friction it takes to make strong character. But by then it may be too late.

Consider your own limits, too. How long can you continue lavishing your kids with attention? At what point will you sit up and say, "What about *my* feelings? Don't they count for something?" If the pendulum swings of history are any guide, parents will not revolt halfheartedly. We will throw off the shackles of our children's feelings a little too abruptly and maybe even do them harm in the process.

Most books that discuss the state of children in our society point out the physical and emotional neglect of children, especially teenagers. How can there be neglect where there is all this AED? Part of it, of course, is that we're talking about different youngsters here. Another reason is burnout. Most parents I know cannot possibly keep up the level of involvement they now have with their children, so they pay too little attention to their kids when they're older. Still another is that the attention we're paying our children is the shallow kind.

Children will always need their parents to spend positive attention on them, to listen to and talk with them. Positive attention is not just the time we spend with children but the time we spend on them, figuring out how to help them become good people. Of course, there are times when kids need more of us, need our pep talks, our discipline, our insight, our presence. But they don't need all of us all the time. On the other hand, negative attention is not just when our child acts up so we'll notice him. It's also when we feel we must be constantly available to our child, that we must do little else but play with him.

I'll admit it hasn't been easy for my family to kick AED. It's a sneaky thing. You think you've got it licked one week and the next week it's back. We've had to deny our children's feelings, that mortal sin of modern childrearing. Just last night, we told our daughters to "leave us alone" while we were finishing dinner. Can you believe how mean that sounds? I cringe. But our girls are learning to wait their turn to speak. They play on their own and take care of each other. Because we are at their beck and call less often than we used to be, they turn more often now to books, to paper and pencil, to fantasy games. In other words, they, more than most kids I know, act like children.

We haven't reverted to grunting communication in our house, nor do we ignore our children. But we have begun to assert our rights and create more balance in our family. I want our daughters to know that their father and I have our own inner lives, and that we have a life together as a couple. Our relationship with them is not all there is. Deep down, I don't think kids really want it to be.

One thought that's helped me battle AED is that we are building a family—not just raising children—and that means helping our kids know their needs are not always paramount. Sometimes one of their sisters needs more of us than they do; sometimes Mom and Dad just need to be alone together, or they need to help a parent, sibling, or friend. It seems to me that as the nuclear family becomes smaller and more mobile, we are not only deprived of contact with our larger families, but also of the opportunity to care for them. We focus all our affection on our spouse and our one or two children. It seems lopsided, even miserly. I guess that's why I'm often nostalgic for the days of larger families. I know they are not practical now for many people, but they taught children, just by their noise and clatter and sheer volume, to shift for themselves or rely on each other, to appreciate what they have. Most parents we know have stopped at one or two. Some of us have pushed on to three, and I know a handful of families who have four or more children. When I recently met a father of six, it was like greeting a visitor from another planet. I bet *his* kids don't have AED.

I'm not suggesting that we all go out and have more babies just so the kids we have won't suffer from attention excess disorder. But we can *think* bigger. We can focus on what our children give to others instead of what they get from us. Remember that quotation from Antoine de Saint-Exupery—it made frequent appearances on posters in college dorms: "Love does not consist of gazing at each other, but in looking outward together in the same direction." We used to apply it to our lovers or spouses. Now we can apply it to our kids. When I think outward rather than inward I lose the nagging sense that I must constantly observe and entertain our daughters. I think about what we, together, can give others.

If you won't make these changes for your own sake, make them for your child's. Kids thrive when left to their own devices. They solve their own problems, develop inner resources, and invent fantastic worlds. I recall playing outside my grandparents' house when I was young. I did it any number of times, but in my memory it's always May, an early summer evening, and we are crawling behind the spirea bushes that lined the far side of the house. Now I realize that we were probably shooed outside because the adults wanted grown-up conversation. But to me those were blessed times, the times apart, and our kids, all kids, need more of them.

4

"It's Just a Stage" . . .
And Other Excuses for Feel-Good Discipline

*"My unhappiness was the unhappiness of a person
who could not say no."*
—Dazai Osamu

In a small classroom of a large, suburban elementary school, 30 students are attending a special class. It's not a required class, but it's recommended if you want to get ahead. At the first meeting everyone is a little nervous, including the bearded, 40-something teacher. He's having a little trouble with the VCR, what we used to call the AV equipment, and when he finally gets the machine to work, the sound and color fade in and out. The students don't seem to mind, though. They are just glad they got in; there was such demand that others were turned away.

The first lesson is on homework. The students scribble away as the teacher talks about learning styles, the importance of study routines, and how to develop "school smarts." The teacher uses the word "research" four times in a half hour. Every time he says it, someone writes it down.

Those who say that education has hit hard times, that students no longer want to study and teachers no longer want to teach, have not been to any parenting classes lately. Because every one of these 30 students (all of whom are 30 and over, I might add) is eager to learn. The "school smarts" they've come to learn about are not their own, but their children's. And the studies they're writing down in their notebooks describe the best ways to discipline and motivate their kids.

As I look around the room at all of us, earnestly scribbling, it suddenly dawns on me why we're here: Making our children "school smart" is only the advertised goal. We are really here to redefine what is meant by good behavior, to wash away the notions we might once have had of our kids behaving as we always thought they would, as we were expected to. We're learning that if we expect too much we might saddle our kids with unattainable goals and damage their self-esteem. We are changing our expectations so that if our children disappoint us, we won't mind too much.

The parents around me are the kind who come to PTA meetings and never miss a parent-teacher conference. Many of them are graduates of other parenting classes. To break the ice, Vince,[1] the teacher, asks us to talk about what our parents expected of us in school. We agree that they stayed much clearer of our homework than we do our children's. They saw it as "our thing" not "their thing." We, of course, are far more involved. Vince explains that we'll be talking about discipline, as well as schoolwork, because the two go hand in hand.

In every class, there's always one student who doesn't quite get it, who goads the teacher a little, even if he doesn't intend to. Many times it's the brightest student, the one who doesn't accept pat answers. In our class it's a no-nonsense father named Steve, a young Kirk Douglas look-alike with ramrod posture and a short haircut. He says that when his father came home he expected him to have done his chores and his homework, as well as to have taken care of his younger brother—"or else."

As soon as Vince hears the words "or else," he springs into action. "You can give consequences instead of punishment," he says, rushing headlong into the next unit of material in a desperate attempt to correct the impression that some children, even children of yore, might have been punished when they misbehaved.

To prove his point, he clicks the button to show a video of a father disciplining his preteen daughter for misbehaving in school. The father in the first vignette comes on stronger than Attila the Hun. You can almost see the daughter's self-esteem drooping as he yells at her. But in the next vignette, the father is quite friendly and lets his daughter help determine her own "consequence." The second vignette is the correct one, of course.

Steve can't wait to comment. "I have a problem with the second scene," he says. "I think the father is making all the concessions and abrogating his responsibilities." The word "abrogate" jars this crowd. It's a strong word, an authoritative word, a word you read but never use.

Vince looks a bit pained upon hearing it, but swallows hard and says: "You have to choose your battles; you must give and take. Besides, it takes time and practice to talk to a child in this new way. You'll catch on."

But Steve doesn't want to catch on. Instead, he presses, "Why shouldn't the father be the leader? In the video the daughter pushes her point and the parent abrogates his power. Kids at seven and eight are running the negotiations."

Vince puts him off with a dismissive "Ah, yes," as if this father is almost too retrograde to handle.

The rest of the class begins talking among themselves, seemingly in strong disagreement with Steve. One father criticizes him for using the word "negotiation": "The way you're talking about children sets up a labor-management analogy, and that's no way to relate to your kids." A tall woman adds that she learned a lot about give and take in an earlier class she took with Vince on family meetings. She implies that Steve isn't really evil, just unenlightened.

By this point Vince is eager to move on. "If you can get what you want with mutual agreement then you don't need leadership. When children feel empowered, there's less reason for them to struggle. The more self-esteem the child develops, the more this will translate into positive behavior!"

Steve smiles lamely. He is defeated, but not convinced.

Feel-Good Discipline

The biggest lesson *I* learned at this class wasn't part of the curriculum. It's that for most parents, feel-good discipline—that modern style of correcting kids in which no one has hurt feelings or is inconvenienced—is still the main game in town. This is true even though there's a growing "spare the rod and spoil the child" movement. This is true even though mainstream magazines more frequently mention authoritative parenting, which combines warmth and understanding with firm discipline. Parents are beginning to realize they'll have to get tougher if they want to raise good children, but the parenting classes—and most of the books and articles—shy away from get-tough recommendations. It takes a while to remake all those videos, after all. And it's far more risky to advise parents to be firm than to peddle feel-good discipline. No teacher wants to condone strict punishment for fear he might inadvertently sanction abuse. It's much easier and safer to promise well-behaved children with very little effort.

The amazing part is that the experienced mothers and fathers in this class (all of whom have at least one child in elementary school) are buying it. It says something about the reach of the new disciplinary doublethink. It has permeated beyond the academy and the scholarly journal, outside the pages of the popular magazines, and into our homes and consciences. We know when our kids are doing something we wish they wouldn't. If we didn't we wouldn't be sitting in this classroom on a Tuesday night when we could be watching *Frasier* instead. But spend a few hours in a parenting class and you'll wonder if what you thought was a problem really is one. You'll hear that your bossy, demanding six-year-old is just "going through a stage" or that your temperamental three-year-old may be a challenge now but has the makings of a C.E.O. Not to worry. You're doing fine.

As I've said before, I'm no parenting expert, no Penelope Leach or T. Berry Brazelton. But I certainly know about failed discipline. I have been embarrassed in grocery store checkout lines and at family weddings, in schools and in doctors' offices. Stuffed full of modern childrearing theory, I have stood by while our kids danced on other people's coffee tables or hid inside racks of clothes in department stores, and all I've done was plead, "You better not do that again, okay?" I know the justifications—"it's just a stage" or "she's always been that way"—and all the other excuses. In short, I know firsthand what happens when we let information and advice get in the way of our own better judgment. And it's not a pretty sight.

Liberty, Equality, Authority!

Discipline is the hardest thing we do as parents. In an era when the right to pursue happiness has become the right to have it, firm discipline means we must make our kids unhappy at times. Instead, we've come to believe what the experts have told us—that guiding children is simply a matter of having a bunch of clever tricks up our sleeves; that it's easy, really, to make kids behave. We just use positive reinforcement, set a good example and, when the going gets tough, we set our timers for one minute per each year of our child's life and hope for the best.

When the easy techniques don't pan out, we're horribly disappointed, even angry. But instead of blaming the advice we've so eagerly lapped up, we seek more of it. One parenting expert has said that more than half the questions he receives in an on-line advice column have to do with discipline. New books on "positive discipline" clog the bookshelves.

The more we turn to the experts, the more confused we become. Because everyone has his own agenda, and even the experts can't agree. Some tell us it's okay to spank, as long as it's done only with an open palm on the bottom of a child two to eight years old. Others tell us we're setting our child on the path to delinquency if we inflict corporal punishment. Some encourage us to use time outs for discipline while others say the best way to change behavior is through positive reinforcement.

What's happened to our kids while we've been figuring out how to control them? I realize that our children aren't usually the ones who become hardcore criminals. So the fact that after remaining almost constant between 1972 and the late '80s, the juvenile crime rate hit a 20-year high in 1992 may not mean much to you personally. Still, it's interesting to note that during a time when crime figures for other ages began to fall, those for ten- to 17-year-olds, kids born in the late '70s and early '80s, when baby boomers began to marry and settle down, began to rise. Although juvenile crime rates dipped in 1995 and 1996, some experts predict even more crime in the next decade as members of the late '80s and early '90s baby boomlet come of age.

Perhaps a better measure of what's happening to our kids shows up in drug-use statistics. Although about one in five teen-agers acknowledge ever using illicit drugs themselves, six in ten say at least some of the students at their school use drugs. Even more interesting is the fact that nine out of ten parents said they'd had a "serious talk" with their teenagers about illegal drugs, but only six out of ten kids said such a conversation occurred. There seem to be some definition problems here, or maybe just some selective forgetting. Anyway, despite the advice and information we consume, we haven't exactly empowered ourselves. A recent survey of teens and drug use concludes: "Many baby boomer parents appear resigned to widespread drug use by their teens,"—and the number of teens expected to try illegal drugs doubled from 1995 to 1996.[2]

Laws tell us a lot, too. In some states, parents are fined or jailed when their children commit crimes. Society seems to be saying, "If you can't control your kids, then we will do it for you." On the other hand, some parents feel so out of control of their kids' lives that they are pushing state legislatures (and even Congress) to enact parental rights bills to protect their ability to rear and educate their children as they see fit. If they're being punished for what their kids do wrong, then they at least want to be sure they can control how they raise them.

It's more difficult to chart the subtle shifts in basic values that children have undergone in the last few decades. No one keeps statistics on the number of little kids who talk back to their parents, but only 12 percent of the parents surveyed by Public Agenda said it was common for children to treat others with respect, and only 17 percent consider it usual for kids to be friendly and helpful toward their neighbors. About a month ago I volunteered in our daughter Claire's kindergarten class, a group of 27 middle-class kids. When I asked one little girl if I could help her sound out a word, she snapped back, "I don't need you; I can do it myself," in a tone of voice that could only have been perfected after much practice at home. And just the other day a five-year-old I know said, "Don't you dare touch that TV," when I asked him if I could turn down the volume. These may be little moments, easily written off to youthful exuberance. But I witness enough of them to think they are symptoms of something deeper, a lack of respect for adults; indeed, a lack of respect in general.

We are confused about discipline for two reasons: Because of the kind of parents we are, and because of what we read, hear, and learn. If one doesn't get us, the other will.

In Chapter Two we talked about what makes us parents who think too much. Some of these traits would make us strong, if only we had them in moderation. But because we have them in excess, they make us weak. For instance, we believe that kids and adults are equal, not just in the "Declaration of Independence" way but in every way. We have been made to think that children are the same as we are from the beginning, rather than realizing that they have the potential to become our equals but aren't yet. This insistence on equality explains much of our foolish and self-defeating behavior, including family meetings where children are asked to decide how they should be punished when they misbehave. Total equality makes discipline an impossibility.

Many of the articles I read about discipline note that it comes from the Latin word "disciplina," which means teaching. I guess teaching is supposed to sound a lot easier than punishing. But this is another example of doublethink. Sure, discipline is teaching if you take teaching to mean everything we do to guide and shape our child. But it's not the same as helping our kid with the ABC's. Equating discipline with teaching ignores its difficulties and its other, less politically correct definitions, such as "punishment" and "control gained by enforcing obedience." It is true that "discipline" is derived from the same root as "disciple." But to have a follower you must have a leader, and we're reluctant to assume command. If anything, we are the followers and our *kids* are the leaders.

This emphasis on total equality between child and adult—along with our fear of hypocrisy—means that we have trouble saying, "Do as I say, not as I do." I don't think we should use this phrase every day, but wise parents must use it from time to time. For instance, should we give up an occasional glass of wine because we forbid teenagers to have keg parties? I would have thought the answer to this one was a resounding "of course not" until I heard some of our neighbors talking recently. One said the best way to stop teenagers from drinking was for parents to become teetotalers. "If they can't drink, why should we?" she reasoned. Others agreed.

Are we so bewildered about basic questions that someone else has to tell us what to think? Apparently so. The National Council on Alcoholism and Drug Dependence sent me a flyer about their new prevention video for parents, *What Should I Tell My Child About Drinking?* "Hosted by Academy Award-winning actress Meryl Streep, the video offers viewers advice both about good parenting and how to discuss alcohol," trumpets the press release. Our grip on authority is so slippery that some of us even need a book such as *Getting Your Kids to Say "No" in the '90s When You Said "Yes" in the '60s,* by Victor Strasburger, which assures us it's not hypocritical to insist that our teenagers postpone sex and avoid drugs and alcohol.

Perhaps it was inevitable. "Question Authority" has always been our mantra, and that hasn't changed now that we're parents. But the authority we question now is our *own*. Because I was indoctrinated with feel-good discipline early in my parent-hood, I'm constantly fearing that I've come on too strong, spo-ken too firmly, set too harsh a penalty. I worry that my kids won't like me, or that I'm squashing their spirit. One day when our oldest daughter was five and pretending to be Mommy interviewing an expert on the phone, she suddenly put her hand over the receiver, whipped her head around, and snapped at her two-year-old sister, "That's enough, Claire. You're way out of line." That was certainly grist for my thinking-too-much mill.

Some parents worry that teaching kids to follow rules will turn them into little automatons, blithely carrying out orders without understanding the morality underneath. Here's one father's lament: "I know all too well about the suspect judg-ment and twisted motivation of some of those who make every-day rules and enforce them. And I know for certain I don't want my sons growing up to be mindless minions of despotic rule," writes Don Oldenburg in *The Washington Post*.[3] He then pro-vides advice from experts on teaching kids to question author-ity. Funny how we can question almost any authority except childrearing authorities.

I realized the lengths we would go to avoid authority a few years ago, when a friend told me about an article she'd read criticizing time out. I was interested to read the article because most kids I know, ours included, aren't deterred by the "threat" of having to sit in another room for a few minutes by themselves. The article certainly was critical, but not in the way I supposed it would be. It lambasted the time out as "an authori-tarian approach [that] can work only among children trained to comply with the power and authority of adults."

What did this article suggest instead? "Give information and reasons. If your child colors on the wall, explain why we color on paper only. Look for underlying feelings. If your child hits his baby sister, encourage him to tell you why he is upset." Other suggestions included taking a parental time out and, my personal favorite, "If your child refuses to take a bath, offer to take one with him.''[4] In other words, don't insist that young-sters comply with your rules. Instead, do anything to keep the peace.

Something happened to my marvelously modern preten-sions the day I read that article, and they've never been the same since. This is what happens when we think too much, I told myself. We become afraid of our children. We want them to like us so much that we're willing to sell their future down the drain in order to make sure they do.

Truth or Consequences

But enough self-flagellation. After all, we can excuse our-selves a little by realizing that never before in the history of childrearing have parents been tempted by the information and advice we have access to every day. And what does this information tell us about discipline? Although there are thou-sands of books and classes, most of them contain remarkably similar suggestions: Set a good example yourself. Correct the behavior, not the child. Ask your youngster why he is angry, and whenever possible let him have a say in how he's disciplined. When children misbehave, let them experience the conse-quences of their actions.

The theory of consequences is a cornerstone of discipline these days. You can read about it in countless magazine articles and books. While it can be a practical and bold tactic in some situations, now it seems the only word you can use for punish-ment. Even the word discipline, Latin root and all, is considered pejorative in comparison. The word consequences has a nice, safe, neutral sound that parents and parenting class teachers seem to like.

You can learn a lot about consequences in parenting classes. When Vince, the teacher I described earlier, talked about logi-cal consequences, one mother didn't look so convinced. She cracked a wry, get-serious smile and said she always uses the same "consequence" whenever her preteen son misbehaves—denying him phone privileges.

"No, no," says Vince. "You must come up with a new consequence for each misbehavior."

Talk about thinking too much—to follow this requirement we'd be thinking all the time. So I raise my hand. "I have some problems with natural consequences," I say, a bit tentatively at first. "It's like we're washing our hands of discipline and letting fate do the job for us."

"You're confusing natural consequences with logical consequences," Vince explains. "With natural consequences you let whatever happens happen. The milk spills, there's no more milk. You run in front of a car, you get hit. But you can't always rely on natural consequences. They can be serious and dangerous, or maybe nothing at all. But with logical consequences, you decide the penalty—along with your child, of course."

"But why should a child determine his own punishment?" I ask, making a point to use the politically incorrect "punishment" rather than the politically correct "consequences."

"Because it's important to let the child have some say. Otherwise the consequence is too judgmental," Vince says.

"But if the child has done something wrong, why shouldn't a parent be judgmental?" I ask, trying hard to keep my voice even.

"You have to keep in mind that it's not winning or losing that's important, but keeping the relationship strong. You don't want to do anything that will damage your relationship with your child. The less you can say, 'Because I said so,' the better your relationship with your children will be," Vince says with a ring of authority. "Besides, if you let children determine their own punishment, they'll devise one far more Draconian than any you could ever come up with."

My head is spinning. What should I worry about first? Being judgmental? My nasty habit of assigning punishments rather than negotiating them? As for the final point, what does it mean that kids go harder on themselves than we go on them? To me it says they want firmer boundaries than we're willing to give them.

At the end of this class session, we talk about how parents

should support their school's disciplinary policy. It's then that Vince makes his most telling comment: "You know, I'm amazed at how disrespectful children are to adults," he says. "Even the little ones talk in ways I would never allow." Apparently, it's never dawned on him that children might be more disrespectful because their parents are less judgmental.

Is It "Just a Stage"?

Underlying most modern disciplinary methods is the belief that we must understand our child's stage of development—what she can do when—before we can discipline wisely. Otherwise we might expect a baby to drink from a cup without spilling her milk or leave a six-year-old alone in the house while we run out to an aerobics class. The implication is that we don't have much common sense, and that if not properly informed, we might discipline our children too harshly or put them in dangerous situations.

First of all, I think parents have a better grasp of what their children are capable of than many experts give them credit for. The books and articles, after all, are written as safely and conservatively as possible. And to prove their worth, they must assume we know very little.

Secondly, expert advice is, by its very nature, more formalized than advice handed down in families or offered by friends. Parents of the past got a sense of what children could and couldn't do from the experienced parents and grandparents around them. "Oh, you can't expect a little one not to make a mess. She'll learn to drink neatly when she's a little older," someone might say in a casual, offhanded way. Now we receive our advice from a book, a research study, or a parenting column like one I recently read in the paper.

"Family Almanac," by Marguerite Kelly, is a syndicated advice column for parents. One week a father wrote in asking for help with his almost four-year-old daughter.[5] He said that while she's usually sweet, thoughtful, and intelligent, she talks back in an ugly tone of voice and can be "shrill, loud, and very rude," especially when her mom's attention is diverted by the phone

or by another adult. In the past he'd been using "gentle reprimands" to correct her because she's "expanding her verbal
skills." But the "gentle reprimands" no longer worked. "How
can I get her to treat her parents with respect?" he asked Kelly.

Since Kelly's reply is rather long, I will quote a few lines and
summarize the rest. I'll also include some of my own remarks in
parentheses. These are the comments I scribble in the margins
every time I read something like this. They can be a little nasty
at times, but I've begun to count on them. They keep me sane.

Kelly begins by saying the little girl "screeches" because she
feels safer with her parents than anyone else, and because four
is "a pretty rowdy age." (The "feels safe with you" line is not
only getting very stale, but it's only half the picture. Sure, kids
can act out more with their parents, but aren't we supposed to
set an example? And if we let them walk all over us, won't they
learn that it's okay to walk all over other people? As for four
being a rowdy age, well, I guess every age can be rowdy if we let
it be.) Instead of exhorting the parents to act wisely, firmly and
quickly, and that there's still time to turn their child around but
they have to get right to it, Kelly tells the parents not to come
down too hard because they don't want to "squelch" their
daughter's independence.

Kelly also said that the girl's behavior would improve if her
parents gave a little time to her when they had time to spare.
"Even if she's playing contentedly, offer to read a book to her
or have a tea party with her." (No modern advice column
would be complete without telling us we need to spend more
time with our child. Kelly even suggests interrupting a child
who's busily playing by herself, thereby guaranteeing that she
will develop attention excess disorder—if she hasn't already.)

Buried in paragraph 11 is Kelly's only tough statement—and
she almost smothers it in qualifiers: "Tell your child that she
must express herself with words—not screeches—when she's
mad, and that they mustn't be mean words because that would
hurt people's feelings, and no one in the family is allowed to
hurt anyone's feelings. A young child will usually obey a 'family
tradition' quickly, even when she's slow to obey her parents."

(In other words, don't insist that your child follow a rule. That would be too authoritarian.)

This letter had no signature, so there's no way to tell if this family was helped by Kelly's suggestions. But I certainly wouldn't be. Kelly totally sidesteps the problem. This father and mother have allowed their daughter to sass and interrupt them. Now their daughter has verbal skills all right, and look how she uses them! Kelly ends her column by recommending a parenting book, which practically guarantees that the child's misbehavior will continue.

I read Kelly's column every week, and sometimes I agree with her advice. But this particular article proves that learning more about *why* kids behave as they do makes it harder to *make* them behave. We finesse things so our kids believe they are always in charge. Yet eventually they must learn they are not always in charge, that their personalities are not always dominant. And eventually we must realize that our job is more than just understanding where our children are; it's taking them where we want them to be.

My husband and I aren't the only parents whose children's "terrible two's" lingered well into their fourth or fifth year. Kids' difficult stages seem to be lasting longer and longer these days. That's because believing that their behavior is "just a stage" has become just an excuse to avoid the difficult but exquisitely important task of disciplining them. We're so caught up in knowing exactly what our children are capable of at any given moment that we're petrified of doing something "developmentally inappropriate" and scarring them for life. There's nothing wrong with learning a little about how kids grow and change, but what's most important, it seems to me, is paying attention to how our *own* child behaves.

Why Parents Need to Say No

Monitoring our children's developmental stages has become very popular in the last decade or two, but the concepts behind it have been around much longer. More than 50 years ago, Arnold Gesell and his disciples were already pioneering the careful observation of infant and child behavior and identifying various milestones with which to measure children's abilities.

Parents still flock to Gesell Institute books such as *Your Two-Year-Old* and *Your Three-Year-Old* for a quick overview of what kids can and can't do at each age. Though groundbreaking at the time, these works have been trivialized through the years. For one thing, we ignore the authors' frequent reminders that children develop according to their own timetables, and the ones in the book are just approximations. So we worry needlessly. "My son must have been about 18 months when I read that by now he should be able to hold a crayon and color with it. And I thought: 'Oh, my God. I never thought of crayons. We don't have any crayons in the house,' " Sue Brickman recalled with a laugh. (Luckily, she learned that her son was coloring quite nicely at daycare.)

More to the point, however, the "ages and stages" we read so much about often become excuses for our children's misbehavior. When a friend of mine mentioned to her pediatrician that her 19-month-old son was spitting, the doctor replied, "My! He's advanced for his age." My friend was looking for guidance, and she received a progress report instead.

I remember how relieved I was when I read that 18 months is a time of "disequilibrium." Our oldest daughter was 18 months old at the time and quite a handful. I only felt good for six months, though, because her "disequilibrium" lingered two more years.

Often, the parent hooked on these developmental charts may decide she wants more information. After all, Gesell focused on behavior and physical development, and we want to know what's going on inside our children's heads. We can explore this fertile territory by studying the theories of Swiss psychologist Jean Piaget. When you read about the studies Piaget conducted—many of them on his own kids—you get the feeling that perhaps *he* was the original Parent Who Thinks Too Much. He was always observing his kids to see what they did and when they did it—all for a good purpose, of course. His theory that children pass through a sequence of cognitive stages to achieve adult intellectual functioning is still considered a brilliant achievement. But because it's so difficult to read Piaget, even in translation, most of us know only the brief, watered-down references to his categories of preoperational, concrete operational, and other stages of mental growth. However, that doesn't stop us from watching our kids to see if they've graduated into concrete thinkers.

On one level, attributing children's misbehavior to their developmental stage may seem the epitome of not thinking at all. But the parents I know who use the "it's just a stage" excuse don't do so idly. They are well-meaning and well-informed. They know their Piaget from their Gesell.

Meanwhile, almost every article I've written lately says something to the effect that once we understand why our kids behave as they do, we can learn techniques to handle them until they outgrow it. But what makes them outgrow it? Certainly not the techniques, which may be derived from useful research but which have been watered down into simplistic bromides.

To explain what I mean, I'll pick on one of my own stories. I wrote "Why Toddlers Need to Say No" when our second and most intense daughter was two. Parents of toddlers are exhausted, stretched, and in need of strength. I knew I needed help handling our daughter's constant stream of "no way, Mommys." Because the subject was such an important one for me at the time, and because I had already written several articles on this topic, I wanted to find something especially useful to say to parents, something that might help them better handle this trying period.

When I collected information for the article, I heard some very cute stories. One psychologist told me about the time her son called out to her from his crib, "Mommy!" and when she said, "Y-e-s-s-s?" to answer him, he snapped back "NO!" A writer who had collected a book of tips for parents of toddlers gave me one suggestion that I thought wouldn't pass muster with my editor but was too novel to pass up: If your child wants to go into a store or restaurant that you'd rather not enter, simply tell him there's a sign posted outside that says, "The pizza ovens are out of order" or "Closed on Tuesday." It seemed a little, well, dishonest, but to my surprise, was left in the published version of the story. Probably because it was non-confrontational.

But, alas, most of the advice I heard was the same old thing. The pediatricians and child psychologists I interviewed told me that two-year-olds must say "no" because they're developing independence and autonomy this year. Their solutions (yawn) included giving kids choices, making sure they don't get overly tired, and limiting the number of times you say no—the standard recipe for failed and frazzled parenting. I had tried all of these with our two-year-old and wasn't getting anywhere.

The piece I finally wrote cobbled together as many tough suggestions as I could find—including one expert who said it was important to say "no" sometimes—along with the cute stories I mentioned above and some of my own strategies, such as asking silly questions to which kids will have to answer "no." (I'd found that this defused almost every sub-tantrum level incident.) But, as usual, I felt that something was missing in the final product, some voice of strength and wisdom, an expert who was willing to go out on a limb and say: "Look, I know all this stuff sounds good, but sometimes you just have to be firm." I never found such an expert, and even if I had, I doubt his comments would have made it into the final published version of the story.

As much as I wanted to believe what I was hearing—that constant nay-saying is a sign of secure toddler development and we shouldn't discourage it—a little voice inside me kept nagging: "This may explain why they do it, but it doesn't explain what we do about it." How do children learn to take no for an answer if we try so hard to avoid saying it? These strategies may buy time but they don't make kids behave. They are tiptoeing around compliance as if it were a sleeping child. Our kids become so used to the strategies and the choices that they don't know what to do when we issue a command.

"The fact we constantly give our children choices means they are very poor at taking sharp orders," said a father of two from

Colorado who I met through a news group on the Internet. "An example would be when we were moving a heavy piece of furniture up from the basement and my four-year-old was in the way. Straining under the piece, I yelled, 'Get out of the way!' He just froze and I repeated the order even louder. He just started crying. All the pleading in the world couldn't move him. He's incredibly bright and sophisticated, but he can't deal with that type of situation at this time."

I should point out that there are practical and commercial reasons why most magazine articles give such predictable suggestions that one of my friends says of them, "I pretty much always know what the happy endings will be before I read the story." Some of the predictability stems from the small space into which the information is crammed: a two-page article, by its very nature, cannot go into great depth. But another cause, and the one more often to blame in the case of such a sensitive topic as discipline, is the "child-friendly" philosophy most publications have today. Editors seem terribly concerned lest anything in print nudge parents toward misunderstanding their kids. Perhaps they are haunted by the spectres of child abuse and legal liability or perhaps they are just responding to trends in psychological research. Whatever the reason, I've had editors remove cute anecdotes, such as one about when our daughter, Suzanne, then a toddler, bit my leg while I was on the phone, because it was deemed "anti-child." The result is like the Emperor's New Clothes. Everyone knows that children try our patience, that some toddlers will even bite your leg if you give them half a chance, but to admit this in print makes one suspect. The result is squeaky clean and unrealistic.

It wasn't always this way. The mainstream parenting magazines used to focus more on toys, games, and birthday parties with only the occasional "why your child behaves as he does" article thrown in. Now it seems like every other article attempts to explain child development to parents. The first such article I remember writing was in 1988. It was a story about how toddlers are incapable of being bad, and that we should understand rather than correct them. I've written scores more since then.

The "ages and stages" apology approach is still in full favor with the big parenting magazines. It's funny how my attitude has changed, though. At first these developmental articles were more interesting for me to write and to read. They had a little meat to them. But now I turn to magazines for those little tips that I might have passed over before, you know, the ten new birthday party games and how to make a drum out of used oatmeal containers. I appreciate these more now because they collect and share information that other parents have found useful. And they aren't telling me how to raise my kids. They leave discipline and other important decisions right where they should be, in my hands.

Read the table of contents of any parenting magazine and you'll see what I mean about the apology approach. I picked up the one closest to my desk last night, an issue of *Parents,* and came up with these titles: "When Your Child Says, 'I Hate You!'—Find out what she really means by these three nasty words," or "Let's Make a Deal—Is your preteen begging for new privileges? Come to the table ready to negotiate and everyone will come out a winner." If you read these articles you will learn that a preschooler's "I hate you" is really a sign of his intellectual growth and that a preteen's request for a new phone line in her room is an opportunity to develop rapport with her. The longer I've been a parent the more these articles seem like balloons ready to pop—or to break free of our grasp and soar into the clouds. The advice they offer has no connection to my reality anymore.

The "Spirited Child"

I know there isn't a conspiracy to make parents *think* so much about discipline that they can't *do* discipline. It's simply the fashion right now to talk about what kids can and can't do rather than what parents should or shouldn't do. And this has turned "just a stage" into just an excuse. But "just a stage" isn't the only excuse in town. There's also "that's just the way she is."

The best way to understand how pervasive this excuse has

become is to eavesdrop on another parenting class. This one is called "Raising Your Spirited Child," and it's filled with parents of children who might in the past have been called "naughty" or "a handful" but who now are called "spirited." Here are some of the words we come up with to describe our kids: "persistent, relentless, active, demanding, badgering, affectionate, intense." Yes, these children give great big bear hugs. Yes, they also give great big headaches. Calling them spirited means we'll concentrate on the hugs and hope the headaches go away.

The class is based on *Raising Your Spirited Child*, by Mary Sheedy Kurcinka, a book which draws on the author's years of teaching "Spirited Child" workshops. In other words, I'm attending a workshop based on a book that is based on a workshop. I find it interesting that this book now seems more popular than *The Difficult Child*, by Stanley Turecki, which I always liked and which was my husband's personal favorite (indeed, the only parenting book he's read in its entirety). But it's no longer politically correct to call your child "difficult."

Barbara, the teacher of the "Spirited Child" class, is humble and efficient. She has a plain moon face and a tired smile. She lets us know right away that she's the mother of a spirited child (which may account for the tired smile). Our first class assignment is to write our names. A minute later Barbara tells us to write them again—only this time with the hand we don't usually write with. "How did it feel to write your name the first time?" she asks. "Natural, like it usually does," we reply. "And how did it feel to write it the second time?" "Hard, like we'd never done it before, like we were children," we say. Pushing a child against his temperament is like making him write with the hand he doesn't usually write with, Barbara says. It's going against the grain; it's a losing battle.

This was a perfect introduction to the class because every week we learn a new way to work around our child's temperament. "When you're having a confrontation with your spirited child, ask yourself, 'Is there something in this situation I can say yes to?' " Barbara advises. Learn to control the environment, to be a "stimulus barrier." "Maybe you just won't be able to take your child to large family gatherings," Barbara says. (I wonder why she chooses family gatherings to omit. Yes, they can be tense, but so can a trip to Chuck E. Cheese.) "Give your child a wide range of feeling words to choose from so that he can describe all his many emotions. Most school counselors' offices have lists of feeling words in case you get stuck," she offers.

We learn some useful techniques—letting tactile children decompress by running their hands through a big vat of birdseed and telling your spirited child she can ask you the same question twice and no more. Better than the advice are the stories. They make us feel better immediately. Yes, our child misbehaves, but not as much as some of the other kids we hear about. One night a woman named Joanne tells us about her four-year-old son throwing a tantrum in a restaurant because the waitress didn't bring the crayons quickly enough. The little guy worked himself into such a lather that by the time the crayons did arrive, he took a swat at the waitress just to teach her a lesson. He ended up in a hallway kicking and screaming. The worst part is that Joanne's mother-in-law was present at this scene. "To her credit, she didn't say anything to me like, 'You don't know how to raise him,' but I know she was thinking it. She raised seven children."

"And none of them was spirited?" Barbara asks, incredulous.

"She used corporal punishment. It's kind of scary," Joanne replies. "But we know that one of her children was spirited because my husband's youngest sister is real sensitive to certain types of clothing." (I should add that tactile sensitivity is a sign of spiritedness.)

"I know what you mean. It seems like there weren't as many spirited children when we were growing up," interjects Michelle, a mother of one spirited child and one baby, temperament yet to be determined. "When I told my mother I was going to this class, she said, 'You were spirited, too, but you knew you had to obey me.' "

During class discussions, we talk about time outs, consequences, and penalties. But every time we get to a really tough situation—what to do about a child who refuses to go to bed or who screams at the top of his lungs because he doesn't want to get in his stroller at the Baltimore Aquarium—I'm struck by how weak the strategies seem. All these techniques and plans have one thing in common—they are dancing around compliance. How do you get your children to obey you? We have the carrots but we don't have the sticks. And we're not going to get them in this class. When one woman admits she took away her daughter's favorite dress for a while as punishment, class members seemed to feel that was too strict. After all, these are *spirited* children. They need special treatment.

Do Parents Matter?

Temperament research has come of age in the last 20 years. And no advice book or article is complete without a reminder to keep in mind what kind of child you have, whether intense or subdued, cautious or impetuous. Though it was initially liberating to parents to think their children were born one way or another, that they weren't solely to blame for a bad temper, this philosophy can, as you see, become yet another excuse for inertia. We are urged to let our kids express who they really are on the inside and afraid to exert any checks and balances from the outside. Instead of saying, "You have a quick temper, and you must learn to control it," we say, "You must be very angry about that."

Any parent who has more than one child knows that babies are born with their own distinctive personalities. But for a long time it wasn't very popular to say so. The political ramifications were too great. If our genes determine too much of who we are, then what about change, what about Head Start and all the other social action policies we'd like to believe in? For that and many other reasons, researchers focused mostly on what the environment did to shape a child's behavior. It was old-fashioned and unpopular to suggest that children might be born with their own unique natures right from the start.

But Stella Chess, a child psychiatrist now in her 80s, was bothered by the status quo. In 1958 she wrote: "Many of the mothers of problem children develop enormous guilt feelings due to the assumption that they must necessarily be solely responsible for their children's emotional difficulties. With this guilt comes anxiety, defensiveness, increased pressures on the children and even hostility toward them for 'exposing' the mother's inadequacy by their disturbed behavior.''[6]

Beginning in the mid '50s, Chess, along with her husband, Alexander Thomas, and colleague Herbert Birch, studied the same group of children from infancy until early adulthood and isolated nine variables from which they could assess temperamental traits—ways of behaving that children were born with and for the most part kept into adulthood. These included activity level, regularity, approach or withdrawal, adaptability, intensity of reaction, threshold of responsiveness, quality of mood, distractibility, and persistence.

Based on these nine temperamental traits, Chess and her colleagues came up with three temperamental profiles or patterns—the easy baby (40 percent), who is positive in mood, regular in body functions, and quick to adapt; the slow-to-warm-up infant (15 percent), who is negative in mood, slow to adapt, and likely to withdraw from new situations; and the difficult baby (ten percent), who has negative moods, irregular eating, sleeping, and elimination patterns, is slow to adapt, withdraws in new situations, and reacts with great intensity. It's this ten percent that are called "difficult" or "spirited." (The remaining 35 percent have such a combination of traits that they do not slide easily into any of these descriptions.)[7]

Research by Chess and by others, such as Jerome Kagan, has given credence to what parents have known all along: that children are born with strong preferences and proclivities, likes and dislikes; that when approached by a stranger, some will cry and others will smile. Knowing that some children are just born harder to handle has reassured hundreds of thousands of parents who believed they were doing everything wrong—to say nothing of spawning the "Spirited Child" cottage industry.

If Chess and Thomas were right, though, and ten percent of babies are born with the constellation of qualities called "diffi cult" or "spirited," then we might suppose that ten percent of children have always been this way. And then we have to ask why we are hearing more about this ten percent now than we did 30 years ago. Perhaps it's because a more permissive childrearing style allows these characteristics to flourish until they're driving us crazy. Easygoing children are less likely to take advantage of timid, uncertain parents. But children with "oomph" roll right over us. If you don't believe me (and I've been rolled over), look no further than the bulging rosters of "Spirited Child" parenting classes.

Chess and her colleagues didn't think everything is innate, however. They believed that a combination of temperament and environment is responsible for the kind of person a child becomes, and the interaction between parent and child is a crucial component of that environment. Chess used the term "fit" to describe this match between parent and child. "Goodness of fit," for example, happens when a child who is slow to warm up to new situations has parents who give her the time and space she needs to fit into them. On the other hand, "poorness of fit" results if her parents and teachers push her to adapt as quickly as the other children.[8]

Though the concept of fit has also been a welcome counterpoint to the behavioristic approach, with its emphasis on conditioned reflexes, it has been a mixed blessing for parents who think too much. It encourages us to focus perhaps unduly on ourselves, which we do enough as it is, and to expect more malleability than we can muster. Let's face it: We can change some of our traits, but not all of them. Selecting a parenting style is not the same as picking out a pair of chinos at Banana Republic.

Our fascination with temperament proves that the more we discover about our child's inborn traits, the less likely we are to interfere with them. Temperament researcher Nathan Fox has observed that in his studies, "Parents usually say, 'This is who my child is.' Depending on what they do or don't do, however, that child's biology is either going to express itself or be moderated. Because [parents are] too busy and it's too hard, most parents today don't intervene, so biology mostly creates the kids' environments."[9] This from a researcher who believes that experience can modify the brain.

Also disheartening to parents is the news coming from the more extreme fringe of temperament researchers, behavioral geneticists, who believe that what parents do makes little difference in the kind of adult a child becomes. They think that personality is determined by the genetic hand dealt at birth, the state of the family, birth order, and other influences. A *Philadelphia Inquirer Magazine* cover story on the temperament research teased readers with the question: "Do Parents Matter?"

Even a parent who thinks very little might feel threatened by this query. What's interesting to me, though, is how we hone in on the immobilizing part of each new bit of research and cling to it. When nurture is the explanation of the day, we are so paranoid about the job we're doing that we can't react naturally. When nature is held responsible, we feel irrelevant.

Yo-Yo Parenting

No wonder the parents I know—Tom and I included—feel so tentative about the childrearing decisions we make. Eventually these dual excuses, "It's just a stage" and "It's just temperament," erode our faith in ourselves as the molders and shapers of young minds and hearts. We feel guilty and insecure when we do take a stand. We become what I call "yo-yo parents." After repeated polite and fruitless requests that our child hang up her coat, take the toys off the stairs, or stop teasing the baby, we explode in anger. There's an up-and-down quality to our interaction with our children made possible by—you guessed it—those parenting books, magazines, and classes.

The dangers of yo-yo dieting are well-documented. It's hard on the body to gain and lose weight, to go up and down the scale. But no one has yet to define, let alone chart, the problems of yo-yo parenting—being a pushover one day and a demon the next. This often happens to parents who think too much, and do too little, about discipline in their own homes. In fact, it happened to me just yesterday, when a skirmish over a clothing choice escalated into a full-scale battle. Had I not started out so "easy," had I been firmer about what our daughter could wear from the beginning, the fight might not have happened at all. When we're not doing what comes naturally—and I do think it's natural to assume control of a small child who doesn't yet know right from wrong—it's easy to waffle wildly between unrealistic pleading and corrosive anger.

Statistics from Sweden, where laws prohibiting corporal punishment went into effect in 1979 and parents are encouraged to inhibit their children as little as possible, show a fourfold increase in child abuse from 1984 to 1994.[10] No one has proven a causal link, but you have to wonder, do parents required to barely restrict their children at all become frustrated enough to strike them?

We have failed to realize that everyone in the family pays the price for our disciplinary doublethink. Children who misbehave are more likely to arouse their parents' wrath. And parents whose wrath is aroused are more likely to feel tired and guilty. If we could only understand that it's impossible to rear children the way most modern books tell us to—that sometimes we have to say, "because I said so," and other politically incorrect statements, we would be stronger disciplinarians from the beginning. The antidote to yo-yo parenting is knowing our own minds and staying the course. But in these times, that's neither simple nor easy.

I didn't write this book to tell *you* what to do, of course, but I will say that Tom and I are much stricter parents now than when we started out—a fact that must be apparent by now. We've cultivated a firm, "I mean it" tone, and we no longer buy into the excuses. I am also resurrecting a discipline technique that was used quite effectively on me as a child, the withering glare. So much can be said with so little. I think we have forgotten this.

When our five-year-old's kindergarten teacher called the other day to say that Claire had cut her hair instead of construction paper while making collages, I greeted our daughter at the bus stop with a few severe words: "You know better than to use

scissors for cutting hair. When we get home you will go immediately to your room." And she stayed there, without lunch, for an
hour and a half. We have also put our children to bed without
dinner, deprived them of treats and toys, and, occasionally,
spanked them. I think often about the word "obedience." It
has all sorts of negative connotations, I know, but we're promot-
ing it in our family. It doesn't mean that our children will never
think for themselves. But it means that now, when they don't
know better, they are expected to obey their parents, who do.

When I mention our own stern techniques, other parents
confess that they, too, are tiring of disciplinary doublethink and
are getting down to business. Eleanore and John Keenan gave
their three-and-a-half-year-old son what they call the "longest
time out"—several hours in his room—for striking his mother.
Now, before you scream "child abuse," know that these are
kind, reasonable parents who had simply had it. They gave their
son a light dinner and assured him that they loved him, but in
taking a tough stand they also assured he would not hit his
mother again. And he hasn't.

Call it old-fashioned. Call it coming to our senses. But whatever you call it, realize that these signs of parental awakening
are all the more remarkable given the child-oriented culture
from which they've arisen. When children are precious and
fragile and overanalyzed, one mistake can take on legendary
dimensions. Our supermarket has several checkout lanes that
are candy-free so that parents won't have to say "No, you can't
have any" to their tots. Our president signed into law a bill
mandating that new televisions be manufactured with a V-chip
so that parents no longer need tell their kids not to watch
Married With Children. The V-chip will do it for them.

Few of the advice manuals I've read let parents know how
hard it will be to discipline children. Indeed, a book's popularity often rests on making punishment sound easy, which is why
you find titles like *One, Two, Three Magic* or *Discipline: A
Sourcebook of 50 Failsafe Techniques for Parents.* Few of them dwell
on how heart-wrenching it is to take away a favorite toy or deny
a long-awaited privilege, or how hard it will be on parents. We

have to listen to the cries and screams; the treats we forbid, say, dinner out, might have been treats for us, too. Yet realistic parents know that these actions must be as much a part of their repertoire as an understanding heart. When my own struggles with discipline are getting me down, I tell myself that it is not supposed to be easy.

The Authoritative Solution

Too often in the past we've been torn between two images of parenting: Either we're flexible, intelligent parents who reason with our children or we're unthinking hooligans who spank our kids. But that may be changing.

For a number of years, spanking has been growing more and more out of favor with the experts. Some have even said that a swat on the bottom or a slap on the wrist is tantamount to child abuse. In his book, *Beating the Devil Out of Them,* psychologist Murray Straus describes spanking as violence against children and says that children who've been spanked are more likely to become depressed and violent people later on. The issue of spanking casts a long shadow, indeed, over the discipline advice found in books, magazines, and classes.

Depending upon which study you read, anywhere from 80 to 90 percent of parents use corporal punishment. But several developments suggest that it's on the wane. Only 45 percent of those who were not spanked themselves spank their children, and younger parents seem less likely to spank than older parents. Anywhere from a quarter to a third of younger parents (those 18 to 29) don't spank.[11] What's happened in the meantime, though, is that spanking has become a flashpoint for an argument about traditional versus liberal parenting.

In a move that bodes well for all parents—though most of us never heard about it—an American Academy of Pediatrics conference on corporal punishment held in 1996 reached a startling conclusion. Though organizers admitted they had a "preconceived notion that corporal punishment, including spanking, was innately and always 'bad,'" though there were as many anti-spanking as pro-spanking types at this meeting, the doctors and psychologists there declined to condemn spanking. This doesn't mean that they all approved of it. And you can be sure that they'll study it further. But they didn't find enough evidence to recommend against it.[12]

This conclusion—or maybe we should call it a non-conclusion—should be especially heartening news for thoughtful parents. It represents a triumph of reason over hysteria. And, though this may not have been the intention, it underlines that decisions like whether or not to spank are private ones we should make for ourselves.

Psychologist Diana Baumrind, of the Institute for Human Development at the University of California, Berkeley, believes that questions such as to spank or not to spank have helped polarize parents into liberal or conservative camps. But she, unlike many experts, offers a middle ground. It's called authoritative parenting. Authoritative parents are firm but warm, demanding but responsive. They may occasionally spank their children, but they also reason with them, especially as youngsters grow older. Baumrind found that mothers who use authoritative discipline strategies have children who are more achievement-oriented, persevering, independent, and friendly than parents who are either stricter or more permissive.[13]

Though Baumrind believes that parents ought to understand child development, she points out that authoritative parents do not use "just a stage" as an excuse. "Authoritative parents view the child as maturing through developmental stages . . . but do not describe this maturational process as an automatic unfolding, emphasizing instead well-timed parental interventions. . . . Because children's wishes often conflict with those of their caregivers, the notion that children can or should be raised without using aversive discipline is utopian," Baumrind writes.[14]

The amazing thing to me is that Baumrind has been writing about authoritative parenting for 30 years, but I only became aware of her research a few years ago. Admittedly, I don't read every journal, but I do read enough articles in both the academic and popular press that I'm astonished I didn't hear about her work earlier. I contacted Diana Baumrind, in fact, to ask her why she thinks her research, which could be so useful to parents, is not as well-known as that of many other experts. She told me that there have always been references to her work, but that the references are increasing rather than decreasing, perhaps because of the focus on "family values."

Part of the reason we don't hear as much about Baumrind's work is that she is reluctant to be interviewed. She feels strongly that parents ought not to be told what to do. As you know, I also believe that you ought not to be told what to do, so I won't suggest that you go read all of Baumrind's studies. I mention her work to show that a few psychologists, educators, and other experts—the best of them, in my opinion—know where the research should leave off and the parenting begin.

Sometimes, though, an idea has met its time. And the fact that you can read more about authoritative parenting now in books and magazines says to me that there's a turnaround in American parenthood. I think we've finally become saturated with permissiveness, have seen what it's done to our children, and crave something better. In his book *Beyond the Classroom*, Laurence Steinberg says that study after study (especially those conducted in the last 15 years) show three things necessary for effective discipline: accepting the child for who he is, supporting his autonomy, and providing firm control. We're finally beginning to pay attention to that last point.

But beware. Sensible ideas are not always pat or easy. They can be complicated. And complication doesn't sell. Now that this research on "discipline styles" has trickled out into everyday reading matter, the "good" parent, the "authoritative" parent, sounds suspiciously like every other parent I read about—a perfect one who never raises his voice and never doubts himself. The point is, you can't swallow a philosophy whole from the pages of a book.

I think we would be better disciplinarians if we were not so hard on ourselves. How can we pay so much attention to our children's feelings yet hold our children totally unaccountable for our own? So many parents I know mentally beat themselves up when they lose their temper with a child. And no wonder, when even articles that talk about tougher discipline include plenty of qualifiers. For instance, a newspaper article headlined "When Parents Take Charge" explains that experts are recanting some of their previous advice and urging parents to toughen up. That there is news in parents taking charge is news in itself. To show that we still have a long way to go, however, the article ends with this quotation from author Nancy Samalin: "If a child says, 'I hate you,' at some point, you're probably doing something right."[15]

Getting to "No"

Now that our third child, Celia, is a toddler, I'm no longer writing magazine articles about "no." I am no longer so brainwashed about a toddler's *need* to say no that I've completely given up my *own right* to say it. I try to put a positive spin on the limits I set, and I keep in mind that our little two-year-old is busily carving out her own spot in the world. But I don't let this information interfere with what I know we have to do, which is to civilize her. We are chummy parents. We started off chummy, and I don't know if we can ever cultivate the seemliness that my parents had raising us. But I don't believe that all is lost. I feel much like this mother quoted by Robert Coles: "I think there are times my little girl is being willful . . . [and] . . . I've got to be willful back! She's headed in some direction that would get her in trouble, get her in trouble with me, so I've got to say 'no,' a big loud 'no,' a 'no' that will bring her *to* (all right, scare her plenty) so she'll obey, right away."[16]

An image that helps me stay the course is to imagine that I have, somewhere inside me, a parental resistance muscle. When toned and in shape, this muscle helps me say "no" with conviction and gives me the strength to let our child go without supper if necessary. At first, it hurts to use this muscle, hurts not only because it's always hard to see our children unhappy, but also because so many cultural messages condemn us for taking a tough stand. But the more often I use this muscle, the easier it becomes. So as our youngest daughter begins flexing her independence muscle, I'm firming up my parental resistance muscle—setting clear limits and sticking with them. And whenever I start thinking, "She's so young. This is only a stage," I tell myself how much easier it will be to shape her now than to wait until she's four or five years old.

Only we can resist the excuses, stop being yo-yo parents, and tone up our resistance muscles until we're firm, fair, and reasonable. We will not do this overnight. And we will always be struggling against voices that tell us to take the easy way out. But we have a strong incentive to make the change: We love our children too much to ruin them.

One night not long ago, Celia woke up at 4 A.M., crying out that she was hungry. To me, nighttime is the crucible of child-rearing, when best intentions often succumb to the primitive urge to go back to sleep as quickly as possible. I knew she'd had a good dinner the night before and a drink of water right before bedtime. She didn't seem frightened or ill. My hunch was that she just wanted a little attention, something I'm pretty stingy with in the middle of the night. So I had a little conversation with myself, then summoned up the most ultimatum-tinged voice I could muster and said, "No, Celia. It's time for sleep. You can have some water."

"No," she said. "Me hungry, Momma."

I thought about how easy it would be to go down to the kitchen, open a box of cereal, pour it into a bowl, splash on some milk. I could be back to bed in no time. "No," I said, catching myself before I enacted this fantasy. "Have some water and go back to sleep." We walked into the bathroom and I gave her a sip from a small cup. She fussed for a while, but eventually curled up in my arms and went back to sleep. As I felt the warm weight of her head on my shoulder, I wanted to replay the scene, to give her anything, to keep her happy every moment of her life. It was that Monday morning quarterback voice, the parent who thinks too much interrogation: "Was I denying her needs by not giving her a midnight snack?" I recalled what Vince, the parenting teacher, had said, that if we don't let our child have a say in the "consequence" we "damage the relationship." If I'd made my decision based on his advice, I would have done just what Celia asked me to do and made her very happy—temporarily. Instead, we struck a sort of compromise. She wanted to eat, I wanted to sleep. But she bent to my wishes by settling in my arms and accepting the water. I bent to hers by getting up at all!

A relationship is, by necessity, composed of give and take. It is a sweet subjugation, this "give" we give our children, and most of us are quite good at giving. It's the "taking" we're not so good at. We pay too much attention to people who tell us our "relationship will suffer" if we stand up for what we know is right. No, I think to myself, the only way the relationship can suffer is if we always give in to our kids or ever give up on them. Otherwise, we sell our relationships short if we think they will be harmed by the simple realities of family life. The bonds we build with our children rest on countless exchanges like the one I had that night, times when, just by doing what comes naturally, we weave yet another row in the firm, flexible fabric of our lives together.

5

Superbaby Grows Up
Living in a Society Where Everyone's "Above Average"

"If children grew up according to early indications we should have nothing but geniuses."
—*Johann Wolfgang von Goethe*

In April 1997, Robin Williams, Tom Hanks, Arnold Schwarzenegger, Rosie O'Donnell, Roseanne, and other celebrities appeared together in a one-hour television special. Their mission was not to battle breast cancer or to save rain forests but to make American parents aware of the tremendous learning that takes place during the first three years of life.

The television special was only one part of a carefully orchestrated media event called the Early Childhood Engagement Campaign, which also included public service announcements, a toll-free number, a World Wide Web site, special magazine editions, and more. The airwaves, cyberspace, and even plain old print outlets were humming with the news. It was filtering down from the universities and the foundation headquarters, from the offices of those dedicated to the future of children. Even from the White House, which convened a similar conference of its own the same month. The message was vital. As the Carnegie report that catalyzed the campaign proclaimed: "How children function from the preschool years all the way through adolescence, and even adulthood, hinges in large part on their experience before the age of three." Cognitive development had become a cause célèbre.

Psychologists have been charting the amazing brain power of infants and young children for years, and it's no secret that the seeds of our personalities are sown early in life. But recent research shows that the sights, sounds, and touches baby receives in the first three years of life, especially language and eye contact, actually shapes his growing brain. It's easy to forget that just a few years ago intelligence and the environment were barely mentioned in the same breath. Now what parents do matters a lot, experts say.

What does all this mean for us? In all fairness, I don't think the Early Childhood Engagement Campaign—especially the program "I Am Your Child"—was aimed at parents who think too much. If anything, it was for parents who don't think enough. But it was difficult to read a newspaper or watch television that month and not hear about it. And because we are information addicts, once we heard about it we wanted to read more, and we began to second-guess ourselves.

"Whenever I read one of those articles about brain development I think, 'Gosh, what did I not do in the first three years of my children's lives that has impaired them?' " says Barbara Bailey, who has a seven-year-old and a five-year-old. "It makes me wish I could just go back and do it over. But if I could go back and do it over I'd probably just do the same things."

Human beings have wanted to understand the human brain ever since we realized we had one, and you can't fault researchers for wanting to shout their latest findings from the rooftops. But the suggestions for parents this research inspires won't come as big news to most of us. We already know how important it is to hold infants, talk to babies, and read to children. How much are we willing to do to help our kids develop a few more synapses?

Superbabies Redux

Most of us are well aware of what has been dubbed the "superbaby syndrome." I wrote an article about it eight years ago. The notion of superbabies sounds outdated now, very "1980s." No parent worth his Piaget would show a baby a flashcard. And the few parents who admit they have a preschooler who can read are careful to qualify their revelations with, "I don't know how he picked it up. I never helped him." No alphabet pushers we. After all, we've read *The Hurried Child,* by David Elkind, which 16 years ago alerted us to the dangers of pressuring our children. We have learned that two-year-old mathematicians and three-year-old readers do not perform better—and often do worse—later in school than their unhurried counterparts. We know that hurried children are stressed children.

We may think we're avoiding the "superbaby syndrome" by sending our toddler to a developmental preschool or by returning that phonics kit we ordered impulsively through the mail. But the superbaby syndrome has grown up, has become far more refined and insidious. It's no longer about babies and flashcards. It's now about educational toys and academic summer camps and daily extracurricular activities and gifted and talented programs. It's about testing and labels and parent involvement. The superbaby has become the smartkid. And children are paying the price. "You should see the fingernails of the children in my classroom," an elementary school teacher told me. "They're bitten to the quick."

The rise of the childcare expert and studies on the importance of early learning have fostered a generation of anxious and competitive parents. It's easy to feel we're falling down on the job if we're not constantly stimulating, enriching, and scheduling our youngsters. We may no longer teach babies to "read," but we can't stop reading about early learning. Isn't it important to understand neural plasticity? Won't we be better parents if we do? And once we absorb all the information, we can't just sit on it. It infiltrates our attitudes in scads of ways, some conscious, some not. This chapter will explore why many of the assumptions underlying the superbaby syndrome are still with us, propose some reasons why, and offer a few ways out of this predicament.

The Boys on the Bus—A Disclaimer

Just because we've gotten the message about early learning doesn't mean all parents have. Barry Kritzberg, a high school English teacher at Morgan Park Academy in Chicago, told me about two pairs of preschool boys and their fathers he observed on a bus one day. Both little boys were asking questions. "How does the bus turn?" "What's that funny thing in the middle of the bus?" One father responded to the questions with a "Shut up" or a "Sit down." The other father gave lengthy explanations about how the driver makes the bus turn and how a long bus needs that accordion-like cushion in the middle to make it flexible enough to maneuver around corners. It was an unusually graphic display of two vastly different, shall we say, parenting styles. And Kritzberg couldn't help but think he saw the beginnings of both a good student and a dropout right there on the city bus.

There are plenty of children who languish without encouragement, whose every request is squelched. And they're not all low-income children. So how can I criticize information on mental and emotional development when there's even one parent who yells "shut up" every time his child asks him a question?

It's complicated, this dance of expert and parent. The problem lies not just in the dissemination of the information but also in how it's received. It's up to us to realize that we *can* have too much of a good thing, that what scientists learn is interesting and important because it furthers the body of knowledge about the human condition. But it cannot tell us about our own unique child, and we must let some of it roll off our backs or we will go crazy.

I remember talking with one mother I know shortly after we had both attended a parents' meeting on the importance of math in daily life. "Sometimes I just don't know what to do first.

The expert said to work math into every part of the day, but I'm already trying to work reading into every part of the day,'' she said, with a bewildered smile. Parents want to do the best for their children. But "the best" is getting ever more complicated and time-consuming.

Consider the results of Zero to Three's national parent poll. Although 95 percent of the parents surveyed said they understand their babies are learning from the beginning, 87 percent said that the more stimulation a baby receives, the better off she is. Sixty percent of parents said they were very interested in information on brain research and how children learn, and nearly half of all parents said they pay serious attention to media reports on early childhood development.

It seems that many parents believe they need expert assistance to help their children reach their full potential. Before we investigate how deeply the superbaby syndrome has permeated our consciousness, let's look at why we want so desperately for our children to succeed.

"Where Every Child Is Above Average"

It makes sense. We are parents who think too much. We are well-educated and expect our children to be, too. Accustomed to academic competition, we gladly accept the fact that we must start our children early—if not by teaching actual skills, then by building better brains that will, in time, learn those skills. But there are emotions at work, too, and parental ambitions, and those are what I want to plumb.

Every year at our school, there is an open house for the parents of rising kindergartners. Last year we attended the meeting for our daughter Claire. I felt a little smug sitting there. A veteran, you know. We had an older child (all of seven!). We were pros. Well, my smugness didn't last long. I sniffed something different in the air, heard more impassioned questions. Within a half hour it was apparent to me that this would be a "faster" class, if you will. Parents were asking how much reading and writing would be taught. I knew that a couple of the kids in Claire's class would be a full year older than she when school started in September, children with summer birthdays who weren't ready last year.

Some school systems have pushed back birthday deadlines to the point that kids must be five by June 1 to start kindergarten in the fall. (It's September 30 in our county.) If the deadlines aren't late enough, parents make up the difference by holding back their sons and daughters to make sure they'll hit the ground running. This "academic redshirting," as it's called, means that children in the same class can be 18 months apart. Older kindergartners make for more academic kindergartens, and academic kindergartens make for older kindergartners.

As the year has gone on, my initial feelings about Claire's class have been borne out. The teachers are sweet and helpful, but the pace is fast. Reading and writing is not a goal of this class; it is a reality. Claire is learning to read and write more than a year ahead of her big sister—but she isn't having as much fun. She doesn't bound home from school singing, "This is the song about colors." A song about colors seems far too basic for this group.

A few months into the school year, Claire brought home Cuddle Bear, the kindergarten class mascot, along with a journal in which she was to describe the weekend she spent with him. Apart from the usual near disaster—Claire came down with a stomach virus that weekend and Cuddle Bear came within inches of being thrown up on—I had my own crisis when I looked at the entries other children had made in the journal. I couldn't help but notice how many kindergartners were already printing their two- and three-page entries quite neatly. Claire can read and write a few words, but nothing like some of her classmates. I knew this shouldn't bother me—in fact, I hated the fact that it bothered me—but nevertheless I quickly assembled excuses: Claire is young for her grade. Other parents must be dictating to their kids—or doing it for them. Maybe these young authors are graduates of "Hooked on Phonics."

Even though I know that pushing children can actually backfire, a part of me still worried that we were wasting Claire's mind, that we ought to be reading to her more. She is a middle child, after all. Had we overlooked her? So I said to my husband, "Why haven't we 'worked with' Claire more? ['Worked with,' of course, is a code word for 'pushed.'] She could write this way, too, if we gave her more encouragement."

"I thought we weren't going to push our kids," Tom reminded me. "They only have a little time in their lives to play and make up pretend games and use their imaginations. That's what we always said."

"I know, that's what I believe, too, but I still feel like we're not doing enough." I was brought up with high expectations and above all, I want our kids to become the best people they can be. That means kindhearted, honest, willing to go the distance for a person or a principle they believe in. If they have a talent, I want them to develop it. I want them to develop their minds, yes, to "be smart." And of course, deep down, I want our daughters to shine. I don't consider myself a pushy parent. But I want everyone else to know how wonderful they are. Doesn't this impulse explain our voracious appetite for research on intelligence, this fear of our children being left behind and becoming less than they can be.

We seem terrified that our kids might be stuck in the middle of the bell curve. We are like the inhabitants of Garrison Keillor's make-believe town Lake Wobegon, where "all the children are above average." I didn't realize until recently the extent to which schools have begun to comply with our wishes. The "Lake Wobegon effect" not only refers to Keillor's story but also to a shocking study in which 49 out of 50 state education departments in this country reported above-average performance for their students.[1]

When the weekend was over, Claire drew a picture and wrote these words in the journal: "I WAS SIK. BUT CUDL BAER MAD ME FEEL BETR." She wrote the words by herself. When she went back to school the next day I was proud of her accomplishments and embarrassed about my own feelings. But I offer my experience to help explain why the superbaby syndrome continues to haunt us.

Some Parent-Teacher Conferences

Whenever I think I'm the only one caught up in the superbaby syndrome, I find I have company. A few weeks ago we had our friends Peter and Annie and their two-year-old daughter, Emma, over to dinner. When the children left the table and we were lingering over our coffee, Annie described their first parent-teacher conference. "We were laughing when we walked up to the school," she said. "We thought this would probably be our easiest conference ever. I mean, what were they going to say—that Emma was coloring outside the lines?"

Well, they weren't laughing for long, Annie said. The teacher got right to the point. Emma could be aggressive with other children, didn't share, and sometimes had tantrums.

At first, Annie and Peter were in shock. They couldn't believe that the sweet, engaging toddler they knew at home was such a monster at her two-morning-a-week nursery school program. A few days later, Annie summoned up the courage to ask another mother what kind of evaluation her child received from the same teacher. "I'm glad you asked me," the woman said. "I think I was trying to block it out." Turns out that her daughter received much the same kind of report, which, you might notice, sounds suspiciously like the portrait of an average two-year-old. How many toddlers do you know who are never aggressive, seldom have tantrums, and always share? That we have preschool for two-year-olds is one thing, that we have conferences for their progress is another, but that we pan them for acting out and not sharing is something else entirely. Peter and Annie felt much better when they realized their daughter was not being singled out. But what does it say about modern childrearing that what happened to them is not an isolated experience?

A week later, I got a call from another friend with a similar dilemma. Debbie had just attended a conference with her daughter's preschool teacher, too, and had been informed that Brittany's speech was not up to par. The teacher said the child should begin speech and language therapy right away. Brittany had just turned four. When Debbie pressed the teacher for more details about her daughter's speech problems, the teacher said that Brittany communicates well but that some of her words were not clear. Even though Debbie knows instinctively that time is probably the only "cure" her child needs, and her husband, Dave, concurs, she feels pressured to sign up for the expensive ($80 an hour) speech therapy sessions. Debbie says she'll feel like a bad mother if she doesn't accept the extra help because that's what the posh private preschool expects of her.

The Scramble for Achievement

It's not just our friends who are feeling the squeeze. And it's not just in preschool. Parents plot their children's education as if it were some intricate battle campaign. Some hire consultants to help place their elementary-age children in the right private schools. The number of such educational consultants in our area has more than tripled in the last five years. Others seek out magnet schools, language immersion programs, or gifted and talented programs. Perhaps in competition with their private-school cousins, public schools offer parents more choices within school districts and sponsor hot lines where parents can ask questions about education.

You could argue that all of this is good for our kids. But not if children feel pushed to make the grade instead of truly learn. Teachers complain that their children want to memorize lists of vocabulary words, but not read; to take the SAT prep course, but not understand their daily lessons. Scarcely a week goes by that our local school district doesn't announce some test results—of students or programs. Of course, higher educational standards are something to celebrate, not lament, but if the mania for testing becomes an end in itself, it could shortchange real education.

In Virginia many parents and educators feel that the push to meet new state standards is making it harder for teachers to teach. "I think we're all worried about the number of tests and that they will take away time from connecting with kids," fourth-grade teacher Cathy McMurtrey told *The Washington Post*. "It could get to the point where all we have time for is tests."[2]

The new standards became so controversial that hundreds of parents and teachers turned out for a public hearing, many of them to say, "It's too much, too soon." Since the state's new plan of study has been hailed as a model for the nation—it meets the president's call for stiff academic standards and several states are borrowing from it—I think this trend bears watching.

It's easy to see these changes as the kind of get-tough plan our schools need. After all, aren't we the very parents who complain that our children can't find Europe on the map or do simple addition problems in their heads. Don't we want higher standards? Of course we do. But if you look deeper than surface remedies this latest mania for educational excellence might just be another face of the superbaby syndrome. Worse yet, if current educational reform is merely a quick fix, then students won't make the inner changes that could really make a difference in how they will learn. Instead of pointing blame at the schools and the students, we ought to ask ourselves whether in our race to push children further and faster, we might not have lost the point of the process.

"This Above All: To Thine Own Self Be True."

Think back to your own pasts, to what made you the kind of person you are. Chances are the respect for learning you have, the need to understand what makes your children tick, for example, comes from experiences that are almost indefinable. Not from any program or plan of study but from moments when your parents or a favorite teacher said something that changed you forever. I remember my mother sitting with my brothers and sister and me and reciting Shakespeare from memory:

"This above all: to thine own self be true,
And it must follow, as the night the day,
Thou canst not then be false to any man."

My mother was no sage on a mountaintop. She was a harried parent of four with a pail full of dirty diapers to wash. For several years, my father's work took him out of town from Monday through Friday every week. But she took time out to talk to us about life and learning whenever she could. The diapers could wait.

At first I had no idea what she meant by, "This above all: to thine own self be true," but I heard her say these words often enough through the years that they became a part of me. I began to say them to myself at times when I needed them, when someone or something was enticing me to be less than I could be. This notion of truth to self was not only an intellectual idea but a moral idea. Moreover, it was an idea that helped me bridge the gap between the two spheres, between the world of learning from books and the world of learning by heart. And, as Robert Coles says in *The Moral Intelligence of Children,* kids need, kids crave, both of these kinds of learning.

It is interesting that these words come flooding back to me now because in a paradoxical way, the more we think about our children's intellectual development, the more we are removed from the source of our own greatest inspiration. It is a checklist kind of affair, seeing stimulation as a matter of one, two, three. By filling our heads with a laundry list of do's and don'ts, we have stilled the voice inside that reminds us what we're all about.

Now that we're raising our own children I realize how much education is a matter of excitement, of offering children a world that is tantalizing in its ideas and its complexity. Even very young children can be entranced by words read aloud, although they cannot yet understand them. So when our first daughter was a baby, I bought what would be the first of many copies of Robert Louis Stevenson's *A Child's Garden of Verses.*

"How do you like to go up in a swing,
Up in the air so blue?
Oh, I do think it's the pleasantest thing
Ever a child can do!"

These are words a child can attach to a favorite activity so that when her legs are pumping and her hair is flying behind her in the breeze, she can recall that poem and feel the words within her.

What I'm talking about, I suppose, is inspiration. Inspiration early and often. Perhaps inspiration can be at least an occasional replacement for stimulation. Children will still have to master the multiplication tables and learn to spell. But they will have, at their core, a love of learning.

The superbaby syndrome works against inspiration. Sure the early years are important, but the more we know about how important they are, the more tense and efficient and organized we become about how we use them. It's like the way you felt when you were first learning to ride a bike. You'd be pedaling along pretty well, and then your mother would lean out the window and say, "That's great, honey," and immediately you'd fall off. Self-consciousness gets us every time.

The Growing (Brain) Season

It was pure serendipity that when it came time for me to write this chapter, the airwaves and newspapers were full of information about brain development. There was the Early Childhood Engagement Campaign, which I mentioned earlier, and Brain Awareness Week, during which time you could download a quiz from the Internet to test your knowledge of this three-pound wonder organ. I'm writing these words during the Week of the Young Child, with its theme, "Early years are learning years— make them count!"

That same month the Society for Research on Child Development held its biennial meeting in Washington, D.C. The fact that 4,600 developmental psychologists from here and abroad were gathering practically in my backyard proved an irresistible lure. I spent a day and a half at the conference, which lasted four days, featured 2,000 presenters, and straddled two large, conference-friendly hotels. If you'd been there, you could have heard the latest scientific theories on brain development, the quality of mother-infant attachment, and prenatal drug exposure. You could have attended debates on violence, depression, foster care, teenage pregnancy, television, and more.

If you'd wandered down to the poster sessions, as I did, you'd have found a younger crowd, livelier discussions and obscurer topics, as these developmentalists-in-training sought to distinguish themselves by finding a subject someone else hadn't already mined. "Variability in Arm Activity and Visual Attention during the Transition to Reaching" was one topic that caught my eye. "Synchrony Facilitated Learning of Arbitrary Vowel-Object Relativity by Seven-Months-Old Infants" was another. They were just two out of hundreds, notable because I hadn't a clue what they were about. The studies were posted up on room dividers and people milled around them. Despite the murky titles, what came across here was not stuffy academics, but good minds at work, a sort of marketplace of ideas. I know there was just as much energy and purpose in the more formal sessions upstairs. But it was here that I could best sense the dedication to a life based on research. This is where it all begins, I thought. From ideas like the ones on these poster boards. They are proven or disproven, perhaps elaborated upon in further research, and maybe someday mentioned in a magazine article or used in a childrearing class. And that, of course, is where parents come into the chain. We *are* a part of it, and we need to realize we are.

A highlight of the child development conference was a speech by First Lady Hillary Rodham Clinton. The purpose of her talk was to challenge scientists to disseminate their research as far and wide as they could. "Make sure your research doesn't stay in a room like this," she said. The room we were in was actually a large ballroom, but we knew that she meant the academy, the laboratory, the place where research takes place. Make sure this information affects public policy, she said.

Think of the assumptions underlying her challenge. She was asking scientists to have a direct impact on the way parents rear their children. I attended another session at the conference which was entirely about "dissemination": How to communicate complex ideas in a world of quick sound bites, and how to reach parents who never read magazines or take classes. I felt as if I were in the enemy camp, learning all the secret plans.

Of course, these scientists are not really the enemy. They are intelligent, well-intentioned people furthering our knowledge of the human condition. They have learned, among other things, that the young human brain is not a fixed vessel into which we pour information, but a dynamic entity from the beginning, especially in the first three years. They know that young brains have far more nerve cells than they need and that the cells that aren't used will die. They've also learned that children who don't play much or who are rarely touched have brains 20 to 30 percent smaller than normal, and that laboratory rats with plenty of toys in their cages show more complex behavior than rats raised in empty, boring boxes. Yes, it is fascinating information, and scientists must feel it would be unethical to withhold it from parents. But should we change our lives because of it? Generations of parents have known that babies need parents to talk to them, to listen to their earliest babbles and respond to them. Children need people they love to show them the world, to point out the colors of the sunrise and the way the wind moves through the trees. Parents may not have realized they were helping babies' brains forge neural connections, but they did know that it made them, and their babies, feel good.

Parentese

One of the things researchers are now discovering is that Parentese, the melodious, high-pitched voice mothers and fathers naturally use when talking to babies, hastens the process of connecting words to objects. Isn't it interesting that something so right for babies is something so instinctive for parents—that it's our voices that babies love, not the artificial cadences of television and radio, but the human voice, with all its warbles and imperfections? We don't have to read in a book about how important it is to pitch our voices higher when talking to an infant. We just do it.

Another noteworthy aspect of Parentese, I think, is how it

thrives in an unself-conscious atmosphere. It flows more naturally when we're not thinking about it. The ease and comfort we feel in the company of our babies is, for many of us, unlike any we've felt before. Here is a little person who hangs on our every word; someone who accepts us as we are. Babies don't know that we're wearing our bathrobes at noon or that we haven't combed our hair all morning. In the beginning, they see us at our worst, all tired out and learning on the job. But babies are infinitely forgiving. They are there, over and over again, giving us chance after chance to love them, to show them the way. So we trust them with our silly songs and our Parentese. And they thrive on it.

I can't imagine feigning Parentese, but inevitably parents will, now that word of its importance has emerged. The more crucial early stimulation is found to be, the more at risk our children are for early overstimulation. If knowing the importance of early physical movement spawned a generation of kids reared on Gymboree, which introduces babies as young as three months to "organized" play, then I shudder to think what kind of activities the new brain research will inspire.

The first book is already out on the subject. *Meaningful Differences in the Everyday Experience of Young American Children,* by Betty Hart and Todd Ridley, details a study that found that the more you talk to babies the smarter they become. It's not too far-fetched to think that the next book on this topic will tell us *how* to talk to babies. Or perhaps some entrepreneur will come out with a device to measure the number of words we speak per hour, a voice-o-meter, so we can be sure we're talking enough.

Windows of Opportunity

A crucial catalyst of superbaby anxiety is the notion that there are windows of opportunity when children should learn various skills, and if they miss learning them then, they may never learn them at all. And in some ways, it's true: A child born with cataracts on both eyes will be able to see if the cataracts are removed before two months of age, but will not if they're left on longer than six months. The pathways carrying the pictures to the brain will not have been properly formed.[3] And although one can learn a foreign language at any point in life, it's much easier to do so before age ten. This notion that there is one best time for children to learn or perfect a skill greatly affects our decisions about our children's education. "We wanted Sarah to enter the Spanish language immersion program because we read that it's advantageous to learn a second language at an early age," said Karen Hastings, mother of seven-year-old Sarah and five-year-old Nicholas.

Knowing that there's always a window of opportunity about to slam shut makes me very nervous, though. After thinking about windows and other brain research for a while, I needed some perspective. So I called Jane Healy, an author, teacher, and learning specialist I'd interviewed several times in the past. I knew she had challenged such sacred cows as *Sesame Street* (in her book *Endangered Brains*) and computers for kids (in her latest, *Virtual Minds*). In other words, she's one of those experts who can put other experts in perspective. So what about all this new brain research? I asked.

First of all, she said, the information isn't so new. "I wrote about it in 1985, and it wasn't that new then." But on the whole, she noted, "We are overplaying the role of the environment. I have been one of the writers who's stressed the role of the environment because the environment can do so much [for the brain].

"What we need to keep in mind," she said, "is that the brain is resilient. In the absence of extreme circumstances—like child abuse or real neglect of language input—all is not lost at the end of the first three years. The brain remains plastic throughout adolescence and even till age 30." In fact, Healy said, "There are people who as adults can learn things they could never learn in childhood. There are hundreds of examples of that."

That gave me hope. Maybe parents like me, parents who think too much, can learn to lighten up. If we were to do such a radical thing—lighten up—which part of the research should we use and which should we ignore? "Your child's cognitive development is secondary to his emotional development," Healy said. "If you're going to put your energy in one place or another, put it on emotional development and language. If the basic foundation is there, most of the cognitive stuff can be worked on later. So work on language, emotional support— loving, cuddling, and hugging—then add as much intellectual stimulation as you want to. But don't get uptight about it or you'll ruin the emotional part."

Super Toys for Superbabies

Hugging and talking. It sounds simple enough. But of course it isn't. In her book *The Superbaby Syndrome,* Jean Grasso Fitzpatrick quotes the mother of a nine-month-old baby who says, "Your Busy Box plays music? Gee, ours doesn't. Where'd you get it? I guess I got the wrong one."[4] To avoid such catastrophes, parents can shop in catalogs such as the one that arrived in my mailbox recently from Kids Club. It brings together toys, safety features, and equipment, everything your child needs to be launched into a well-stimulated life. There is a foam desk for "little execs" (ages one to three); an activity center, where "everything baby touches makes something happen"; and "foot finders," black-and-white striped socks with a ladybug and butterfly to "encourage foot-eye coordination." A toy is no longer just a toy; it's a learning tool.

I noticed one brand of infant toys emblazoned with a gold star from the American Academy of Child and Adolescent Psychiatry. "Sassy" brand toys are "designed by child development experts to help your baby learn and grow in four developmental areas—moving and exploring, communicating and talking, thinking and learning, interacting and feeling."

Consider the mobile. This delightful baby toy once featured pastel lambs or bunnies, but that all changed after research showed that infants prefer staring at black-and-white patterns, bull's-eyes, and faces. Now if you look at the baby toy section of an upscale store you're likely to see double from all the black-and-white stripes you're forced to endure.

For preschoolers, there are foam letters for the bathtub and counting games and spelling games. There are those ever-popular and ubiquitous teachers' stores. Did they have these places when we were kids? I always thought teachers got supplies from big, dark closets. But even if there were teachers' stores decades ago, I have a feeling they weren't as spiffy as they are now because the target market has changed considerably. A chain of these stores sent me a catalog recently. It listed the opening of seven new locations and a World Wide Web site, along with its alphabet charts, unifix cubes, and incentive stickers.

In fact, outfits like Zany Brainy and Noodle Kidoodle, two chains of high-end toy emporiums on the East Coast and parts of the Midwest, blur the line between teachers' stores and toy stores. Whenever I enter Zany Brainy (and I try to enter it as little as possible due to the cash I leave behind), I'm hit with a graphic display of what modern childhood is all about. It's a seductive place—lots of good books, child-size shopping carts, videos, and toys, all displayed for touching. There are no tacky toys here. Everything is developmentally sound with just enough of an educational angle that you don't feel guilty spending lots of money. It's a superstore designed to soothe the worries and empty the pocketbooks of parents who think too much.

Booking It

Toys are not the only way our neuroses are showing. Take reading, for example. Curling up with a favorite book and a little child used to be a pleasant, low-key pastime. But now it's a brain-boosting activity, one that even the most conservative educators recommend without reservation. Nursery rhymes and simple stories impress upon growing brains the cadence of the spoken word. Reading begets readers. Perhaps because flashcards, workbooks, and other avenues to achievement have been questioned, parents are even more eager to do a good job at reading.

But, alas, reading to children isn't as simple as it used to be. What books should you read? And when should you begin? There are so many board books for the under-24-month set that first-time parents assume babies will actually sit still to listen to them. These parents are again surprised when, a year later, the same children request a story read aloud every 15 minutes. How much of this is love of literature and how much is AED only the discerning parent will know for sure. Reading aloud has become so politically correct that books such as *A Bedtime Story,* by Mem Fox, and *The Extraordinary Gift,* by Florence Langlois, have as their morals the importance of reading to children.

Meanwhile, bookstores have found that one surefire way to lure parents inside is to promise story hours and children's book groups. Libraries offer so many storytellers, puppet shows, and other book-related entertainment for kids that adults find it difficult to browse in peace. Bookfairs are a can't-miss fundraiser for schools. A front-page story in our newspaper recently detailed the amazing allure of a chain letter for kids' books. People who would pitch any other kind of chain could not pass up one that promised to improve youngsters' minds.

Once again, the problem is not that we read to our kids, but the fuss we make about doing it. If one story is good, we reason, then four must be better. As proof of our obsession with the quality of our children's reading, note the many books that either review children's books, such as *The Parents' Guide to the Best Books for Children,* by Eden Ross Lipson, and *Books to Build On,* by the Core Knowledge Foundation; or encourage parental involvement, such as *Raising a Reader,* by Paul Kropp, or *Keeping Kids Reading* by Mary Leonhardt. There's a Children's Literature Web site, which clocks 3,500 hits a week, "Children's Literature: A Newsletter for Adults," and the Chinaberry Catalog, a folksy, annotated compilation of books for children and parents.

We insist that the pleasures of literature be extended to even the youngest readers. For the baby who has everything, there is *Babybug,* a magazine for children two and under that costs five dollars per issue. A precursor to *Ladybug* and *Cricket, Babybug* is a "board magazine" that comes wrapped with instructions for parents: "Some children may notice in the picture that the boy's shoelace needs to be tied. If not, point it out." The editors are careful to add a disclaimer: "This shouldn't be a 'test,' but rather a relaxed, enjoyable time to have fun with Babybug." But they give themselves away when they say, "We hope you and your child enjoy *interacting* with Babybug." Does one "interact" with a much-loved story?

It seems to me that kids do just fine with a random collection of printed material. If there's a jumble of books and magazines around, kids can pick out what they like, even if it happens to be adult poetry or an old *National Geographic*. Or maybe I'm just saying this in self-defense. Books are everywhere in our house: crammed into shelves, piled beside beds, and stacked on top of tables. People give us old, cast-off volumes; I pick up out-of-print titles at library book sales; and we order books through the school. The titles are not all politically correct. Some are old volumes of chauvinistic fairy tales I enjoyed as a girl. And others are hopelessly out of date. I believe we have an astronomy book published before Pluto was discovered. But whenever I begin to worry about the disorganized condition of our library, I tell myself that children are resilient creatures, and they will find what they need.

And then there is the matter of how much we should read to our little ones. Tom and I must have read two hours a day to our firstborn. Yes, it seems to have worked, she loves to read now. But why should we spend so much time reading *Charlotte's Web* to our kids that we have no time left to read Charlotte Brontë to ourselves?

The Other Ten Hours

Has the superbaby syndrome, newly fueled by the latest brain research, had much impact on childcare? How could it not? The fact that so much happens to babies before the age of three is bound to make the parents of young children who work outside the home think and think again about being away from their little ones. At the very least, it will make us listen all the more carefully to what experts have to say about the effect of childcare on the mental and emotional development of young children.

I heard the latest word on childcare at the child development conference I mentioned earlier, when researchers there reported on the largest study to date.[5] Scientists tracked over 1,300 children in nine states—and hope to follow these same children until age seven. Their conclusions were that the balance of power still rests in family life and that it's the quality not the quantity of daycare that matters. It's how much a provider responds to your child, talks to him, sings to him, reads to him. It's all the subtle stuff you'd expect, quantified as best it could be.

Most of the reporters at the press conference announcing these findings were women. "What would I tell a mother who's trying to decide how many hours of care her child should have?" asked one, anxiously. The new report does show that the mother-infant attachment weakens a bit if the child has lots of daycare in the first six months, and when one of the researchers said that, in a low-key way, you could almost hear the alarm bells sounding in nearby ears.

It just so happens that this press conference was held on a Friday, the day I recently added to our daycare week. In order for me to write this book, our youngest daughter is now in care four days a week rather than three, more than either of our other daughters ever was. I know firsthand why parents want "answers" about daycare, why we pay such close attention to study after study. One says, yes, daycare is okay. Another says, no, it's not. Still another one, this one, says it's okay as long as it's good. But what is good? No one really knows. The bottom line, of course, is that we must figure out what "good" is for ourselves.

The prevalence of daycare *has* changed the way we rear children, though, and it does feed the superbaby syndrome, which is why I mention it here. There are 12 million kids in childcare. Half go to centers and half stay with family or in other informal care, according to the Child Care Information Exchange. Daycare, especially if it's at a center, is by its very nature more organized and efficient than most parents are. Yet when I see at-home parents trucking their kids from one activity to another or working parents replicating on weekends a frenetic weekday-like schedule in their quest for quality time, I think maybe all of us are subconsciously competing with hired providers. Daycare has fostered the superbaby syndrome by making us think of ourselves more as teachers than parents.

In our quest for stimulation, aren't we, whether stay-at-home or working parents, giving up the very things that make us special? Isn't one of our chief advantages the fact that we don't have to be "stimulating"? We can give our kids a refreshing and creativity-inducing haphazardness; we can give them normal life. As I mentioned in Chapter Three, children who are in daycare all day seldom see adults washing windows or balancing checkbooks or doing other tasks that don't pertain directly to them. They quickly gain the mistaken notion that big people are present solely to tend to the needs of little people. It's not that parents can't compensate for these mistaken impressions. My point is that daycare is contributing to the superbaby syndrome by changing the way we look at childrearing. The more we analyze what goes into good childrearing (and daycare has certainly made us do that), the more we've decided that "stimulation" must be part of the package.

It's interesting that although many experts say children benefit from the social life and stimulation of quality center daycare, many working parents seek out family daycare providers. Maybe it's because it's more affordable, but I'd like to think it's because when kids are with family, or in a baby-sitter's house, they are more like children used to be, and if left alone, they will find their own stimulating activities. They will make a bunny out of an old plastic container and a bunch of cotton. They will draw pictures of sailing ships and blue skies. They will listen to the same song 15 times without stopping.

And then, when they are back home with us, they will be ready for what I think they need from parents—not quality time but downtime. What they miss when they're not with us is who we are, is the way only we know how to be. So on Saturdays, Sundays, and Mondays, and in the late afternoons and evenings of our weeks, I try to give our kids home life—with all its confusion, inadequacy, and inspiration—all the songs we can sing, all the stars we can see, and pie crust we make together, from scratch.

Get Ready, Get Set, Get Ready!

Perhaps the new brain research will make preschool passé. After all, if the first three years are all *that* important, then four- and five-year-olds are a bit over the hill. When the Clintons had their own brain conference, the president announced he would expand Early Head Start enrollment by a third. Early Head Start was created in 1994 to bring the same kind of services to very young children that Head Start has given preschoolers.

As it stands now, of course, preschool is anything but passé. Enrollment among three- and four-year-olds has quadrupled in the last 25 years. Almost a third of children under school age are enrolled in organized group programs. At least 20 percent of those include children under three. That's double the percentage 15 years earlier. For many children, preschool has become the beginning of the rat race—a rat race that starts much earlier than it used to.

For some parents, enrolling a child in preschool is as simple as signing up with a local program held in the basement of a nearby church. But in the big cities and affluent suburbs of this country, getting into a good preschool is as fraught with tension as applying to college. Big city parents who choose private schools, for instance, must test and enroll their child in a prestigious nursery school to increase his chances of being accepted into a top-notch grade school. Every fall, newspaper articles appear about the angst of getting a child into one of the East Coast's more exclusive preschools, places where kids stand a 300-to-one chance of being accepted and parents pay up to $10,000 a year if they are.

But to earn this privilege, parents must begin searching in the fall, apply in the winter, and wait until spring to find out if the little tyke "made it." They must fill out applications for two-year-olds that require character descriptions, lists of hobbies, and letters of reference.

Most of us will not experience the angst of parents who must enter a lottery even to get an application to a desirable preschool. But the point is, most of us do assume our child will go to preschool, and we spend quite a bit of time deciding which kind and which one. We begin agonizing about our children's education when the little guys are two or three instead of when they are five or six. By the time our kids earn their graduate degrees, they will have been students more than 20 years.

The big deal we make out of preschool is early evidence of how much we feel that the education of our children rests on our shoulders. Look at the book titles: *You Are Your Child's First Teacher*, by Rahima Baldwin, or *Awakening Brilliance: How to Inspire Children to Become Successful Learners*, by Pamela Sims. Over and over again, we hear the message: If the job is to be done right, we must do it ourselves. In one of the parenting classes I attended recently, our final exercise was to write, on a three-by-five card, what we would say to a teacher we were briefing on our little student.

If we can't get the help we need from a teacher or principal, then we must go outside the system to a tutor or a learning center and buy the help we need. Tutors have always been available to help struggling students. But the tutoring and learning centers of today are as much for average and above-average students who want to get ahead as they are for below-average ones who want to catch up. No one keeps figures on the number of tutoring centers that have opened in the last decade, but their increased presence in our midst is proven by the fact that two tutoring associations were founded in the early 1990s. Tutors fill important needs in a superbaby society. They help kids who cannot make the grade, and they ratchet up expectations. By the time kids are in high school, some parents pay college consultants to advise students on which activities to' take, which to drop, the colleges to which they should apply, and how to package themselves for admission.

Teachers' Stories

Before I was a writer, I was a teacher, but that was many years ago, before the full flowering of the superbaby syndrome. I wanted to know if experienced teachers would agree with my observations. Do they see parents who carry the weight of the world on their shoulders? Do they think the lasting legacy of the superbaby syndrome is threatening the way teachers teach, students learn, and parents raise their kids?

Barry Kritzberg, who noticed those two boys and their fathers on the bus that I described in the beginning of this chapter, has been teaching almost 25 years. A rigorous but much loved high school English teacher, he has a way of making Camus come alive. But he sees parents progressively more interested in how to get their kids into college than in how to help them get the most out of high school. "Parents are looking for shortcuts and prescriptions," he says. He tells the story of being cornered at a social gathering once by a woman he did not know but who knew he was a teacher. She asked him how her sons might improve their SAT scores. When Kritzberg told her, "They should read widely, in as many disciplines as possible," she wasn't satisfied. "But shouldn't they memorize vocabulary words or take a Stanley Kaplan course?" she pressed. "No," Kritzberg persisted. "Their time would be better spent reading books." The woman then admitted that her sons' English teacher had told her the same thing. Parental attitudes like these explain why students are willing to learn thousand-word vocabulary lists, but not read a book.

This is high school, though, and I wondered if these attitudes develop earlier. So I talked with Sue Hall, who's been teaching for 18 years, most recently first grade in Fairfax County, Virginia. She's a warm and funny woman who's launched countless first-graders into the big school. I asked her to tell me about the parents she sees now.

"I see parents' intensity increasing every year," she said. "I think 20 years ago parents had high expectations for their children, but they allowed teachers to teach. Now what I see more and more of is parents who want to be involved and are very well-meaning, are very well-read and well-versed, but they really would like to design the curriculum for their children."

Our county school board recently floated the idea of asking parents to buy expensive laptop computers (at a special discount price of $1,800 each!) for sixth-graders to use at school. There was an immediate outcry against the notion, but it's significant that the idea was even brought up at all. Do children really need this stuff? Have children really changed?

"As I say at every back-to-school night and have for years, the volume of materials that children must learn today is many more times the amount that we had to learn. For one thing, we didn't have to worry about being computer literate when we went to first grade," says Hall. "But the one thing that hasn't changed over time is that a six-year-old is still a six-year-old. No matter how much more information we have to pour into their little minds, they've only had life experience on this earth for six years. So we have to be very careful in balancing that. I think in parents' zeal to have the very best for our children sometimes we push them too much."

Before she became a teacher, Hall was a pre-med student, so she has a lot of 25-year-old medical textbooks around her house. She uses these to make a point: "A little knowledge is dangerous," she says. "When I or my kids have a symptom I refer back to these books. For one thing, they probably have a cure for whatever it is now and I'm not even aware of it. But this reminds me of some of the parents I have. They read a book, but they don't practice the profession. They don't have anyone else with whom they can compare the knowledge they gain from books, so they take this knowledge that has been generalized and never meant to describe a specific child and become an 'expert' on their child."

When Hall said this, some thoughts that had been bobbing around disconnectedly in my head suddenly came together. Reading books about childrearing can rob us of confidence, can make the easy difficult and the difficult easy. We've already talked about that. But they can also make us think we're experts on everything connected with our kids, even things we know very little about. Of course we understand our own children better than anyone else. In that sense we are the true experts. But can we claim to be better versed in education than the men and women who toil away at the profession every day?

There are people who would answer yes to that question, and many of them are homeschoolers. I mentioned homeschooling in Chapter Three, and I do think that attention excess disorder is part of why it's so popular now. However, homeschooling is also a product of a superbaby society. It is a way to drop out of the competitiveness while still pushing education.

Susan Tullington began teaching her seven-year-old, Kevin, at home because he didn't want to go to school. But once she began to homeschool, she became more and more sold on the idea. Homeschooling helps a child learn to be a learner, Susan said. You, the parent, are not as much a teacher as a "resource person." You point your child in the direction he wants to go. It was while talking to Susan that I began to see our positions as points on a line, as a continuum. Some parents consult experts for almost every aspect of raising children. Others feel that the more they control, the better off their children will be. They say, if we're casting off some childrearing experts then why not do away with teachers, too?

Many parents decide to homeschool their children because they feel schools are usurping parental duties (even as teachers claim that parents expect them to raise their kids). Some homeschoolers hope to create a more godly environment for their children; others merely hope to create a saner one, less pressure and competition, fewer tests. I respect parents who homeschool, but my instincts tell me that our kids will be better off with someone else teaching them to read and write and compute. Teaching is an art, and like most arts, is perfected by practice. Some of the more earnest parents I see remind me of student teachers, idealistic and naive, filled with book learning, untested and untried. But unlike student teachers, we will never have a way to put our knowledge to the test. Unless we home-school, of course.

Learning Styles of the Not-Yet-Famous

In his 1983 book *Frames of Mind,* Harvard educator Howard Gardner proposed the theory that children learn in many ways, that they have seven forms of intelligence: verbal, logical-mathematical, spatial, musical, kinesthetic, interpersonal, and intrapersonal. Traditional classrooms reward verbal and logical-mathematical intelligences more than any other, and children whose capacities fit neatly into those two learning styles tend to excel in school. Gardner and others have tried to make educators more aware of the many ways children learn and have founded schools based on multiple intelligence principles. I think it fair to say that even though most schools still base their curriculums primarily on verbal and logical-mathematical approaches, there is greater awareness of the many ways kids learn.

The theory of multiple intelligences is sound and much needed. But it's easy to see how parents could abuse it, especially parents of superkids. "Sometimes this knowledge about learning styles allows parents to make excuses. I see a great deal of that now," Sue Hall says. "Parents may say something like, 'He's a kinesthetic learner,' which is a nice way of saying, 'He's hyperactive.' Or they might say, 'You don't take my child's individuality into account. He's really "gifted and talented." He's just an "alternative learner." ' A good teacher always looks at each child as an individual. We do take that into account. You can't make excuses from a definition in a book."

In *The Superbaby Syndrome,* Fitzpatrick presents Gardner's theories as a balm to parents who might have thought their child would never make the grade in the logical/analytical arena. The multiple intelligence way of being smart, she says, "more fully appreciates [children's] unique talents and inclinations, rather than just branding them 'very bright' or (perish the thought!) 'not particularly bright.' "[6] What Fitzpatrick thought would broaden parents' viewpoints and release them from the traditional intelligence trap, which made sense at the first wave of the superbaby syndrome in the '80s, has been commandeered by parents eager to find evidence of intelligence in any arena. Now any child can be gifted. If not in the traditional way, then interpersonally or kinesthetically or musically. With multiple intelligence as our ally, there's no end to the little geniuses we can create. But this attitude often puts us at odds with teachers and school administrators.

Many of us grew up in the post-sputnik, "Why Johnny Can't Read" era, and we are the products of an educational system that has been trying to purify and improve itself ever since. We have our own less-than-sterling memories of school. Now we're armed with books and studies and good intentions and we're determined to get something better for our kids. So we don't stand behind the teacher and the system, as our parents did. If our child comes home complaining of a bad grade, we don't tell him to accept it or help him do better next time. We go in and demand a better mark. "When kids don't make the grade, parents say, 'It must be because the classroom is not stimulating,' or the teacher is not stimulating their child," Hall says. It's become the responsibility of the teacher to stimulate instead of the responsibility of the child to learn. Barry Kritzberg has had parents beg him to improve their children's grades because the poor marks they did earn are bad for their "self-esteem." No wonder grade inflation has become such a problem.

The Gifted and the Derailed

During a phone conversation, a friend of mine eagerly confided, "The letters have gone out." The "letters" were not from a college or prep school. They were the official notification of acceptance into the gifted and talented program, fondly known as GT.

Parents have always wanted their children to excel, and it's easy to say that GT programs are just another expression of this universal desire. And yet, making the cut seems so important now, and it happens so early—in elementary school rather than middle or high school. I offer the GT hoopla as further proof of the superbaby syndrome's lingering legacy.

Some gifted and talented programs give bright kids enrichment in the classroom right along with "average" students.

Other programs pull GT kids out into separate classrooms, even separate schools. Parents whose children make the cut are glad for the extra attention and stimulation. Without it they feel their youngsters would languish in a sea of mediocrity and would not reach their potential. Parents whose children don't make it feel their kids are deprived of the extra resources (field trips, special programs, more individualized attention) showered on the GT kids.

GT certainly brings out a competitive streak in parents. They begin to gear their kids up for this program in kindergarten and continue throughout the early grades. So crucial is the appearance of academic success to some parents that they hire tutors for their "gifted and talented" child. At this point you might wonder whose interest is being served. As Elkind points out in *The Hurried Child,* "The desire to say that a child is in one of these 'gifted and talented' programs has pushed many parents to put their children in such programs even when they really do not belong and cannot keep up. Such youngsters are doubly humiliated by their failure within the 'gifted and talented' class and then by having to leave it and rejoin the regular class."[7] As for the exclusiveness of GT, there are so many "gifted" children in our area that there's a large organization dedicated to their needs and concerns.

At the other end of the gifted and talented spectrum, but closer than you might think, are the large numbers of children diagnosed with attention deficit disorder or other learning disabilities. There have always been children who can't pay attention, who bounce off the walls with energy. That such behavior can be tied to a brain disorder is very reassuring to parents. But like any other valid discovery, this one can also be misused. Parents may cling to a diagnosis of attention deficit disorder because it provides an excuse for failure.

ADD affects an estimated six percent of children under age 18. The number of ADD cases doubled from 1990 to 1995, and the production of the drug Ritalin tripled during that time. Some mental health experts believe ADD is a fad disorder and that kids are being diagnosed with it because it's a quick fix for frustrated parents and overtaxed teachers.[8]

"So many parents will come in and say, 'My school wants me to get an occupational therapy or developmental evaluation for my child,' " says Maryland pediatrician Linda Goldstein. Often she tells the parents, "Your child is doing okay. Maybe he's not great at everything but no one's great at everything." While some parents come to her just to get the referral for specialized evaluation and treatment, others, she says, want a "reality check—they ask me, 'Am I nuts for thinking my kid's pretty good? The school is making me nervous.' "

A few weeks ago I sat in a room with a number of parents and parenting professionals. We were at an unusual conference that featured speakers versed in spiritual as well as psychological issues. We could have talked about most anything, yet the conversation in our small group drifted toward attention deficit disorder. One participant, the principal of a Montessori school, said that six out of a class of 12 first-graders at her school were recently diagnosed ADD or ADHD. She wondered whether these children might be suffering from something deeper and more all-encompassing than a learning disorder.

Another group member, a psychotherapist, discussed research which showed that stress in a family increases the chance that a child has ADD. We wondered aloud if pushing children to excel in school and activities might be contributing to the epidemic of ADD. Specialists in learning have certainly not ruled out the power of the environment. "Children who come from overly permissive—or overly bossy—homes may have particular problems internalizing motivation and behavioral controls,"[9] says Jane Healy. The more intellectually competitive our society, the more we need the sanctuary of a diagnosis such as attention deficit disorder.

Testing . . . Testing

An eight-year-old begins worrying in February about the standardized exam he's scheduled to take in May. He asks his mother what would happen if he had to go to the bathroom during the test and wonders whether he should get his pencils ready four months ahead of time.

Tests are an unavoidable part of modern academic life. Though we decry them, especially when they're "wrong," achievement could not exist without them. Schools administer tests to confirm learning (or lack thereof) and to separate children into categories: gifted, normal, "special." But critics of frequent testing note that children learn more about passing tests than they do about the subject matter itself. A friend of mine told me about a child she knows who always got A's on his spelling test but forgot how to spell the words the next week. When his parents brought up the fact that their son had little or no retention, the teacher pointed proudly to his test scores. "But look, he's getting '100s' on his spelling tests." "Yes," his mother replied. "But he's not learning how to spell."

Testing stresses children by pushing them to perform. It's a departure from the normal day, and even little kids know that a lot rides on it. Even more frightening to equal-opportunity-minded Americans is that tests are often used to label kids early, before they've had a chance to prove themselves.

Testing has changed considerably since we were kids, says Jane Healy. Then, the IQ test was used as a "scientific crystal ball, virtually capable of predicting a child's future on the basis of a one-hour test."[10] Fortunately for all of us, teachers no longer depend upon a single test to grade a child. They rely on several tests and, of course, upon a child's performance in the classroom.

We are well rid of the IQ tyranny, but perhaps we have gotten rather too much of the upper hand over tests. In some school districts, if parents don't agree with test results used to determine giftedness, they can have their child privately retested to show that, yes indeed, he can make the cut. Tests have also become more, shall we say, accessible. For example, SAT scores were just "recentered," which means that the College Board decided to base its average score on the performance of students who took the test in 1990 instead of 1941. A 508 on math a student earns now would have been a 484 on the original scale, and a 505 on verbal would have been a 428. I can't help but think that changes like this, as well as rampant grade inflation, are further evidence of the superbaby syndrome's lasting legacy. If we can't make kids smarter, we'll make them seem smarter.

Assessing school performance is a product of this same mentality. School districts want to be sure children are learning. They are pressured by smart, anxious parents who want their children to have optimal educational experiences. Some school districts now issue "report cards" which measure (and pit) one school against another. When the New York State Education Department for the first time issued report cards of school districts, one school principal felt it necessary to hold a meeting with real estate agents, who worried that mediocre scores in a neighborhood school would make it difficult to sell houses in that area.

Our kids and our schools aren't the only ones being tested. Parenting classes often use quizzes to help us decipher our "parenting style." However we look at it, the prevalence of testing, the casual way we toss around names like "Iowa" (the test, not the state) and "Otis-Lennon," signifies a deeper difference in the way we visualize our children's minds. No longer do we imagine an uncharted land, a bit mysterious. Now we visualize gray matter deepening and furrowing, growing more textured, synapses humming with messages, our child Ivy League bound.

Why Parents Help Johnny Learn to Read

Parents who think too much may be a pain around testing time. But they are quite valuable the rest of the year. Most of us feel it's essential to be active and visible in our kids' schools. We may choose a co-op nursery school, join the Parent Teacher Association, even take on those unpopular fund-raising jobs. We volunteer in our children's classrooms, in the office, cafeteria, or library. We attend workshops to learn about new types of math or reading instruction. We want to learn what our kids learn, to know what they know.

Districts strapped for cash and staff use parents to monitor hallways, take attendance, and tutor reading. Parents sell candy, wrapping paper, and entertainment coupon books; or they collect cereal box tops or cash register receipts to raise money for computers, uniforms, even teacher salaries. Sometimes parents donate their labor to build a playground or install computer cables to link schools to the Internet. Sometimes I wish the school would just ask us for a generous donation in September and be done with it.

I'll admit I'm probably in the minority, though. Many parents love working in their child's school. They want to keep an eye on what their kids are doing and ensure they have a high-quality learning environment. They've read the studies which show that children do better in school when parents are involved in their education, and they don't want to take any chances. Their definition of involvement seems to include being physically present in the school building for hours each month.

And then, there is parental peer pressure. The rise in dual-career couples means that fewer of us have the time to be "room parents," to make calls to organize who's working at the school carnival. Parents who are willing to pitch in feel there is even greater pressure for them to do it all. But they may soon get some relief, as school districts have begun playing upon the guilt of those who don't volunteer. An ad in a Lexington, Kentucky newspaper shows a proud parent and the words, "Being a volunteer makes a difference to this mother." The ad was sponsored by the Partnership for Kentucky Schools and boasted the slogan: "Education. Make it your business." The very existence of that slogan, and the reference to the volunteer's full-time job ("although she has to take personal or vacation time to volunteer at school during her normal working hours, her employer is always agreeable to her special schedule needs") makes it clear that no longer is it enough to join the PTA and check your child's homework at night. Now you're urged to take a personal day to volunteer in the classroom or chaperone a field trip.

In exclusive private schools, which you might think would

require little of parents other than the $10,000 or $15,000 a year they shell out to send their children there, parent involvement is an even greater given. As James Atlas writes, "Boy, am I busy! What with serving as a sommelier at the Fathers Who Cook dinner, attending 'the first Class VII Parents in Action Meeting,' lacing up my kids' Chargers on Great Skate Night at Wollman Rink, attending a performance of 'Iolanthe,' and hawking raffle tickets for the school fund drive door to door in our building, who has time for work? Sometimes I fret: Which stocks are tanking while the broker from Goldman, Sachs is at his daughter's basketball game? What perp is on the loose while the district attorney organizes the Father-Daughter Breakfast? Can the citizenry of New York City afford to have the parents of school-age children keeping these indentured-servant hours?"[11]

Maybe we volunteer in our kids' schools because our parents didn't work in ours, and we want to assert our independence from them. Think back to your own parents. Though PTA membership was higher when we were kids (it peaked in the early '60s), parents didn't work three hours a week in the library. We knew our parents were behind us, but teaching students was the teachers' job, learning was our job, and unless there was trouble, parents were barely in the loop. I can remember my mother coming to school about twice a year, once for the annual parent-teacher conference and the other because I'd forgotten my lunch. It was not that the teachers couldn't have used some help (there were 60 children in my first-grade class), but the separation between home and school was almost as sacred as the separation between church and state.

Now we have school programs designed to teach students *and their parents* the importance of math. (Haven't we served our time in the prison of arithmetic?) We have projects that are ostensibly the child's responsibility yet cannot be completed without parental help. We have, in short, lots of busywork. Perhaps we ought to busy ourselves with other things.

Isn't it possible that more is expected of parents because parents expect more for their children? If so, then the guilt placed on parents who can't measure up to the volunteer requirements (either implied or self-imposed) can be traced right back to—you guessed it—our nasty habit of thinking too much. The title of a recent workshop I attended at our children's public school tells the tale: "Parents on Board: Building Academic Success Through Parent Involvement." Instead of seeing this as our *child*'s school experience, it's something we're doing together.

Earnestly Extracurricular

We live off what is known as a "cut through" street. While indistinguishable from any other quiet suburban drive most of the day, from 3:30 to 4 P.M., vans and station wagons begin their afternoon trek down the street to shave a few minutes off their trip to the nearby elementary school. School is dismissed at 3:45 P.M., and it's difficult to make a four o'clock soccer practice or piano lesson unless Mom picks you up and takes you there. So we've gotten used to a mini rush hour on our sidewalk-less suburban lane.

We push our children in many ways other than academic ones. Perhaps because we recognize that children have different styles of learning or because we want our kids to have many chances to shine or because we see younger and younger athletic champions and musical prodigies, we are encouraging children to find their passion and find it early. We want to stimulate not just our children's neurons, but their fingers and their feet and, above all, their artistic and athletic prowess. We want to enrich them—and we do, often to the point of saturation.

Maybe we're so impressed with extra activities because they hold out to us the promise of a perfectly adjusted child. "Your child gets more out of childhood at Gymboree," reads one brochure. A competitor's reads: "The Little Gym's *unique, non-competitive* [their emphasis] curriculum and environment offer children the opportunity to love themselves as they are," says a brochure. "The building of self-confidence and self-esteem is truly the key to success, both now and for the future." Inside is a schedule of classes for children aged four months to 14 years and this lofty "mission statement": "To promote the Healthy and Successful Physical and Mental Development of the Children of the World."

A mother at the bus stop the other day said that her five-year-old was now taking karate three days a week. "I thought it would be a few years before I was driving her around to activities all the time," she said, a tinge of frustration in her voice. "She used to take karate only one day a week, but she's been taking it for a couple years now and she has three friends who are all moving up to the next level, too." It was plain that this mother had reservations about involving her young child in such a schedule. But she seemed reluctant to say no.

Parenting newspapers are filled with ads touting art classes, soccer leagues, gymnastics, tai chi, you name it. Just so we won't feel guilty that our children are wasting time on these activities, they are pitched for their educational value. An ad for a karate school says, "Karate Teaches Kids A Lot!" and includes a karate "report card." Discipline A+, Confidence A+, and Attitude A+.

Activities begin when children are born. I've already mentioned Gymboree, and there are plenty of music and movement classes for toddlers. I know a two-year-old who takes horseback riding lessons. By the time a child is in preschool it's not uncommon for her to have dropped out of more activities than we ever took. "When you're a parent you want to give your child everything you didn't have as a child," says Tiff Wimberly. Of course, there are a lot of activities that weren't even available when we were young, so to work in all these classes, children must start early. "Nobody wants a beginner on their team," says Colleen Sullivan. "If kids haven't had a couple years of baseball by third grade, nobody wants you." Imagine that, washed up at eight!

By school age, the pace picks up considerably. "I see children on five different soccer teams, two basketball teams, and who play the violin *and* the oboe. Plus, they're on a hockey team and doing ballet," Sharon Davis-Holmes, an elementary school principal, told me. "I'm exaggerating a little now, but you know what I mean. Somewhere along the line, I think everybody has lost their minds. How much enrichment do kids need? When do they get a chance to do what they want to do?''

Summer School

Activities that are called classes during the school year become "daycamps" in the summer. Here's a pitch from a private school in Indianapolis: "Arts, crafts, games, stories, and nature are all a part of our integrated theme-based camps designed to hook your child's interests at his or her developmental level." Once camps were places to romp and play, ride horses, and make lanyards; now they must have themes and contain the word "developmental" in their promotional literature. Choosing a camp has become such a production that some parents and kids visit a number of them the summer before—much like the traditional college scouting tour.

An article in our paper one of the first days of vacation was headlined: "Play's the Thing: Children's Days Are Often Booked Solid. So When Do They Learn to Goof Around?" In it parents waxed nostalgic about their own unfettered childhoods and experts asserted how important it is to give children a chance to play on their own. But they should only do this 20 to 30 percent of the time, cautioned one of the authorities. Take out your stopwatches! The article's final irony was a box at the end telling parents how to leave their children alone. It was entitled: "Playtime Pointers for Parents."[12]

Don't you wish you could give your kids what you had? Safer streets and a neighborhood full of playmates. A world that doesn't require adult-organized activities but where games well up from the collective unconscious that is childhood. The other day it struck me how little our girls jump rope. When I was a girl the jump rope was our constant companion. These were beefy cotton ropes, thick but soft. My friend Elaine would hold one end and I the other and her kid sister Phoebe would jump. Then we would switch places. On the playground a line of girls would wait to jump. If we could find two ropes we'd jump double dutch. After school we'd collect as many kids as we could find (and there were over 20 of us in one block), and play Wiffle ball in someone's backyard. Nostalgia has a way of erasing the bad times. But I still remember the mean dog named Colonel who terrorized the neighborhood and how lonely I was the summer that my friend Barbie went away with her family. Even with the bad memories factored in, we had a good time.

Now we're suspicious of regular, unplanned fun. It seems a rather flimsy platform on which to build a future life, and the idle months of summer have been rounded up into the superbaby corral. Increasing numbers of schools offer summer "homework," reading lists and vacation classes. Tutoring centers pelt us with flyers to encourage business in June and July. "This month we are offering $20 discounts on diagnostic evaluations for new students," read one of these flyers. "Don't let the summer slip away. Call now!" I guess no summer is complete without a diagnostic evaluation.

Meanwhile, some school systems already have year-round school and others are considering it. Yes, I know most parents work and kids need to stay busy. I know our kids must compete in a global marketplace. There are forces at work here that may be beyond our control, yet it seems to me that summer is still essential, even the poor imitation of summer we now have. It is the time when kids touch bottom with boredom and suddenly come up with great plans, brilliant ideas, a backyard circus. It is when they finally clean their rooms because they have nothing better to do. One summer a particularly enterprising lad we know, who's now almost grown, re-bottled his mother's perfume and sold it door to door. Nothing like that could happen if there were year-round school. Has the superbaby syndrome made us think we can do away with boredom?

How Quickly It Goes

In the introduction to the revised edition of *The Hurried Child,* David Elkind says the reason there are still superbabies, even after mothers and fathers learned about the stress that pushing kids causes, was that superbabies make life easier for parents. "We are going through one of those periods in history, such as the early decades of the Industrial Revolution, when children are the unwilling victims of societal upheaval and change," he said. When we think of our child as a "superkid," we can "hurry the little powerhouse with impunity."[13] We feel we're doing right by him even as we force him into an adult-like world he is not yet prepared to enter. We cling to this myth because it is reassuring to us in our busy, pressured lives. Our children are so bright, so talented, so esteemed.

The myth of child competence we've created may temporarily assuage our guilt, but it won't work forever. I'm sure there's no conspiracy to shove our children into early adulthood by pushing their intellectual and extracurricular development. The lasting legacy of the superbaby syndrome has many causes and many cures and some cures (the multiple intelligences theory, for example) that twist back on themselves and become causes. Once again, it's up to us to think our way out of this mess, to approach our children's development with wisdom and maturity, to keep our eyes on the big picture.

I am talking with first-grade teacher Sue Hall again. She's telling me about her two sons. One's in high school, the other's in college. So old, so fast. Our daughters are much younger, but they are old enough—and I am old enough—to know the truth of her words, to feel it in my bones. "Parents come in, and they're so intense and uptight. I just want to shake them and say, 'Have you any idea how quickly this will go?' " It's that old truth, the biggest cliché of childrearing ("Enjoy them now, they grow up so fast") but still the ultimate, all-too-fathomable reality. Isn't that what we are up against? Time and its constraints. Time and its opportunities.

One of the most significant findings in the Zero to Three poll of parents was that half of them said they end their days feeling they've spent less time with their kids than they wanted to. Some (20 percent) said they'd spent a *lot* less time, and others (27 percent) said they'd spent a *little* less. But whether a lot or a little, many parents go to bed with a nagging sense of incompletion and loss.

How are some parents avoiding the powerful pull of the

superbaby syndrome? By not hiring a tutor or assuming their child has a learning disability when he brings home average grades; by not feeling desperate when other kids *appear* (that's a key word) to be passing them by. My friend Maureen reminds herself three or four times a week that her sons do not need to be involved in sports every season. "These activities erode the family," she says one night during our book group. She's decided that her family is better off with less, and she's sticking with it, despite the peer pressure (on her kids and on her as well) to do otherwise. Attitude adjustments like Maureen's are difficult to make because it's hard not to think your child is losing out. To keep the faith, we can remind ourselves that we're changing for our kids' sakes—and that we haven't a moment to lose.

Even Hillary Clinton came close to admitting that information can make parents think too much: "My fear is that parents will feel even more guilt and anxiety because they're not doing enough," she said in her speech at the child development conference. And in fact there are plenty of fine parents who have not read, and do not need to read, any books or magazines on what makes children thrive. They do not know the latest theories on cognitive development. But they are teaching their children to respect themselves and others. They are showing their children the books they love and the world around them. They are, perhaps, the modern day inheritors of that stubborn Yankee self-reliance that Ralph Waldo Emerson describes: "If the single man plant himself indomitably on his instincts, and there abide, the huge world will come round to him."

What are the gifts we want to give our children? What kind of people do we want them to become—perpetual learners or prodigies who flare up and burn out? Perhaps we ought to think about the purpose of the enrichment programs, the tutors, the computers in kindergarten. Do we want our children to value education as an end in itself, or do we teach them, from the beginning, that education is merely a means to an end: today, a GT class; tomorrow, a big income and expensive home?

Tulip Buds

As I finish writing this chapter it is springtime in Virginia. I slow down on my ho-hum daily drives. I want to look at each papery dogwood blossom, each shimmering azalea. Surely, spring is extravagant. Like the young brain, it puts forth far more than it needs to. Soon it will take some of its bounty back. The bright colors will fade. "Nature's first green is gold/Her hardest hue to hold," said poet Robert Frost.

Today I'm noticing tulips, and I decide that I like them better before they open. Tulip buds are elegant and purposeful, and what is so grand about them, I think, is the sense of potential they evoke. A closed tulip is two plants, really, the one you see before you and the one you know will follow.

Our children are buds, too, more potential than actual. Though I don't buy into the analogy that we must leave them alone and let them unfold on their own, it struck me the other day, looking at a row of particularly fetching tulips, that all this research, all this angst about neural pathways and learning styles, is making us miss the point, the glory of our children being not yet formed. The great miracle of potential.

Instead of carrying this potential like a great weight upon our shoulders, why don't we delight in it. Do our best, of course, but then simply enjoy it. We will worry sometimes about whether our kids will bloom as we would like them to. But should we do it so much, and with such intensity, that we forget things can change in a day?

As it stands now, we no longer trust ourselves or our abilities to sense what our children need, so we read books that tell us exactly what growing brains require. We have lost faith in our teachers' ability to teach, so we hire tutors. We have lost faith in our children's ability to derive meaningful lessons from random daily living, so we construct for them strings of perfectly scheduled days.

For many modern parents, the only good tulip is an open tulip. A closed one makes us nervous. What if it doesn't bloom? What if it's nipped by frost? Yes, it's true, these things can happen. But they happen no matter how devotedly we plant and water and feed.

Children have been blossoming for centuries without our constant pruning and intervention, but now that we know more about what makes them bloom, we are at risk for fouling up the process. The knowledge is here. And because we are intelligent people, dedicated to being the best parents we can be, we can't pretend as if it doesn't exist. But we can say to ourselves, "Yes, that is fine, that is interesting," and then keep right on raising our kids the way we see fit. We can push through the peer pressure, ignore the parents who say, "Edward didn't go out for select soccer? But why not?"

We can trust in the secret potential locked in each child, a potential that we notice, nourish, and sometimes, just pray will emerge. Our child may not be gifted and talented. He may not make All-State Band. But he has something no other child has had before or since. And that is what we celebrate.

6

Are We Making the World Too Safe for Our Children?

Keeping Independence and Trust Alive in a Scary World

"Courage is resistance to fear, mastery of fear, not absence of fear."
—Mark Twain

I can still remember those first trips to the playground when our oldest daughter was a toddler. I would imagine every grisly possibility: She would be bumped off the seesaw, dragged underneath the merry-go-round, pushed from the top of a slide. It was as if I'd taken her to a Roman coliseum instead of the local tot lot. Gradually, I got over it. I told myself that generations of children survived playgrounds and, with vigilance on my part, our child would, too.

Imagine my surprise, then, when I began to read that there are hazards in playgrounds—and for that matter in almost everything—of which not even I had dreamed: mulch that's too thin, swings spaced too close together. Articles on playground safety fanned the flames of safety-consciousness. Down came the turrets and hideaways. Up grew the weeds. Meanwhile, kids spent even more time watching videos or playing in padded, climate-controlled indoor playgrounds with names like the Discovery Zone.

When I first heard reports of dangerous playgrounds, I felt vindicated in my wimpiness. But then I came to my senses. Playgrounds are no more dangerous than they've ever been. It's we who have changed, we who have become so obsessed with making the world safe for our children that the suits of armor we provide them are as dangerous as the world we're protecting them from. It's we who have become so worried that we finger-print our kids, that we wake in the night shivering from fears we can barely remember in the morning. But they are vivid in our dreams, these visions of abduction and death and injury. We are parents who think too much. So of course we obsess about safety.

We worry about birth defects, sudden infant death syndrome, toys with small parts, collapsing playpens, drunk drivers, deer ticks, and unnecessary immunizations. If we aren't fretting about the lead dust in the mini-blinds, we're worried about the strangulation risk posed by their cords. Children are so afraid of meeting a "stranger," and adults so leery of appearing to be one, that a grown-up will drive past a neighbor child walking to school along a busy highway rather than offer to give him a ride. Self-ordained safety consultants crawl around the houses of first-time parents looking for unplugged outlets, loose crib slats, and other dangers. Pediatricians coined the term "fever phobia" because they see so many anxious parents measuring every rise and fall of their child's temperature. When we aren't worrying about physical dangers, we fret about whether our kids are meeting some psychological or intellectual standards, real or imagined.

Whenever parents gather, it doesn't take long for the topic to turn to safety. This has been especially true recently because of the abduction and murder of two sisters from a small rural town in Virginia. The tragedy had a particular resonance here because it was a local story, and because some attempted kidnappings in our area a couple weeks later gave it added weight.

"I was one of the parents who felt that statistically the number of children who are kidnapped and harmed is so small that I wouldn't let myself worry about it," said Linda Falkerson, who has a three-year-old daughter. "But when it happened to the Lisk sisters, I was truly depressed for days. Then two weeks later, when the children were almost taken from the hardware store, my whole mind-set was turned around. I've gotten very scared." Parents are afraid to let children out of their sight and they wonder aloud what their paranoia is doing to them. They can't stop imagining their quiet suburban neighborhoods pierced by unimaginable horror. Suddenly it seems as if we're under siege, as if a bogeyman waits around every corner. The mood among parents I know is somber and wary, and I write this chapter with a heavy heart.

Of course, we demand safety for our children. If our child is not safe then it doesn't matter whether he's potty trained or diapered, well-behaved or wild, GT or ADD. So understandably, safety is foremost in our minds. A recent *Newsweek* poll showed that parents' greatest worry was that their child would be kidnapped or the victim of a violent crime. A *Reader's Digest*/Roper survey of good places to raise kids found that parents' number one need is a low crime rate.[1] Protecting one's young is instinctive parenting at its most instinctive. So how can I fault it?

Because the information revolution that has transformed the way we discipline and educate our children is also changing the way we think about their safety. In trying to smooth all the rough corners of life, we're denying kids the chance to brave their own dangers and develop their own judgment. Our fears rob children of independence. There are so many places they can't go, so many things they can't do. The constant watchfulness hurts parents, too. Worry is debilitating. It forces us to micromanage our kids' lives. It tinges our joy with vague, numbing fear.

In our urgent pursuit of the perfectly safe childrearing environment it's easy to forget that more children are hurt by family members than by strangers (roughly two-thirds of the 662 children under five murdered in 1992 were killed by their parents);[2] that most accidents can be prevented with common sense; and most of all, that we have souls to care for as well as bodies, that there is such a thing as moral courage and it's not built by keeping the world at bay.

The Safety Trap

You might say we've gotten caught in a safety trap. We don't like being in it, and we know we should get out. But we don't know how. My friend Marianne Vakiener and I had a talk about that one warm afternoon. Marianne is one of those people who makes me feel like a bold parent, and there are not many people who can do that. When I told her our oldest daughter was about to go on an overnight camping trip with her Brownie troop, Marianne marveled at my bravery. She has gone on field trips with her eight-year-old, David, since he was a toddler in Mother's Day Out programs, and from the sound of it, it will be a while before he goes on an overnight camping trip without having one of his parents as a chaperone. "Yesterday, David's class had a field trip to the zoo. I couldn't go on the bus with the class because siblings aren't allowed. The only way I could go is if I drove myself there. So I got in my car and drove me and the baby [her three-month-old] there, figured out where the bus was going to let the kids out, met David and his classmates, stayed with them a couple hours, and then David got on the bus and went home. Now exactly how much was I protecting him?"

Marianne realizes that she takes on these chaperone gigs because she thinks her son will be safer if she's nearby, that her presence provides a sort of talisman against evil. One day a few years ago, when she was conducting a leadership workshop, her husband decided to drive himself and their son down a heavily trafficked interstate to an amusement park. Marianne was beside herself with worry. She was convinced that something would happen to them on the way. So her husband, Paul, said, "Marianne, do you really think David will be safer if you're in the car?" And, without skipping a beat, she said, "Yes, I think he will." She knew it didn't make much sense—and it still doesn't. She goes on the field trips anyway.

When I asked Marianne why she is so safety cautious, she said she believes it's just something she was born with. But I happen to know that she reads a lot, too. Here's Marianne on children crossing the street: "I read about this research. It was done somewhere out west. It says that until children are about age ten, they don't have the ability to accurately perceive the distance and speed of approaching vehicles. So even though we live on this quiet little street, I don't want my son crossing it."

Here is Marianne on play dates: "Whenever David is going to a friend's house to play, if I don't know the parents, I'll call them up and ask them if they have any guns in the house. This is really hard to do. But every time I read about a child accidentally killed with a gun he's always playing at somebody else's house. And you know, I've asked three families so far and two of them have had guns." They assured her that the guns are locked up, and she assured them that this is her own problem, her own paranoia.

But it isn't just her own problem. It's everyone's problem. Not the guns, although of course they are a problem, too. But how we deal with them. How do we raise our kids safely in towns where people don't know their neighbors and in a time that seems so much more dangerous than the one in which we grew up? I've told other friends that Marianne asks about guns. They gasp in recognition and say it's something they thought about but haven't had the courage to do. The fact that we don't know the families of the kids our children play with, don't know if their parents are careful people—all these gaps make us want to ask. Our need to know is emblematic of our safety-consciousness. It speaks volumes about our fears.

Is the world really less safe than it used to be? And if it isn't, then why are we so protective? Are our children more precious to us than we were to our parents or they were to theirs? What does our protectiveness say about us as mothers and fathers? What does our quest for safety do to our peace of mind, and how does it affect our children's childhood? Finally, can we keep our kids safe and still keep them whole?

Numbers and Pictures

Talk to parents about safety and you end up talking about danger. We worry because the world in which we're raising our kids seems much more dangerous than it used to be. The headlines and the photos stare at us every day: A child is shot on his way to school. A toddler wanders from his house onto a nearby highway. Or we hear stories: A man in a battered silver car is seen lurking around the bus stop; a friend of a friend's baby drowns in the bathtub. These are what we remember; these are the pictures that run through our minds when we can't sleep.

But the numbers tell a different story. The child death rate, the number of children ages one to 14 who die every year, has been falling lately. In 1985, 34 children out of every 100,000 died; in 1994 only 29 out of 100,000 died, according to the 1997 Annie E. Casey Kids Count survey. The same survey shows a decline in the infant mortality rate, from 10½ per 1,000 live births in 1985 to eight per 1,000 in 1994. Another study shows that death from car crashes, drownings, and fires for those 19 and younger dropped by 39 percent from 1978 to 1991.[3] As for our greatest fear, abduction, most children are taken by family members during custody fights. Detailed studies of nine years of FBI homicide numbers show that from 52 to 158 children are kidnapped and murdered each year. The chance of a young child being grabbed and killed by a stranger is literally one in a million.[4]

Yes, kids are still dying needlessly. The same study that showed reductions in deaths from accidental causes showed that deaths from murder and suicide were up 47 percent in children 19 and younger. Guns were to blame for many of these deaths. In fact, home ownership of guns increases the risk of suicide among teenagers and young adults more than tenfold and more than triples the risk of homicide.

In 1993, the most recent year for which records are available, 6,900 children ages 14 and younger died from what are now known as "unintentional injuries." We are discouraged from using the word "accident" because most of these deaths are preventable. In fact, the number of children's deaths due to injury dropped 14 percent since a safety organization called the National Safe Kids Campaign began in 1988. Seat belts, smoke detectors, and bicycle helmets are lowering fatalities, too.[5] Awareness is saving lives.

But the closer we get to zero deaths the closer we get to zero tolerance. We avoid not only the patently unsafe but even the slightly risky. We act like John Irving's character Garp, running down the street of his suburban neighborhood in a futile attempt to catch speeding cars. What I feel on the playground is what many feel about life in general: that anything can happen, that no measure is too extreme to keep kids healthy and happy. In our quest for security, we have become number crunchers, tallying up our own private calculus of safety: the latest vehicle crash numbers, the age at which our chance of having a Down's syndrome baby equals or exceeds our chance of having a miscarriage due to amniocentesis, the crime statistics of various cities.

The Evening News

If you look at the numbers, then, by many measures kids are safer than they used to be. But we have trouble believing it. Our early warning system is amiss, so that we feel on the alert even when we don't need to. We act on impulses that originate not from our immediate environment but because of something we've seen on the evening news or read in the paper. Don't you check your doors more carefully the night you've heard about a kidnapping—even if the kidnapping was 600 miles away?

Consider the extent to which we're bombarded with reports of atrocities committed against children. Seldom a local news show passes without a heartbreaking story of a youngster shot in a drive-by shooting, the peeling lead paint in an old school, or a child injured in a car crash. In an analysis of 100 newscasts of 55 television markets in 35 states taken on a single day in February 1997, the Rocky Mountain Media Watch found that 72 of the lead stories were about crime and disaster. Almost half the news (42.6 percent) was about violent topics.[6]

If a child is involved then it seems that story always leads the newscast. A friend of mine who worked for a national health organization once confessed that when he used to write press releases, "Newsworthy invariably meant an article about a risk to children. I knew that if I came up with something about pollution or secondhand smoke injuring children in some way I had a surefire seller."

Our newspaper is full of child abuse and abandonment stories. I realize that since I live near Washington, D.C., a hotbed of murder and gang violence, my experience may be a bit skewed. But don't we all receive postcards of missing children in the mail or see pictures of them on our milk cartons? Because our world is smaller now, bound together by media, computers, ease of travel, we really do "feel the pain" of our neighbors. And sometimes, we feel it so much we think it is our own. It's difficult not to worry about murder and mayhem with those milk carton images, their faces blending ever so subtly with our own children's, staring at us constantly from the refrigerator and the breakfast table.

So we protect our children by keeping them busy in organized activities. Instead of letting them catch crawdads in the creek (What if they fall in? Kids can drown in a few inches of water. And who knows what's in that water anyway? Probably chemicals from the lawn service our neighbors use) we take them to the local pool. It has chlorine and lifeguards. And if we've read up on mortality statistics, we know it's relatively safe. Most childhood drownings occur in residential pools—not in public or community ones.

A few summers ago many of the mothers on our street did not allow their children to play in the big, berry-lush meadow at the end of our block because they were afraid their little ones would be bitten by ticks and contract Lyme disease. I know that Lyme disease is a hazard, but we do not live in a heavily affected area, and the chances of contracting the disease are slim. If children dress properly and are inspected after their return, they shouldn't have to give up one of summer's greatest pleasures. But the kids do not know it is a pleasure because they've never experienced it. The tick scare, like many of our too-safe attitudes, has siphoned a lot of the richness from life.

Linda Falkerson helped clean up the paths in her community's woods. The other day at a neighborhood meeting she overheard a mother say that her daughter had recently asked when the paths would be ready for hiking. "I didn't want to tell her: 'Never,' " the mother said. And yet "never" was this mother's decision. It didn't matter if the brush was gone, or even the poison ivy. The woods would remain off limits simply because they're the woods. "We live in a very safe neighborhood with just two miles of community woods, yet people are afraid to go in," Linda said. It's not as if anything bad has ever happened there, but something could. And those "somethings" happen often enough that we cry for the victims and then redouble our own efforts to stay safe.

Unfortunately, people play on our fears, which intensifies our protectiveness. An industry survey shows that 67 percent of new buyers of cellular phones purchase them for safety reasons.[7] An advertisement for a security system shows a happy baby snugly buckled up. "As a responsible parent, you never drive without a car seat. But you don't have a home security system?" Susan Smith buckled her two sons into their car seats—but then pushed the car into the river. She originally blamed the deaths of her sons on a car-jacker. She knew people would believe her if she pinned the crime on a stranger.

It is the quality of the violence that so unnerves us now. It is the heartless, soulless, bottomless, random pit of violence that makes us quiver even though the statistics may say our children are safer. Disaster strikes when we least expect it, so we feel as if we're never doing enough. The bogeyman who could reach out and grab our child is a sometime kind of guy. Just because he isn't here now doesn't mean he won't be later. We must always be on guard against him.

Ironically, however, the quality of the violence may actually be proof of a safer environment. When our kids aren't outside playing, they are often "safely" inside, watching television and learning that violent actions don't have tragic reactions. When children learn from the comfortable world of televised murder that death is immediately followed by happy people munching potato chips, they learn that violence doesn't matter, doesn't hurt. They learn to disconnect themselves from their actions.

Our kids are not growing up with an "evil empire," an ultimate enemy, as we did. Their basements have no bomb shelters, and they aren't putting their heads under their desks in school drills. The baby boomlet peaked about the same time that jubilant protesters were tearing down the Berlin Wall. Evil is more ambiguous now, more diffused. Although kids are amply counseled when bad things happen, I wonder if they hear a more ominous message than we intend, if the anxiety we feel is rubbing off on them. Do they hear the urgency in our voices? Do they notice the creases in our foreheads? Our children may not know that we're more worried than we should be, but they may be learning too soon that evil doesn't just happen across the seas and the mountains in another place, far away. It happens everywhere.

A *PDR* in Every Home

We worry about our child's safety because we're convinced the world is a dangerous place. That's only one part of the equation, though. We also overprotect our children because we know so much more than our foremothers and forefathers. And we know more because there's so much information available to us. This is especially true when it comes to children's health advice. One woman in an Internet news group on parenting books recommended a slew of health manuals—from an anatomy coloring book ("Although you'd expect it to be silly . . . this is an excellent anatomy book, far easier to use than Gray's Anatomy, and with much more useful detail") to the *Physicians Desk Reference* ("No household should be without a *PDR*").

It's the same impulse—to learn everything there is to know—that gets in the way of disciplining and educating our children. When it comes to health issues, though, most of us are really in over our heads. So we buy books like *Take Charge of Your Child's Health,* by George Wooten and Sarah Verney. Every time I try to "take charge" of our kids' health by reading up on a symptom, I find a more dreadful disease than I could ever have imagined. Still, I think the "take charge" attitude gives a broad hint of what's behind our need to know, and that is our need to be in control. Ironically, though, we need experts to help us get there. So we buy our medical guides, read our magazine articles, and take our cardiopulmonary resuscitation class. We interview three pediatricians before we find one who fits our qualifications and we write up a "birth plan" to make sure that we have bonding time immediately after the baby is born. We buy our expensive, heavy cars and we stake our claim to sanity.

But the kind of control we have is not unlike those limited "choices" we offer our kids. "It's time for bed. Do you want to wear your blue pajamas or your red pajamas?" The really important decisions are often out of our hands. The pediatrician you pick seems never to be on duty when you bring in your wheezing toddler for an emergency visit. The baby is born with meconium in the fluid and whisked away for an immediate checkup so you don't get to hold her right away.

I know that control is part of today's self-help medicine trend with its at-home pregnancy tests and do-it-yourself blood pressure cuffs. But every time I see one of those otitis-media kits I think about how it's even hard for an experienced physician to diagnose an ear infection, so why do we think we can do it? And if we're not actually making the diagnosis, we're pushing our pediatrician to make one. "Why does Sean have this cough? Could he have a sinus infection?" Or "Why isn't Sarah sitting up yet? Do you think she is developmentally delayed?" Pediatrician Linda Goldstein says she gets many calls from parents worried their children aren't meeting certain mileposts they've read about in books or magazine articles. "When you have an essentially healthy child, you focus on any little thing that's not perfect." I asked her what kind of parents tend to worry most. "Parents who read a lot," she said.

Of course, there are times when we must seek a second opinion or challenge a medical verdict. We all know cases where it's only through parental persistence that a mother avoids a cesarean or a child's illness is properly diagnosed. We have to trust our hunches and beliefs. But we have to trust our doctors, too. At least some of the time. After all, we spent enough time choosing them.

Isn't the secret here knowing when to let go? Americans "have come to believe that no one gets sick anymore just because of bad luck. Instead, we see health as largely a matter of doing the right things, with the corollary that illness is a failure of some sort," said Marcia Angell, MD, the editor of the *New England Journal of Medicine*.[8] I think parents now are especially prone to take the illness of their children as a personal failure. Our kids are growing up in an era when vaccinations make many diseases obsolete, when researchers are finding the genes that cause cystic fibrosis and other chronic conditions.

This expectation of health and safety is such an acknowledged fact that the first lines of *Parenting Young Children,* the STEP workbook, says: "For centuries, parents felt they'd accomplished a great deal if they managed to raise a child to adulthood. If their children survived disease, accidents, and violence, parents had succeeded at their job. Today, children have the benefits of modern medicine and technology." Parents of the past learned early on that fate had the upper hand when it came to their children's health and safety, but we are tantalizingly close to feeling omnipotent. And maybe that's part of our problem.

The Issue of Our Times

In 1996, *Mothering Magazine* devoted an entire issue to the subject of vaccination, which it announced on the cover as "The Issue of Our Times." The article included detailed information on how vaccines work, the risks and benefits of each type, and the advantages and disadvantages of vaccinating or not vaccinating your child. The special issue featured a panel of various medical experts, both mainstream and alternative (though two out of the five were homeopaths), and raised the question whether public health measures were stripping away our freedom of choice. People take articles like these very much to heart, says pediatrician Goldstein. "Every time there's an article or a television report on the safety of vaccines, we'll go through a period where there are a lot of refusals."

Vaccination is indeed a complicated and telling issue. The fact that there are now vaccines for relatively minor diseases such as chicken pox perfectly illustrates the theme of parents protecting their children from every discomfort. It also points out the impossibility of perfect protection because children vaccinated against chicken pox may need a booster shot later on, or may not develop as strong an immunity against the disease and so may contract it (or a related disease, shingles) in adulthood, both of which would be more serious than contracting chicken pox in childhood.

Of course, the biggest objections are raised against vaccines like the DPT (diphtheria/pertussis/tetanus), especially the pertussis part of the vaccine, which carries a slight risk of causing brain damage and death. Most parents who oppose vaccines do so because they want to care for their child as they see fit. They don't want to be swayed by larger public health concerns. But they are only able to make such decisions because they live in a country where most people immunize their kids. If more parents did not, and if polio and pertussis were the scourges they once were, these parents would not think twice about the decision. If vaccination is the "issue of our times," it's the issue of thinking too much.

"Parents must arm themselves with as much information as possible," pediatrician Jay Gordon wrote in the article. "What it boils down to is the fact that there are some risks involved in getting vaccines and some risks in not being vaccinated. The risks on both sides of the coin are probably very small, and it is up to each individual family to take a responsible, intelligent look at the issue." Notice he says that the risks are small, but that "parents must arm themselves with as much information as possible."[9] When will we realize that the ammunition—the overabundance of information—can be an enemy, too?

The Precious Child

So we worry about safety because we think our country is more dangerous (even though it isn't), and because we read a lot more and want to be in charge of our children's health (even though we can't be, totally). But there are other reasons for our overprotectiveness. Today as I was leaving our care-giver's house after dropping off our youngest daughter, I found on the front step a crust of the cinnamon toast Celia was eating in the car. She must have dropped it as she walked in the door. Those of you who are sentimental fools like I am will probably guess how I felt—the crust of bread, the child who was just chattering away to me in the car, gone now for the day. I'm off to my spare bedroom office, to the cold company of a computer screen. Well, okay, sometimes I bound out that door. I am glad to get to my work, relieved to take a vacation from the "No way, José's" (Celia's current favorite expression) and the relentless-ness of a two-year-old.

But it struck me this morning that another reason we worry so about our children's health and safety is that so many of us are away from our kids much of the day. For what is vague worry if not abstract care? It is a bit like sackcloth and ashes, a pen-ance for being gone. That sick feeling we get in our stomachs when we read about a child who was hurt while in another's care drives us on to greater guilt. It makes us a bit irrational at times, so that we do all sorts of things—put a secret camera into a teddy bear to check up on the new nanny—because the ulti-mate end of our children's safety justifies any means we choose to accomplish it. Our children's absence makes them doubly precious, and we are doubly worried.

Are there other things about us as parents that make us sense our children's preciousness and their vulnerability more in-tensely than our parents did ours? Perhaps because we have fewer children to worry about? Or because many of us are older and more familiar with the tenuousness of life? Maybe it's better to have children when you're really young and less burdened with your own mortality—and theirs. I'd like to think the wisdom we bring to the job compensates for our protectiveness, but sometimes I wonder.

Historians of childhood can't actually measure the love parents felt for their youngsters in the past, at least not in any absolute, quantifiable way. But in her book *Pricing the Priceless Child,* Viviana Zelizer traces the evolution of children from economically valuable to emotionally priceless. As families moved off the farms and as child-labor laws forbade children to work in factories, she says, kids became economic liabilities rather than economic assets. And the less valuable they were as income producers the more valued they were simply for being children, innocent and harmless.

As late as the eighteenth century, parents still passively accepted the death of their offspring, and mourning was minimal. But by the nineteenth century, there was an outpouring of sentiment when children died. There were special coffins, tender poems, and manuals that told parents how to cope with a "vacant cradle." By the twentieth century, parents were not only mourning the deaths of children, but were taking active steps to save their lives. Children's hospitals, the distribution of safe, wholesome milk for poor children, and the establishment of the U.S. Children's Bureau in 1912 all showed a new respect for young life.

Ironically, just as better sanitation and healthcare began to make a dent in the juvenile mortality rates, accidents became the leading cause of death for children five to 14. In big cities swollen to bursting with immigrants, thousands of children playing street games vied for space with a burgeoning number of cars and streetcars. From 1918 to 1922 the number of vehicle fatalities for five- to 14-year-olds almost doubled. But child death was no longer something parents—or other adults—accepted as God's will. In fact, crowds would mob the drivers of vehicles that killed a child, whether or not they were at fault. The occupants were lucky to escape with their lives.

Zelizer analyzes economic and cultural changes—child safety campaigns, children's life insurance, wrongful death judgments, and adoption agency fees—to show how children's lives became priceless.[10] These outward signs may not reflect the depth of feeling individual parents possessed, but they do show the transformation of social values. Perhaps ours is the strangest and most dichotomous chapter of this story. For at the same time that it's become difficult for low-income parents to raise a healthy child, middle- and upper-income parents make safety a fetish—and a multimillion-dollar industry.

Safety Sells

Sometimes it pays to be a pack rat. The other day I dug out my old Perfectly Safe catalog. It's about five years old, I guess, measures five by seven inches, is printed on uncoated paper and illustrated with simple drawings. It lists about 100 items, many of them costing less than ten dollars. It was interesting to compare it with the Perfectly Safe catalog I received last month, which is two inches taller, printed on slick paper, has photographs instead of drawings, and lists 200 products. Though you can still find some gadgets for under ten dollars, there are many more high-ticket items. The adjustable fireplace guard sells for $89.95, the pool alarm for $119.95, and a CPR Prompt rescue and practice aid, which talks you through actual or practice emergencies—"something no family should be without"—will set you back $100. Interspersed with the products are quotations from *The Perfectly Safe Home,* by Jeanne Miller, who is also president of the Perfectly Safe Company. Compare these two catalogs and you'll see that safety sells even better now than it did five years ago.

The Perfectly Safe catalog is big on locks: potty locks, drawer locks, refrigerator locks, VCR locks, medicine cabinet locks, and a generic lock that fits ovens, dishwashers, and microwaves. You can also order window guards, do-it-yourself lead-testing kits, and a $20 bath toy that gives you a digital display of the water temperature. Along with some legitimate new safety innovations, such as "choke tubes" that allow you to test whether a small toy poses a choking hazard, there is a curling iron safety holder for $25.95—"developed by a grandmother whose grandson was severely burned by a curling iron."

There are two thoughts that come to mind when I flip through this catalog. One is that the perfectly safe environment seems designed so parents will never have to say no: a vast array of gates, an enticing collection of stove knob covers, a product made to "prevent your little toddler from pushing the buttons on your television set." If only we could do away with streets, then the word "no" could truly be retired.

My other thought is that many of these products have less to do with our children's safety than with their comfort. Meditate for a moment on knee protectors for babies that "make crawling safer and more comfortable . . . like crawling on a cloud" or a reflective sunshade to place over your child's car seat so it doesn't get too hot in the summer. Everything is designed so that not only will our children never be in any real danger but they will never even suffer minor discomfort. My old catalog listed roller skates with a special tab that ensures children will not go too fast. (These, by the way, came in an adult model, which makes more sense.) It's difficult to walk the line between comfort and safety, to keep kids from harm yet still allow for the bumps and bruises that teach them to think twice next time. And these products aren't making it any easier.

What the Perfectly Safe catalog tells me most of all is that even if we aren't aware of our paranoia, merchandisers are. You'd think safety would be more a matter of saying "no" to things—from baby walkers to sweatshirts with drawstrings. But entrepreneurs have come up with lots of ways to say "yes" to safety rather than saying "no" to risk. Why shouldn't we part with a few dollars to protect our youngsters? The seeming prosperity of the Perfectly Safe catalog and the presence of stores like the Safety Zone, which carries protective merchandise for kids and adults, underlines the fact that safety has become a commodity, a product we buy instead of a condition we create. The theme for this year's Safe Kids safety awareness campaign is "Gear Up!"

There are so many decisions now to make about protecting our children that many of us feel compelled to read a book called *The Childwise Catalog* to figure out what we need. If you want to buy a cradle, diaper pail, toy chest, gate, tricycle, bicycle child carrier, or even balloons and party favors, you can turn to this book to decide which ones to buy. It's more than just a *Consumer Reports* for kids' paraphernalia. It's a bible of safety information with a definite mission: "We believe that the more you know, the better prepared you will be to head off an unfortunate and painful event for your child," say authors Jack Gillis and Mary Ellen R. Fise. Of course it's difficult to argue against a book that can save lives, as this one can and does. But at what point does our safety consciousness turn into paranoia?

The authors urge parents to "become safety advocates," call government agencies if they find unsafe products, and share information with other parents and friends. These are not outlandish suggestions, but they imply that raising a child is so fraught with peril that only through careful consideration and wise purchasing decisions can we do it right. The authors themselves worry they've given parents this idea. In the afterword they write, "One of the potential 'hazards' associated with a book like this is creating the impression that the fun and excitement of buying for your children is a landmine of doom and gloom. . . . Buying for your children does not have to be an anxiety-ridden proposition."[11]

Maybe not. But before there can be a slew of safety products—and a book to help parents make sense of them—we must think we need them.

Don't Forget the Toilet-Lid Lock

"Have a Safe Trip," teases the headline in *Parents Magazine*.[12] But that scarcely seems possible after reading the article that follows. Here are some of the suggestions: Call ahead and ask the hotel manager if the tables have sharp corners so you'll know whether to bring corner bumpers from home. Pack a nonskid bath mat, half a dozen outlet covers, and of course, a toilet-lid lock. Tie window cords out of reach so your child doesn't strangle himself with them. Place floor and table lamps out of the child's grasp, move chairs away from windows, and ask the management to lower water temperature to prevent scalding.

It's a typical parenting magazine story. I've written a couple like it. The writer and editor know that the article may prevent an injury or even save a life, so they want to be very, very thorough. But as our obsession with safety grows and magazines reach for topics not yet covered, readers end up with advice that ranges from the paranoid—packing toilet-lid locks—to the obnoxious—asking the hotel management to lower the water temperature. We seem to expect everyone around us to be as alarmed as we about the horrible dangers lurking in the ordinary hotel room. Wouldn't children's safety be as well-served by a simple reminder that hotel rooms are not childproofed and to keep a closer eye on your child when you're in unfamiliar terrain? But that would be a very short story.

In the same issue of the magazine in which the travel safety article ran there were also updates on babies and antibiotics, news of a playpen recall, a diagram for installing a clip that keeps a car seat snugly in place, a short piece on safe baseball equipment (including spongier balls, safety-release bases, and face guards for batting helmets), an update on tuberculosis, a discussion of whether parents should be present in the emergency room, a tip on how to make Pedialyte taste better, information on a nondrowsy allergy medication, four steps you can take to make your child less likely to get hit by a car, three steps you can take to make sure your child doesn't fall out a window, and an article on how a child caught salmonella from a pet iguana. On the next page a doctor answers questions about whether it's safe to cover a baby with a blanket, the causes of bad breath, and what to do about pinworms.

With the possible exception of catching salmonella from an iguana, these topics are useful and important. (I say "possible" because the article informs me that lizards, iguanas, turtles, and snakes infect 25,000 children five and younger with salmonella each year.) If you own the type of playpen being recalled, you need to know it. If you let your five-year-old cross the street unchaperoned, you need to stop it. Each of these articles individually contains worthy information. But when you put them all together (as they were in the magazine) they convey the impression that the world is a dangerous place and parents must be constantly on guard.

No wonder the magazine also contained this reader's desperate query: "I can't stop worrying. I'm the mother of a happy, healthy baby boy. But I can't help worrying about his health constantly—that he'll get sick or hurt, or even die of SIDS. I'm driving my family nuts, and I call to check on him so often that my boss has told me to cut back on personal calls! Sometimes I think that my fear takes away from my really enjoying my son. Are there other parents who have advice on how I can overcome my anxiety?"

Of the nine responses to her request that appeared in a later issue, not one suggested that what this anxious mother really needs is to stop reading magazine articles. Even if she did stop reading them, she could find plenty to disturb her in newspapers and on television. A recent trend in newspapers is seasonal safety. Thus we have cautionary tales of tainted candy, poisonous mistletoe, or the hazards of undercooked Easter eggs. Summer, of course, is riddled with dangers. As reliable as June roses are the scary articles about how many children will drown this summer and how important it is to purchase pool alarms and life preservers. Last September I heard on the radio a story about how kids' backpacks should not weigh more than ten to 15 percent of their body weight. Aha! A new hazard. A back-to-school hazard. At least it takes our minds off some of the more terrible events that could befall our kids.

Sometimes I create an imaginary conversation between an editor and reporter: "We're running low on kid safety stuff," the editor says, a tinge of desperation in her voice. "Well, we have that story on hazardous shopping carts," the reporter offers. "No, that's old news," the editor shouts. "Well, what about the piece on garage door openers. There's that new study, you know, the one that shows lots of the older models can crush a child," the reporter stammers. "Just what we need," the editor replies.

Some of the information out there does a great service; it alerts us to simple steps we can take that may save our children's lives. But even those helpful articles can make us think too much—unless we can manage to turn off the worry after we've done as much as we can, to realize that worry takes the joy out of raising kids and that kids need us to be joyful as well as watchful.

For instance, the "Back to Sleep" campaign, which encourages parents to put their newborns to sleep on their backs rather than their stomachs, has saved the lives of thousands of infants who might otherwise have died from SIDS. This is wonderful, but what if your baby won't go to sleep unless he's on his tummy? When our two older daughters were born, the current wisdom favored tummy-sleeping. By the time our youngest arrived, back-sleeping was preferred. It was difficult to put Celia to bed on her back and not think about why I was doing it—to reduce the risk of sudden infant death syndrome. It seems that taking steps to alleviate a risk makes us think more about what we're avoiding. To a great extent, we're prisoners of our own success. Would I trade risk for worry? You bet. But not to the point where my environment would be totally safe—and I would be abysmally anxious.

Perhaps we can begin to treat stories on kids' health and safety with the same kind of caution we would some immunizations. They can do much good if properly used. Otherwise, they can hurt us. Editors at the magazines I've worked with take their role as advisers seriously because they realize how much parents rely on them for basic information. Articles are checked and double-checked for accuracy. But editors know that tragedies and adversities (especially adversities overcome) sell magazines. Readers gobble up stories about children with rare diseases whose parents are scarching for cures. The chances of our child having such diseases are minuscule, of course. Yet the stories are so compelling that we find ourselves checking our kids for symptoms. Even if we know the slim odds of our child's having a Wilms' tumor, the very fact we're reading about a child who has one makes us wonder if our child does, if our child might.

Caution: Warning Labels Do Not Make Products Safe

Our protectiveness is triggered in a number of ways. We are cautioned in school newsletters, through posters in the doctor's office, and with the carefully worded labels that appear everywhere—from kids' playclothes ("This garment is not flame-retardant. It is not intended to be sleepwear") to a plastic sled ("Wear a helmet, have no more than three riders on at a time, don't ride standing up, avoid trees." And in case the user is from another planet, "This product does not have brakes"). I'd like to hone in on labels for a moment because they reveal something important about our worries.

Labels aren't merely a phenomenon of kids' products, of course. In winter our brown paper grocery bags come with a warning that we not use them to dispose of fireplace ashes. Because kids require extra supervision, though, juvenile products are even more carefully labeled. My favorite is a Batman costume with this warning: "Parent: Please exercise caution. FOR PLAY ONLY: Mask and chest plate are not protective; cape does not enable user to fly."[13]

The warnings have become so ridiculous that it's easy to treat them as a big joke, as absurd proof of a litigious society. But what do they say to our children? A playground near us has this sign plastered on a ladder: "DANGER: If this equipment is erected over asphalt, gravel, or packed earth, falls can result in injury or death." Would that inspire you to climb to the top?

Excessive product labeling has become a sort of white noise we tune out whenever possible. We ignore the age limitations on toys, figuring that our two-year-old is above average and would enjoy a more advanced puzzle—never mind that the pieces are small enough to choke on.

Some of the most alarming evidence that we're tuning out warnings and instruction labels is how many car seats are poorly installed. In one spot check conducted in our county recently, 95 percent of cars had improperly installed car seats. Perhaps parents can't understand the instructions, speculated the officer who did the check. It's true, some car seats are difficult to figure out. But I think the officer was being kind. My theory is that we think the mere presence of a warning label—or a safe product—protects our kids. No parental effort required.

In some ways it seems as if we're paying lip service to safety. We're too busy to check and make sure that the seat belt is threaded through the right part of the car seat or that we have clips if we need them. We just mentally check off, "yes," we have a car seat, and our child is buckled into one. That it might not be properly latched, that in the event of a crash it would prove a very lethal missile indeed, we're too busy to consider. Has the expert-oriented culture convinced us that reading about something is the same as doing it?

In the last eight years, we've had three very different toddlers poking around our house, and I've learned the hard way that there's nothing like hands-on supervision, whether that's double-checking the car seat or keeping an eye on the swingset. I don't mean we have to hover. But one of the least protective things we can do, I think, is to assume we have safety all sewn up.

When our daughters played with a bowl of marbles at a friend's house a few months ago, I watched our youngest like a hawk, convinced she would put one in her mouth. I was scrutinizing her face so closely that I didn't notice she was stuffing those marbles into her diaper as fast as she could. Safety experts say that most toy injuries occur because of the way children are playing with toys rather than any inherent defect in them. But the children I know almost never play with toys as they're intended. They're always turning a bottle into a rocket or a stick into a sword. Caution is infinitely simpler and more low-tech than we are led to believe it is. It doesn't require fancy gadgetry or lists of instructions, but it does grow out of the most important information we have—knowing our own child, inside out.

The End of Independence

What has overprotectiveness done to our kids? For one thing, it seems to have made them more physically cautious. Marianne Vakiener's eight-year-old son will not cross the street without her. What about bike riding, I asked Marianne. Does David ride his bike? Not much, she admits. Their street has no sidewalks and David is not allowed on the nearby forest preserve paths unless his mom or dad is with him. Parents in our neighborhood feel the same way. Our streets have no sidewalks, cars often go 20 miles above the posted 25 miles per hour limit, and the risk isn't worth it. Parents feel bad that young children can't enjoy this simple childhood pastime, but they can't in good conscience allow them to do it.

One day while I was sitting in the home of Karen Hastings, whom you met in the last chapter, and her husband, Steve Hazelton, the doorbell rang. It was a neighborhood pal of Steve and Karen's children, asking if they could come over and play. Steve went to the door. I heard a whispered conversation. The children wanted to play, but only if their dad went with them. Steve gently tried to coax his kids to undertake a solo excursion, but without success. A few minutes later he rejoined our conversation. "What you just witnessed is Sarah not wanting to be adventurous on her own," he said. "I'm thinking, maybe I did something, I was too restrictive or something when Sarah was younger and now she's not confident. She doesn't have the confidence to think she can go have fun and doesn't have to have mom and dad with her." Steve is a stay-at-home father, and he gives his children as much or more freedom than most parents. But he, too, has been affected by the recent climate of fear.

"I was just getting to the point where I would let them ride their bikes by themselves to the old playground a few streets down and around the corner. And then that stuff happened with the Lisk sisters. That was enough to make me change," Steve says. "It made me think, maybe Sarah and Nicholas are too young. When we were kids, we lived in a rural area in Maine. I'd think nothing of hiking through the woods and riding my bike through the fields and doing all that stuff at an early age, and now it's like we feel we've got to protect our children so much."

Chris Anderson also thinks she may have created some paranoia in her two daughters by trying to raise their consciousness on safety issues. "I feel bad about having done that to my kids. I've made them very afraid in hopes that they will be careful." (I must interject here that I know her daughters and they certainly seem active and full of life.) What seems to make more of an impression on her kids than her own warning is independent confirmation of what she's said. For instance, her nine-year-old daughter Rebecca often balked at sitting in the back seat of the car. But one day she picked up the newspaper and read a story about how air bags can kill kids sitting in the front seat. Afterward, she told her mother, "I didn't understand before why you wanted me to sit in the back seat, but now I do."

Air bags are a good metaphor for our approach to kids' safety. Many parents bought their cars or vans because they had air bags, which are credited with saving 1,900 lives since 1986. But the angle and force of some air bags' deployment has been held responsible for the deaths of 39 children since 1993,[14] and the National Transportation Safety Board recently recommended that states require children to sit in the back seat. It's a sound recommendation, but perhaps we're overlooking the real message—that we can't make anything totally safe.

In time most of us outgrow the fierce feelings of physical protectiveness we feel when our children are infants. Our babies learn to crawl, then walk, then run. Along the way, they skin their knees and bruise their legs and get their fingers pinched in doors. They go to preschool and then big school. They want to play soccer, so we stand there and watch while a ball is kicked in their face. They want to go camping, so we send them off into the woods with a tent, some buddies, and a scout leader. Eventually, we even let them drive a car. Nature has quite thoughtfully arranged it so that kids grow up and away from us gradually and gently enough that most of us outgrow our fears along the way. Even Marianne admits she's caved in on some safety issues. She was originally not going to let her son ride the bus to school and now she does.

In some ways, however, our early protectiveness may cast a longer shadow than we intend. In our house, I've noticed that my wimpiness has made our kids less likely to take risks and do for themselves. It took my two older daughters years before they'd climb up on the counter to get themselves a glass or a bowl from the cupboard—probably because of my frequent warnings to "be careful."

Keeping kids safe often means denying them independence. "Our block has no kids, and there are plenty of barriers with yards, fences, and such," says Ron Lord, who with his wife, Jenny, is raising two daughters, ages 11 and 14, in suburban Washington, D.C. Still, he finds it amazing that "our kids have never, in the eight or nine years we've lived here, gone to a friend's house by themselves. They've never said, 'I'm going over to so-and-so's,' and then just gone by themselves." I know of kids in seventh or eighth grade who won't even walk two blocks to school. They're old enough to do it. But by now, they've gotten so used to being driven that they don't want to walk. One of the ironies of keeping our children physically safe is that we often keep them physically inactive and thus less fit. Almost 11 percent of children six to 17 were overweight in 1991 (the last year for which statistics are available), according to the National Center for Health Statistics. That's more than double the five percent of overweight kids in 1965.

Another irony is that by keeping our children on such a short tether when they're young we can't give them independence by degrees. Kids often graduate from being driven around by their parents to driving themselves around—without the intermediate stages of "walking independence" or "biking independence." When freedom arrives, it comes with the flourish of squealing tires.

I don't want to give the impression that all kids are cowering inside, afraid to leave their houses. We have friends who, more than most parents we know, try to buck modern trends in child-rearing. Barbara and Bryan de Boinville have two children, Madeleine, nine, and Charles, six. To help their oldest develop independence, Barbara sends her a few blocks down the street to buy milk at the grocery store. So unaccustomed are people to the sight of a child on her own that they stop Madeleine and ask, "Little girl, where's your mother?" Says Barbara: "I feel confident that these little errands aren't unsafe and that they are appropriate for her to do at this age." She wouldn't send her daughter to the store if she didn't feel that way. Yet Barbara is most assuredly out of step. Some mothers in her neighborhood won't even allow their school-age kids to walk five doors down to the bus stop by themselves. To keep our kids safe, we have enmeshed ourselves in their sports activities and other after-school pursuits, and we have made it so they're seldom allowed the thrill of completing a simple errand on their own. We're so insistent on boosting our kids' self-esteem yet we're overlooking one of the best ways to help them get it—facing fear.

Wild Places

Merry-go-rounds and seesaws have no place in the playgrounds of the future. Even swings are on the way out. "Swings are going to be very scarce, and high swings are going to be gone," according to Jay Beckwith, a playground designer. The reason: It could cost up to $10,000 to sufficiently pad the area around the swings so they're safe enough to meet increasingly stringent codes.[15] Two years in a row, our neighborhood association has voted down the purchase of a couple of pieces of playground equipment for the common land at the end of our street because of potential injuries and litigation. When we focus on keeping kids safe, we avoid the negative, rather than embrace the positive. I think about this especially when our children are kept inside to play. They are losing touch with the natural world, with landscapes that are not fashioned expressly for them, but which challenge their bodies and imaginations.

Even when parents do expose their kids to challenges, they are carefully controlled versions of once wilder adventures. For instance, there are now indoor climbing facilities where kids as young as six wear helmets and harnesses as they scale 30-foot walls at birthday parties. At least they're getting some exercise, but am I the only one who finds this kind of controlled risk-taking a sad commentary on the state of childhood today?

Gone are the wide open spaces of childhood, the wild places to explore. They're all hemmed in now, and we hold the keys. As naturalists Gary Paul Nabhan and Stephen Trimble write, "It is clear that we need to find ways to let children roam beyond the pavement, to gain access to vegetation and earth that allows them to tunnel, climb, or even fall."

What's interesting about kids and the out-of-doors, Nabhan notes, is that instead of feeling the power of the wilderness from the vantage point of a grand vista, kids feel it most when they're building little forts and hidey holes in the brush. When his kids wish to gain a sense of wildness, of animal comfort, "they choose not the large, but the small."[16] Preschoolers observed playing on a half-acre playground spent over half their time in three small refuges tucked under dogwoods, junipers, and Scotch brooms. They seem to be creating their own safe places by playing in these shelters. Children will seek their own sanctuary, if we give them a chance.

Stranger Danger

Perhaps the greatest price kids pay for our paranoia is the fear of strangers we impose on them. In our attempt to make the world perfectly safe, are we making our kids think it's more treacherous than it is? The litany begins before they can talk: "Don't talk to strangers, don't talk to strangers, don't talk to strangers." That message is pounded in, year after year, as the information we give them becomes more and more graphic. In well-child visits, pediatricians talk about good touching and bad touching. There are books and videos for kids about "stranger danger," too. On the Safe Child Homepage of the World Wide Web, parents can read this advice: "One of the primary ways children get hurt with strangers is by being friendly and helpful." So much for good manners. We're teaching children to be unkind and unhelpful for safety's sake. And speaking of the World Wide Web, I've been reading a lot lately about the newest threat to children's safety, the dangers that lurk on-line. So accordingly, there are a number of articles and pamphlets that tell parents how to keep kids safe on the information highway as well as devices such as Net Nanny that block access to undesirable Web sites.

There has been much debate about whether it "takes a village" to raise a child. Our village is riven with suspicion. Our kids don't have the advantage of other caring adults because we are too wary of them. Parents are afraid to help other people's children for fear that they might be taken as potential abusers. Our newspaper ran an article a couple years ago about a woman driving to work at 7:45 one chilly weekday morning who came across a child walking down the highway. The woman offered the girl a ride to school—not without thinking about it a long time first of course, weighing whether or not she should—and the girl accepted. When the woman noticed she had driven the child five miles, she wrote her name and number for the girl to give her parents. Tell them to call me; I'll be glad to give you a ride to school again if you need it, she said.

But the woman worried. Did she do the right thing? She wrote a newspaper columnist and asked him. He consulted others. *Did* she do the right thing? Ought she to have picked up the girl? A spokeswoman for the county police said the woman risked being charged with a crime but probably wouldn't have been because investigators are trained to sniff out Good Samaritans from potential abusers. The principal of the middle school the child attended said the woman was in error. Never pick up a school-age child walking alone, she said. Instead, call the police and report it.[17] That such a simple act as giving a child a ride to school should prompt such guilt, uncertainty, and need for expert opinion is a good illustration of how paranoid our society has become. Do we trust officials only because we can't trust anyone else?

Listen to the lament of a one-time clown: "Almost immediately upon joining the circus, for example, I was given a list of things I couldn't do: If a mother asked me to hold her child or if a child asked to sit on my lap, I had to say no. In my first month an adolescent boy asked if I would sign the back of his hand since he couldn't afford a coloring book. I happily obliged. A mother nearby snatched her daughter's hand and said loudly, 'Never let a strange man do that to you.' "[18]

For years, parents have been puzzling out how to make kids street-smart without making them world-weary. Some fear is necessary, especially in a society where family and kinship ties have broken down and there are, quite frankly, more "strangers" to deal with. So of course, we must admonish our children to be careful. But what if we make them so insensitive to others' feelings that kids aren't polite to little old ladies in grocery store lines even when their parents are right next to them?

Keeping in mind the price our paranoia exacts may help us keep matters in perspective. Some precautions seem legitimate. Two counties in Maryland recently passed laws that require a safety lock to be sold along with each handgun. A neighborhood near us has put up street signs that read, "This is a kid protection area. We call 911." The mother who started the campaign describes herself as a "child-safety advocate" and hopes that other communities will follow suit. But we should question the growing number of childproofing businesses, the absurdly strict "zero tolerance" policies of schools, and other semi-hysterical outcomes of a safety-conscious world.

Safety as Morality

Go to a parenting class or read an article about discipline, and you will find there's one time when most experts agree it's okay to spank a child—if he runs into the street or otherwise endangers himself. This is from *Parenting Young Children:* "Of course, there will be times when 'no' is the necessary and wise thing to say. For example, if a toddler is reaching for the burners or knobs on the stove, his parent might say, 'no—never touch the stove.' "

I've noticed that for me, and for many parents, about the only time my voice rings with true authority is when I'm correcting our kids for a safety violation—for riding a bike without a helmet or dashing away from me in a parking lot. The reason, of course, is because I mean what I say. My voice lacks that certainty when I'm telling the kids to pick up their socks. Admittedly there is something clear-cut about a child darting into a street. I don't need to run a score of discipline theories through my head. I don't have to ask myself, "Am I choosing this battle wisely?" or "Should I give my child a choice?" I just do it. But there was a time, and it wasn't all that long ago, when parents were just as sure that their children shouldn't talk back to them. It seems we are teaching our children that the only evil is a lack of caution. Safety is the only moral absolute.

In our urge to be risk-free we let the other lessons, the lessons in moral courage, pass us by. "Courage may be taught as a child is taught to speak," said Euripides. Like a second language, valor is best learned when young. If we can concentrate on making kids strong, on giving them the courage to admit a failure, to stand up for a child everyone else picks on, then we'll have less time to worry about what could go wrong with them. We can teach our children to be good, rather than teaching them to be safe. After all, to be good often means taking a risk.

It is not only safety that coddles our children, but also comfort. And many times, the two are so tangled up together that we can't give kids one without giving them the other. For instance, there are now hundreds of indoor playgrounds across the country, what is called "pay for play"—a few dollars an hour for access to padded tunnels, ball jumps, and arcade games. There are several reasons why indoor playgrounds appeal to today's parents, but one of the main ones is that they provide a safe haven. "We don't let our kids play in the front yard. They can't ride their bikes around the neighborhood, play kick the can," one Discovery Zone owner observed. "There is something reassuring about knowing your kids are protected, knowing where your kids are. You can sit down and have a cup of coffee, read the paper and know your kid is safe."[19] Enter an indoor playground and you'll find an environment so sterile as to seem institutional. Some playgrounds let parents leave the building to run errands—as long as they wear beepers and their kids wear a wristband sensor. Safety from abduction has a price. It's called freedom.

Sixty Bucks a Chromosome

As potentially harmful as our overprotectiveness is to children, I think it's hurting parents more. The anxiety begins before our children are born. A few chapters ago, I talked about how the modern experience of labor and childbirth makes us focus attention on our child-to-be and constantly analyze if we're doing the right thing. Articles advise us to seek preconceptual checkups and genetic counseling. Advertisements urge us to buy ovulation kits and pregnancy testers. Undoubtedly, fear of malpractice is a primary reason that doctors order so many maternal serum alpha fetoprotein (AFP) tests, amniocenteses, and ultrasounds.

Even to understand what these tests mean requires that an expectant couple do a lot of reading. And then, when you've read about all that can go wrong, not only with the baby but also with the tests that tell you about the baby, the nine months of pregnancy can really become a nightmare.

When Cathy Cotter, who lives in Skokie, Illinois, was expecting her first child, "We had just bought the house and I was walking around with the Orkin man, not knowing I was pregnant." Convinced that her first child was exposed to toxic chemicals, Cathy moved out of the house for a while to ensure the safety of her pregnancy. When her son, David, was born fine and healthy, she stopped worrying—for a while. But now she is pregnant again and concerned that a drug she was taking when she conceived the baby may pose a risk. Cathy is an economist and well-versed in statistics. She knows that many tests have a high false-positive ratio. Nevertheless, when an important measure of her AFP screening test came back abnormally high she decided to have an amniocentesis. She and her husband, Miloš, even asked for an early report on one of the chromosomes. "It's 60 bucks a chromosome, so we just did one," Cathy said. Luckily, that report and the final one came back normal. Now Cathy is only slightly edgy that the amnio performed to rule out the risk may have caused another, graver danger to the baby she carries, the risk of miscarriage. Either way you look at it, worry has been as much a part of her pregnancies as maternity clothes.

You would think that as routine blood screening of fetal abnormalities becomes easier and more reliable, our worries would fade. But that doesn't seem to be the case. Instead, each new technology creates the opportunity for countless agonizing, individual decisions. And once the tests are available, it's difficult to say no to them. As Barbara Katz Rothman points out in *The Tentative Pregnancy,* the tests are "bargains of fate." Women say, " 'I had the test, I did everything I was supposed to do.' The unstated hope is that the gods will do their part if you do yours. Or, on another level, if you do have a child with a disability, it won't be your fault if you 'did everything.' "

I think it is in these formative months of our lives as parents that we develop this "safety at all costs" attitude. We may balk at the fetal monitors and the (still) high rate of cesareans. Yet they are the legacy of our concern. They are the by-products of parents who think too much about safety. The Public Citizen Health Research Group cites undue reliance on the electronic fetal monitor as the main reason for the overprediction of fetal distress. If doctors relied solely on electronic fetal-monitoring to decide whether to perform cesareans, three women would have unnecessary ones for every one who needed one.[20]

What We Have Lost

Though these are, I hope, the waning days of diapers in our house, our two-year-old and I have discovered something delicious—baby powder. She asks for it by name now, "Want powda, Momma," and I gladly oblige. It wasn't so easy a few years ago. I'd written an article about bathing and diapering newborns, about how talc particles from the baby powder can lodge themselves in baby's lungs and cause pneumonia, and I'd become terrified of the stuff. What if the baby did ingest some baby powder, and it did lodge itself in her tiny bronchioles? I would never forgive myself. So I was a baby bottom purist from the beginning. Nothing but a diaper and a sparing amount of ointment if a rash seemed imminent. But at some point in our third daughter's young life, I decided to live dangerously, and I used a small amount of powder from a sample size container I'd gotten from the hospital years ago. Amazingly enough, Celia survived!

I could cry for all the tender moments I've missed. To pat a baby's clean bottom and to smell that baby powder smell is one of the activities that makes motherhood come clear somehow. And to think I've been abstaining from it out of fear. You know you're in trouble when using baby powder becomes a risky adventure. Using the stuff is a way to symbolically reclaim the pleasures of parenthood I've lost due to a misguided protectiveness.

I can't remember exactly when this dawned on me, but I can remember the shock of realizing that just because a baby is born perfectly healthy she won't always be. Maybe it was the first sniffle. Or even earlier, during those early weeks when I fretted about whether Suzanne was getting enough milk. Here was this new little slip of a person for whom we were solely responsible. It was the realization that hits all new parents sooner or later— that the fears of parenthood are infinitely more numerous and powerful and long-lasting (let's just admit it, they're eternal) than the fears of pregnancy. In fact, these fears would destroy me if I did not rein them in somehow.

I often wonder if the rounds of pregnancy tests, especially the invasive ones, the surge of anxiety at any twinge of abnormality, make it easy to develop a "safety at any cost" attitude. We feel no price is too high to make sure our child is healthy in utero. Does this attitude carry over into raising children, as well? For instance, some parents use the fears they have of leaving their babies alone with a new provider as an excuse to hire private investigators to monitor them or, as I mentioned before, to use tiny hidden cameras to do the same. A *Washington Post* article recently reported that sales of these "nannycams," as they're called, have increased fivefold in six years. Parents check to make sure the nannies aren't abusing their children, to make sure they're not spending all their time on the phone or in front of the television set.[21]

In our quest for the perfectly safe environment aren't we a little like residents of gated communities? Give up on the rest of the world, just keep our own family safe. Buy that larger, safer vehicle so that if, by chance, we do have an accident, there's less chance that *we* will be hurt. Maybe if we took some of the energy we expend fortifying our own families and used it to make society at large a little less dangerous, we'd all feel safer in the long run.

Striking a Balance

While some people can take safety information for what it is, can do what they think is necessary, and let the hysteria run off their backs, others find that no matter how much they do, no matter how many safety gadgets they buy and install, no matter how many health articles they read, they worry anyway. Plainly, safety is an issue that cries out for balance. We can't go cold turkey and get rid of it entirely. We must always provide a protective environment for our children. But we must balance our need to shelter our kids with our duty to propel them out of our arms and into the big wide world. They want to be at the top of the slide, crawling across the monkey bars, on the edge of our peripheral vision. If we smother them with concern they will lose that urge to explore.

A friend at a party who heard I was writing this chapter implored, "What's your advice? How can we keep our kids safe without making safety an obsession?" This friend and her husband and daughter live in a nice section of Washington, D.C., but there have been armed robberies all around her neighborhood and a few miles away poor children are often killed in drive-by shootings. Plainly, she has made her trade-offs. By choosing to live in the city, she has chosen stricter supervision, pricier schools. But I know parents in the suburbs, where conditions are safer, who are as worried as she is.

There are no easy answers to the dilemma of danger. But we can try to figure out what's making us afraid. We can keep our common sense even when it's buffeted by horrible news stories. We can figure out what we absolutely have to do and then not do anything else. Here's how some parents stopped thinking too much about safety:

Barbara de Boinville not only sends her nine-year-old to the grocery store alone but also lets her six-year-old son make a solo trip into the five-and-dime to buy some candy while she waits outside. "Charles is a shy child and I think it helps him to ask for the Starbursts himself, without me there, and to give the cashier his dollar. You know we always hear how important it is in a city to walk as if we know where we're going. Well, I want our kids to have that kind of independence, to have that kind of swagger in their step."

Another mother strikes her balance this way: "We take sensible precautions such as wearing seat belts in cars and bike helmets when biking," says Judy Tyrer. "We locked up all poisons when our children were toddlers. We blocked off all electrical outlets and turned down the water heater. These are common sense issues. But we don't spend a lot of time worrying about 'what if' and seeing danger on every street corner. And as for safety products, well, our children sleep in all-cotton long johns rather than 'safe' pajamas. We have warned them to be sure and not smoke in bed," she adds with a smile. "Mine is the kid at the top of the tree, or climbing 20 feet up the cliff face. I'd rather see a child with a bruise and self-confidence than one who is uninjured but afraid to try new things. I will not teach my children fear."

When finding your personal balance point, you may want to consider your own strengths and weaknesses. I, for instance, am a wimp. I have to push myself to take physical risks, so I keep in mind that I worry too much about our kids falling down the stairs. I also try to distinguish between safety and comfort whenever possible. Something in me recoils when I see the vans lined up at the corner waiting for the school bus. I'm more likely to make our kids walk in the rain and the cold than in pleasant weather. It's not just plain contrariness. It's because I want them to have a little hardship in their lives. I want them to know discomfort if for no other reason than to appreciate comfort when they have it. Yes, there are limitations. I cannot send our girls to the store for a quart of milk; the store is miles away down a busy, four-lane road. But I can make countless small decisions that will let them know that although their lives are safe, they are not always going to be easy.

One mother of four I know, Cynthia Merrill, wrote an essay about a white-water rafting trip she took with her family that gave them a chance to face fear together: "I felt the tug and rush as the water's frantic grip caught and hurled the raft, jerking us first one way then the other. . . . As we surged ahead, completely powerless, I watched my 11-year-old, Emily, go over. She was dragged under the surface, then up, her helmet bobbing like a cork. Seconds later I saw her feet swing up pointing down the current. She swept by us and landed in the shallows next to the bank where she grinned and waved, making her sisters squirm with envy. . . . By the time we reached our takeout point and stepped once more onto land, I felt satisfaction and sore shoulder muscles, fatigue and triumph. Listening to the sound of our slow, soggy, sneaker-squishing gait, I knew we had shared an adventure and learned how facing a challenge together can multiply the fun. Sitting in a diner on the road back to the city, I looked around our table and saw reflected on bright faces that special, shared joy that sometimes kindles within a family."[22]

Letting Go

Our children tell us who we are—or at least who we'd like to be—and our preoccupation with safety has made me think that we don't trust our own judgment, that we're pretending that pain is not part of life. For our sakes, and our children's, we must come to terms with discomfort as well as suspicion, but most of all, with the fact that there is evil against which even the most well-protected are defenseless. This sounds like a real downer, the ultimate in fatalistic remarks. And yet, there can be strength in confronting this truth. After all, that is what many religions do—not deny evil, but give us the courage and hope to endure suffering.

When I look at myself and the parents around me I think we

have lost the ability to trust in a power higher than ourselves. That is why we must question vaccines, that is why we must spend thousands of dollars on safety equipment. Perhaps we cannot give our children trust because we have none to give. What parents in the past were forced to acknowledge all the time—lack of control over life and death—is something we can often ignore. But when we can't ignore it anymore, we cannot admit our powerlessness either, because we have forgotten how. We have lost the habit of trusting despite incredible odds. We want our children's lives to resemble a well-mulched playground.

"I've found that people with some faith do a better job at parenting," Nashville pediatrician Betsy Triggs said to me when we were talking about the kinds of parents she sees most in her practice. "Because maybe they realize that we, people, are just little specks anyway. I think people who have stronger faith have less of that control issue. A lot of parents seem to think that if they do things just right then their child will be happy all the time."

A child cries out in the night. We go and comfort her, we bring her a glass of water, a calm voice, maybe a night-light. Who hasn't been awakened in the night by a plaintive cry or by a little hand tugging on our blanket. "Mommy, I had a bad dream." Children have their own private fears that we cannot fathom, cannot follow. In the last few weeks our oldest daughter has taken to staying up late worrying about school. She's a conscientious student and fretted for days about how she had colored Arizona blue instead of yellow on a map in social studies. Remembering something I once learned while writing a story on stress, I suggested that Suzanne imagine the letters S-T-O-P. Dress up each letter, I told her, then put them all on a float in a Mardi Gras parade. Let them file past your mind's eye, over and over again. S-T-O-P. S-T-O-P. S-T-O-P. Let those letters tell you to stop thinking, stop worrying.

Sometimes I use this trick myself. After I've comforted one of the girls in the night and can't go back to sleep, when I've just heard about a tragedy in the news, or when something else has got me going, I imagine those letters in their gaudy colors (the gaudier the better). I let them parade through my stubbornly sleepless mind. I cannot get rid of the nightmares that prey on our children, any more than I can banish the evil that still roams the earth. Sometimes all I can do is lie in bed and think of those crazy letters making their way down Bourbon Street. S always wears a big, floppy hat. T is trim in tie and tails. O is overweight, of course, and fancies loud print muumuus. P is dressed as a harlequin. Eventually, I fall back to sleep.

A Separate Peace

In his novel *A Separate Peace,* author John Knowles writes about what happens to a group of boys in the early days of World War Two. The book used to be a staple of high school English classes and when I was 16 years old it was my favorite book of all time. I dug it out recently and reread parts of it because I remembered it was about goodness and evil and how there is no safe haven except the peace we find in ourselves.

In this passage, the narrator, Gene, describes what happens when boys of his age entered the service: "When they began to feel that there was this overwhelmingly hostile thing in the world with them, then the simplicity and unity of their characters broke and they were not the same again." When they experienced "this sighting of the enemy . . . they began an obsessive labor of defense." They "constructed at infinite cost to themselves these Maginot Lines against this enemy they thought they saw across the frontier, this enemy who never attacked that way—if he ever attacked at all; if he was indeed the enemy."

When I first read this I did not know that the Maginot Line was the chain of fortifications built along the eastern border of France after World War One, a defense which was supposed to make the country impregnable but which Germany outflanked during World War Two. When we studied the book I learned that Knowles used the Maginot Line as a symbol of the defenses we build against enemies that never attack us the way we think they will because the real enemy is within us.

By the time Gene becomes a soldier, his best friend has died, the result of injuries he sustained in a fall from a tree after Gene jostled the branch he was standing on. It was from jealousy and a sense of failing his friend, "just some ignorance inside me, some crazy thing inside me, something blind, that's all it was," that makes Gene shake the branch, he says. But because he did shake the branch, he enters the war knowing he was capable of this terrible deed. "I never killed anybody and I never developed an intense level of hatred for the enemy. Because my war ended before I ever put on a uniform; I was on active duty all my time at school; I killed my enemy there."[23]

We do not live during wartime. Today's privileged kids are growing up healthier and safer than parents of the past could ever have imagined. But even this is not enough for us. The separate peace we need to make is with the fears that threaten our sanity. We, too, have built a Maginot Line. It is made of air bags and outlet covers, books and catalogs, and an obsessive wariness of strangers. But these enemies often take different forms than we think they will; they trick us with their disguises.

Of course we protect our children. How can we do otherwise? But we can give them moral as well as physical courage, we can realize that what Palladas wrote in A.D. 400 is true still: "Life is a perilous voyage." Perhaps a little less perilous as the centuries wear on, but still majestic in its unknowns. The best guarantee we can give our children is that the world is, on the whole, a manageable place, that they can make their way in it and we will help them. That is the courage we give them. That is the peace we give ourselves.

7

PC Parents

How Commercialism Has Changed Us—and Our Children

"The world is too much with us, late and soon.
Getting and spending, we lay waste our powers.
Little we see in nature that is ours.
We have given our hearts away."
—William Wordsworth

At the Right Start Store parents can buy a video monitor for $299.95 or a patented air-circulating sleep pad that guards against sudden infant death syndrome for $129.95. Parents tired of brushing little teeth can purchase a battery-powered plaque remover for kids for $19.95. And for those hot walks in the summer, there's the clamp-on stroller fan for $14.95.

Parents who think too much are parents who buy too much. We consume information and we consume things, lots and lots of things. From "tinkle targets" for potty-training boys to talking encyclopedias on CD-ROMs, there are thousands of products available now that weren't when we were kids. In fact, parents have fueled entire new markets in minivans and camcorders. There's almost nothing, it seems, that we won't buy for our kids.

Generations ago expectant parents prepared for the new arrival with a cradle and layette. Today we feather our nests with a humidifier and a baby monitor, a breast pump and a baby swing, a shelf full of books, a year's worth of magazines and countless other products that mark us as enlightened parents with solid incomes. And this is just the beginning.

I don't consider my husband and I big consumers, but our house has been filling up with kid stuff for almost nine years. When our oldest daughter was a baby we kept most of her toys in the playpen, which was located in one corner of our living room. By the time our second child was born, toys and baby gear were spilling into the kitchen, dining room, bedroom, and basement. Soon toys were cutting such a wide swath across the living room floor that we could barely walk out the back door without tripping over Duplo blocks or bits and pieces of Mr. Potato Head. In desperation, we decided to turn the dining room into a playroom. We moved our table and hutch into one half of the living room and the dining room became a kids' sanctuary. Our girls now have the only playroom I know with a chandelier. It's as if we're spotlighting those toys and paying them homage.

Because parents are such avid consumers, Disney films now earn billions of dollars, Toys "R" Us is issuing VISA Gold cards, and countless basic services have redesigned themselves for little customers and their parents. A few years ago, when the circulation and advertising revenues of other magazines were dropping, parenting magazines were still going strong, fueled by lucrative advertising and strong circulations. When few others were buying, parents were. We still are. We stock our pantries with Goldfish crackers, chocolate cereal, Sonic the Hedgehog pasta, and other kid staples. We fill our bathroom shelves with Jungle Care soaps, shampoos, and other kiddie toiletries, made for extra-sensitive skin and extra-plump wallets. When it's birthday time we entertain our little ones with everything from magicians to moon bounces, puppets to ponies. We buy computers for preschoolers, phones for middle schoolers, and new cars and pagers for high schoolers.

We are selective, image-conscious consumers, choosing products that reveal our good taste and set us apart from parents of the past. Take clothes from Baby Gap, for instance. These are high-quality cottons which wear well, but I don't think that's the only reason we favor them. It's because they're clean-cut, understated, and androgynous. They are clothes for no-nonsense, express-train-to-adulthood kids. Sometimes it feels like we're just along for the ride.

What Money Has to Do With It

For decades, bringing up kids has been evolving from something instinctive, personal, and private to something studied, impersonal, and commercial. I would like to have kept money out of the picture, to have kept our discussion of modern parenthood on a lofty plane. But I can't talk about parents who think too much without talking about what happens to us because we think too much. And one of the things that happens is that we get taken to the cleaners. A safety consultant to tell you how to childproof your house? An educational consultant to get your child into a private grammar school? Music classes for babies? Let's face it: We are older and more affluent when we become parents. We buy into expert remedies. We hate to say "no" to our children. We are a marketer's paradise.

Doting parents have always been easy prey for advertisers, but what's happening now is far more intense and far more structural. Think back, if you will, to your own childhood. Did your parents have three different kinds of strollers? Did they enroll you in a soccer clinic when you were in kindergarten? Did you go shopping at a toy warehouse every few weeks? Of course not. This is not to say our parents spent no money on us. Between 1950 and 1987, spending by parents on children rose faster than disposable income.[1] It was the postwar consumer culture in which many of us grew up that began the tide of consumerism that is threatening to drown us now.

A new mother spends $6,000 on her baby in his first year of life, and companies eagerly dole out gift packs in the hospital to hook you on *their* brand of formula and diapers before you fall for Brand X. It's not just baby gear new parents are buying. There's the Mommy and Me exercises and the breast-feeding class. Bearing a child seems to unlock a torrent of other consumerism, too. "Research shows that new parents borrow money for furniture, a new house, major appliances, a new car or a color TV, so marketing efforts need not be limited to baby shampoo and diaper rash remedies."[2]

Lately, the amount we've spent on our children has increased exponentially. It now costs $145,000 to raise a child to age 17. That compares with $120,150 in 1990 and only $25,229 in 1960.[3] These numbers are from an official report prepared by the Department of Agriculture, which measures increases in such basics as housing, food, and medical costs. It doesn't include college or nitty-gritty details like these: Parents with kids under six shop for toys nine times a year and buy 127 percent more than their household share would indicate.[4]

We Get What We Pay For

Why do we spend so much money on our children? One quick and easy answer, of course, is that we live in a consumer culture and the "buy, buy, buy" message is everywhere. In fact, there's a store near us called Buy Buy Baby. But this begs the question. Raising a child was not always such an expensive proposition. What makes us such spendthrifts?

One reason we buy so many things *for* our kids may be that we buy so much advice *about* them. During pregnancy or maybe even before, we're buying books and magazines that tell us whether we're gaining the right amount of weight or what we'll need on hand when baby is born. It's not that we never ask a relative or friend for advice, but we don't feel we have a "certified" answer until we get tips from an expert. And where do we find these certified answers? Often they're in a magazine, sandwiched between ads for minivans and infant formula, and as much a part of the consumer mentality as the products they adjoin.

We buy discipline techniques from a book that costs $12.95, or if we're not the do-it-yourself type, from a class that runs $56 for four weeks. Even if we ask a real human being our questions about childbirth or nursing or teething, chances are that human being will be a doctor, nurse, lactation consultant, therapist, or other professional, and we'll have to pay for their advice, too. Our consuming begins, then, when we seek answers to some of the most basic questions about parenthood.

So we start off buying ideas. And after that it's easy to buy other things—toys and gadgets and lessons and memberships. Surely we buy because we no longer know how to make or to make do. I am not particularly "crafty," but as soon as I knew we were having each of our babies I got this strong urge to crochet. So I bought some yarn soft as silk and a crochet hook and went to town on the simplest (indeed, the only) afghan pattern I know—one great big square. The girls love these blankies. I've told them since they were babes that I thought about them the whole time I was making them. So even though I bought everything else we needed, doing that one little bit of handiwork made me feel I was starting our children off right, with something old-fashioned. As they get older I hope they will realize that these imperfect creations—and all the gorgeous quilts and sweaters made for them through the years by loving relatives and friends—have symbolic importance. They remind us of a time when hours were more abundant than they are now and people made things instead of buying them.

Think of what parents pay for now that they would never have considered paying for in the past: childcare, playgrounds, childbirth classes, even conception and childbirth itself. It's as if we don't trust anything we get for free, as if the expensive, packaged item is somehow more reliable and familiar.

The Trophy Child

A new father sent in this observation to the "Metropolitan Diary" column of *The New York Times*. "On a crisp, sunny Sunday on the Upper East Side, my wife and I are walking on 79th Street, baby carriage ahead. In that neighborhood, as all moms and dads are aware, every parent checks out every other parent to see whether he or she has the correct brand of carriage, stroller, or baby pouch that speaks volumes about status." He then goes on to describe how he and the other father gave each other sidelong glances, went "Rumm, rumm" as they "revved" up their baby buggies and were about to have a friendly little drag race with their expensive strollers when their wives shot them dirty glances and the antics were over.

We're certainly not the first parents in history to show off our kids. But we seem to show them off more intensely, perhaps because we have fewer of them and more money to show them off with. And those high expectations that we talked about earlier make us buy more, too. We want our little one to have the best of everything. Whatever the exact cause, the crass consumerism of the 1980s is not dead; it's flourishing in baby stores across the country. In some cases, we've waited years and invested thousands of dollars to have a baby. So it's no wonder that we treat our offspring as a "trophy child," someone we're proud and amazed to have, someone we want everyone to know we have, not unlike the way an older husband displays his younger "trophy wife."

I don't want to demean the love we feel for our kids. But as a generation of parents we dote on our kids so incessantly and spend money on them so freely that we leave ourselves open to this criticism. One friend says her husband never got over the fact that he was driving an old Subaru worth $200 while his firstborn was being wheeled around in a $400 Aprica.

The suburbs of big cities are particularly prone to this baby worship. Ads in a local parenting publication lure us with "extraordinary handpainted furniture, murals, bedding, accessories . . . storybook rooms that bring wonder and whimsy to your child's favorite places" or "arts and crafts projects personally addressed and mailed to your child every month." Sales of kiddie designer clothes are up as much as 20 percent in pricey stores in Manhattan, Los Angeles, and Miami. A woman who's married to a Wall Street junk-bond trader rationalizes the $20,000 she spent last year on her two-year-old daughter's wardrobe by saying, "I can afford it, so why not?"[5] It's not just that we dote on our kids, but we dote on them shamelessly.

The trophy child is valuable not just for himself but also because of what we've given up to have him. Well-paid women and, occasionally, men, are giving up months and years of income and career growth in order to stay home with their little ones. Also, because we're older parents, I think we're more startled by the demands a child makes in our once efficient existence. We want friends to know what we've gone through to have this bundle of joy. We boast in painful detail how many hours we spent in labor and how little we slept the first month. Later we'll regale our childless friends (or anyone who will listen) about baby's first ear infection, toddler negativity, and the preschool selection process. We constantly try to trump our neighbor's story. An Internet chat group on this topic was called "More Devoted Than Thou." Who lost more sleep? Whose labor lasted longer? In my cynical moments, I wonder if parenting classes don't exist primarily to give moms and dads a chance to talk about the sacrifices they've made to be parents.

Guilt

I can't write about our consuming habits without talking about guilt. And I can't write about guilt without talking about the two-career family. We spend money on our kids because we cannot spend time on them. For many of us there is no choice. We work because we must, either for the money or because that is just what we do. It is a part of us. Whatever the reason, we want make up to our children for our absence, and it's often easier to do that with possessions than time. Half the parents surveyed by Public Agenda believe it's common for parents to equate buying things for their kids with caring for them.

Mary Scott, a mother of two daughters I've quoted earlier, used to run a daycare center. She told me about the little treats parents would bring in for their children when they came to pick them up. Inevitably the treats wouldn't quite measure up to what the child had in mind and would end up being thrown across the room. "I tried to encourage parents not to bring treats. You know, today they want a Snickers and tomorrow a Porsche," Mary said. But parents brought them anyway.

After she had her first child, when she was still working in an office, Chris Anderson would bring little surprises home to her daughter. Now that she's been staying home with her children for almost a decade, Chris talks about how much easier it was to work outside the home. "You'd ask someone to do something and they would do it. Then you'd take the money you earned at your job and spend it on a gift for your child or on advice about your children or on childcare. It's easier to spend the money than to do the hard work of struggling with your child."

In her book *The Time Bind,* Arlie Hochschild makes the point that "the village has gone to work." The support systems people used to receive at home are now in the workplace. In her research at a company she calls Amerco, she found that employees higher up the corporate ladder made less use of the part-time option. Money was not an issue, but prestige was. They were getting something from their jobs that they didn't get at home. When you do a good job at work, you get recognition. When you do a good job at home, your children scream at you. The temptation, then, is to spend more hours at work because spending time at home is complicated and messy. As a result, "children are becoming temporal bill collectors, wanting more time from us than we can give," Hochschild said in a radio interview. "Sometimes it's tempting to give a child a gift instead of time." So we sign our kids up for fancy camps and pottery classes and we hire party planners to organize their birthday galas.

But the guilt that pushes us to purchase is more pervasive and insidious than the kind that drives working parents to compensate with things. It is something all parents share, that frantic and sweaty-palmed feeling that other people's kids are passing ours by, that we haven't done enough for our kids, that we're just one step ahead of failing them. I remember how I felt when an acquaintance of mine told me about her preschool search. I wasn't even sure yet that I wanted to send our oldest to preschool, I hadn't yet "researched" that question, yet I felt left behind when I realized this gung-ho mom had already visited schools, paid deposits, and otherwise thrown herself into the preschool rat race.

As this story shows, and many other examples second, we consume to join the club. We want to belong and we want our children to belong, too. Buying for our babies is one very important way we embark on parenthood, and it sets the tone for future consumption. Our kind of buying is purposeful, scientific, and time-consuming. As parents who think too much we can't just rush out and buy the first thing we see. We have to look it up in *Consumer Reports*. I can remember deliberating for what seemed like hours between a Fisher-Price and a Gerry potty seat.

As children get older, there are many other items they have to have and many other services we want to provide them. Consider the fact that perfect teeth are now a requirement and braces are the rule rather than the exception. Parents shell out thousands of dollars for "stage one" orthodontia, which can begin as young as age seven and which prepares the parent for the monetary shock of "stage two" orthodontia later on. One father had this to say about his family's orthodontic decision: "We went to two dentists, plus we read all the books on it. If we don't take care of this problem our daughter's jaw will jut out. Society is competitive, and I don't want her to look back 15 years from now and say, 'Oh, my mom and dad could have done something and they didn't.'"

Many of the topics in this book can be seen through a commercial lens. Look at the way books and magazine articles encourage us to attend to our children, to notice their every interest and whim. When that joins forces with a consumer culture, we feel duty bound to buy developmentally appropriate toys for our babies and toddlers, and to find the right kinds of activities and classes for older kids. All of this costs money, especially if we let kids pick and choose, dabble and drop out. "My kids always decide they don't like an activity right after the refund period is over," said one exasperated mother I know.

Or consider the impulse to keep our kids safe and healthy that we talked about in the last chapter. That leads some parents to very strange and expensive habits. For the child who has everything, there is Cryo-Cell. "Your wise decision today can protect your child tomorrow. Cryopreserving your newborn's umbilical cord blood stem cells at birth could provide a vital lifesaving medical benefit," boasts the ad for Cryo-Cell. A brief description of the company informs me that it offers storage of umbilical cord blood stem cells, which research shows can be used in much the same way as bone marrow to treat leukemia, lymphoma, and other diseases. All this for only $50 a year plus a one-time processing fee of less than $200! If you'd like protection "in bulk," so to speak, you can make a single lifetime storage payment and buy true "peace of mind."[6]

Ah! Peace of mind. Isn't that what we're buying with so many of these activities and products? Peace that says our child will not be left behind by more privileged peers. Peace that says if our child contracts some terrible disease he will not have to undergo a harrowing bone marrow transplant in order to treat it. Of course, we cannot protect him from the terrible disease. Nor can we assure that he won't be bypassed by other, more privileged kids. But of course, we can try.

Kiddie Consumers

If it were just parents buying for kids it would be one thing, but the biggest story in advertising and marketing now is not what we are buying for our kids but what kids are buying for themselves—or badgering us to buy for them. It should come as no surprise that our kids have noticed and tried to emulate our all-consuming example. Chris Anderson knows this for a fact. "When I was still working part-time, my husband or I would always bring our daughter a little something home from work. It was so cute and she loved getting these presents. But we built a constant need in her to get stuff." Now her firstborn, Liz, is 12, and her "solution to any problem is to consume something. The other day Liz said, 'I can't do my report on Fort Wagner because I looked through the computer programs and I can't find anything I need. So we need to get a new program.' I feel somewhat a failure because she's thinking that things should be a lot easier than they really are." But these complaints are small potatoes compared to a fifth-grader in New York City who came home one day and asked her mom why they didn't own a helicopter.[7]

A few months ago on the radio I heard an ad for a children's allowance kit, which included a book, stickers, and an "investment folder." It was "parent-tested," the ad said, the "winner of two parenting awards." Since hearing that ad, I've noticed a plethora of books and articles on kids and money management. Parents want to know when they should start giving their child an allowance and how much they should give. Banks use stuffed animals, mock branches in schools, and no-minimum savings accounts "to get more accounts and to bring children—and their parents—into the branch often."[8] I suppose piggy banks are out of favor in an economy which needs kids to buy early and buy often.

According to a private kids' marketing firm, the income of five- to 14-year-olds increased by 150 percent in five years. In 1991 kids' income was a little shy of 11 billion dollars; in 1996 it was 27 billion.[9] The fact that kids' money is even called "income" says a lot about the state of kiddie consumerism.

What do kids do with their money? Spend it, mostly. Out of the 27 billion dollars they have, six- to 14-year-olds are responsible for 24 billion of direct expenditures. They spend over 7 billion dollars on food, almost 7 billion on play items, and billions more on clothes, movies, videos, books, music, and magazines.[10]

Product tie-ins are a great money sink for the younger generation. One researcher figured out that a family of four could easily spend $325 on a Disney film, but only ten percent of that total would be spent seeing the movie itself. The rest would be spent on spin-off products, including birthday plates, cups and napkins, backpacks, lunchboxes, costumes, books, drawing kits, T-shirts, pajamas, sneakers, and Burger King Kids' Club Meals.[11]

Even products as old and venerable as the Easy Bake Oven have succumbed to product tie-ins. For the first time in its 33-year history it now features brand-name mixes for Dunkin'

Donuts and M&M cakes. The Dr. Seuss empire, which was forbidden territory as long as its creator, Theodor Geisel, was alive, is now open for business. Already you can buy a talking Cat in the Hat. Can Yertle the Turtle pj's be far behind?

Our children's world is saturated with commercialism and brand-name awareness. By the time a child is 20 months old she will be able to recognize a few brand names, and by the time she's seven she will view 20,000 commercials a year. Twenty percent of the time kids spend watching Saturday morning cartoons they're bombarded with ads coaxing them to buy the toys, stuffed animals, and games they see on screen.[12] Perhaps most distressing is that the characters they get to know and love on screen are the very enticements used to make them buy. Thus kids are caught in an endless cycle of watching and consuming. Whether it's ads for the latest "Jurassic Park" movie or this year's cool jeans, children think they've gotta have it, or else.

If television, radio, and print advertising weren't enough, the World Wide Web is luring children with animated sites peopled by the likes of Ronald McDonald, who pitches a personalized, game-filled campaign for their interest. Some companies start e-mail conversations with kids in which they solicit information about cool words and favorite sneakers. Alcohol and tobacco companies entice kids with games, chat rooms, and messages that tout smoking and drinking. Many schools use lesson plans devised by major corporations.

Sending our kids the message to buy, buy, buy makes it even harder for us to delay their gratification. Toy fads sweep through kids' lives with regrettable regularity. One month it's Tickle Me Elmo, the next it's Beanie Babies. Our kids are growing up in a world where last year's hit cartoon merchandise lies forlornly in the clearance section, crowded off the shelves by this year's models. It's a world of style over substance. A whole generation is learning that nothing lasts, that nothing is worth lasting.

To keep kids buying, toys are made to fall apart quickly. My husband says our playroom looks like a battlefield, so many doll body parts are strewn across the floor. As grown-ups, I think we have forgotten how much our universe was shaped by the sense of permanence and familiarity toys gave us when we were small. When I was growing up, my brothers and sister and I had fewer playthings but sturdier ones. Because the toys in our house survived from one birthday to the next, they became a part of our emotional landscape. We measured our growth against them, year to year. Our children are being deprived of that birthright. It's no wonder that kids I know sell their stuffed animals at garage sales without shedding a tear. I believe that youngsters reared with a procession of replaceable toys will also find it difficult to become attached to people or things later on in life. When children have such a tenuous connection to the world around them, we're all the worse for it.

Maybe I'm strange, but I've always wanted our kids to avoid money as long as possible. They'll have to deal with it soon enough, so why bother them with it now? The tooth fairy is their most reliable source of income, and at a dollar a tooth, they're not exactly amassing a fortune. Still, it's touching that they consider $11 a king's ransom.

Dreams for Sale

One of the defining traits of childhood is that children are removed from the working world. Child-labor laws, which kept kids out of factories, and compulsory education, which put them into schools, guaranteed little people a time and an occupation of their own. Childhood is a relatively recent invention in the history of humanity, and, according to some thinkers, it's an increasingly endangered one.

In *The Disappearance of Childhood*, Neil Postman argues that the electronic media, especially television, are largely responsible for the unraveling of childhood. In the Middle Ages, before the printing press was invented and literacy widespread, children and adults were privy to the same secrets and there were few distinctions made between them. But Gutenberg changed all that.

"From print onward, adulthood had to be earned. . . . The young would have to become adults, and they would have to do it by learning to read," Postman says. Television, on the other hand, is a world accessible to both child and adult. It is a world of pictures, not of print. "Electric media find it impossible to withhold any secrets. Without secrets, of course, there can be no such thing as childhood,"[13] Postman concludes.

In the 15 years since *The Disappearance of Childhood* was published, Postman's vision has seemed increasingly prophetic. Children are being changed by television, particularly by the advertising on television. In the average 21½ hours per week that two- to 11-year-olds spend watching television, they are absorbing the gotta-have-it values of a commercial world. Though commercial television-viewing is down slightly from its high in the mid-1980s, kids often spend that excess time viewing videos or playing on a computer.[14] We've already talked about how advertisers reach kids on the Internet. And as any parent can attest, there are commercials on children's videos, too, especially promos for upcoming movies.

The point is, our media-saturated kids are exposed more to someone else's imaginings than they are to their own. Which is why I think the greatest casualty of a commercialized childhood is our children's fantasy lives. We have stopped giving kids the quiet and the space to invent the world all over again. We have stopped being the creators of our children's childhood and are letting Disney and Mattel do it for us. We've let kids see the movies before they read the books. There are many young children (and even some adults) who have no idea that *The Little Mermaid* and *Beauty and the Beast* were fairy tales before they were videos. So when they create their own magical world, it's not as far-out and personal as it might have been. Instead of magical goats who fly like whirligigs, there are "my pretty ponies" with "combable manes and tails." It's difficult for our kids to get a dream in edgewise these days.

The Nag Factor

Marketing to kids came of age as we did. The baby boom generation showed advertisers the power and autonomy of the youth market. When boomers began to have children, the possibilities seemed endless and market researchers used increasingly more sophisticated methods to learn as much as they could about what kids wanted to buy. "This research, ironically, embodied and applied the same 'helping' philosophy that modern psychology had urged for contemporary parenting: find out what children say they need and then help them get it."[15] In other words, while some psychologists were studying children and telling parents how to raise them, other psychologists were studying children and telling businesses how to sell to them.

According to a Nielsen survey, parents toy-shopping with their kids spend $30 per shopping trip whereas parents shopping without their kids spend "only" $22. This may not seem like much of a difference until you multiply it by nine shopping trips a year and then by the seven out of ten U.S. households that buy toys.[16] No wonder there's now a term, "nag factor," to explain the purchases made when kids badger us till we buy.

Even more shocking is the fact that children will influence about $200 billion in adult purchases this year. It's as if kids have tired of pestering us to buy them the small stuff, the latest action figure or computer game, and have moved on to more challenging requests—having their say about the choice of family minivan. "Ten years ago, it was cereal, candy, and toys [being advertised to kids]. Today, it's also computers and airlines and hotels and banks," Julie Halpin, general manager of Saatchi and Saatchi Advertising's Kid Connection division told *Business Week*. General Motors will tap the "back seat consumer" market by showing previews of Disney's Hercules on a VCR inside the Venture minivan when it's pitched in malls.[17]

So kids are hot properties because they have not only their own dollars to burn, but also their parents'. "We're relying on the kid to pester the mom to buy the product, rather than going straight to the mom," says Barbara A. Martino, a vice-president in Grey Advertising Inc.'s 18 & Under Division.[18]

Because kids' consuming habits seem to change with the wind and retailers and advertisers want to understand and penetrate this mercurial market, newsletters tout them onto the latest trends (Nikes are in, Timberlands are out) and the hottest toys. (Tamagotchi and its clones, those electronic "pets," are the latest on the hype horizon, though by the time you read this, they will probably be long gone.) Youth-oriented marketing firms conduct observational research to see which toys kids like and how they play with them. Or they bring 100 kids together in a panel to track what's hot and what's not. Kids' opinions are also recruited by telephone and through computers.

While this is distasteful to us, the truth of the matter is that we're partially responsible for it. It's not just Big Bad Business preying on innocent children. The nag factor works because we're often too busy or too guilty to say no to the toy lawnmower that blows bubbles, the oversize athletic jacket with sports team logo, or even the extra options in the van. Children want things more often than not because we've taught them to want them. We make kids consumers because of what and how much we buy. Consumerism is changing childhood because we've invited it to.

PC Parents

To find out why, I think we have to take a deeper look at why parents consume, at our habit of turning to others for advice because we've stopped trusting ourselves. The information overload has made it easy to consume (and conform to) other people's notions of how good parents behave.

Though we think we're free, we often behave according to prescribed patterns of behavior, parental peer pressure. I think we may be more susceptible to it than parents of the past. Because we want to be less like our own mothers and fathers than parents used to, we pay closer attention to each other. We're not unlike teenagers who want to break away from the old folks and be free, but the harder they try to be individuals, the more like each other they become: same baggy pants, same baseball cap worn backward. In our efforts to be less like our own parents we are surprisingly similar to each other. We try to be original by giving our kids unique names and then find out that other parents have picked the same unique names for their children. Baby name books have been around for many years but a recent invention is the baby name book with attitude, an example of which is *Beyond Jennifer and Jason,* by Linda Rosenkrantz and Pamela Redmond Satran. This guide contains paragraph-long explanations (somewhat tongue in cheek) of why you might want to choose Katharine rather than Catharine or Geoffrey rather than Jeffrey and how to discern whether a name is upwardly or downwardly mobile.

One of the main things that marketers and advertisers prey on is our desire to be the "right" kind of parent. The commercialization of childhood has made appearances all the more important, and modern childrearing is now the perfect vehicle for political correctness.

When you think about political correctness, you usually think about avoiding racial, gender, or other stereotypes, and indeed, most of us are politically correct parents in that we encourage our children to be open, sensitive, and fair-minded. We also pick nursery schools that forbid sugary snacks, and we edit fairy tales so that the princess saves the prince. On the surface, at least, our efforts seem to be paying off. I've heard a little five-year-old lisp, "I'm gonna be a Native American for Halloween."

But the kind of PC'ness that infects parenthood is psychological as well as political. It's following expert advice to the letter. It's being constantly on guard lest we slip up and say or do something forbidden, such as cooking the breakfast we think is best rather than giving our child a choice or enforcing a punishment rather than giving a consequence. In the past these would not be grievous errors. But today we're made to feel as if they can make or break our kids. A child denied choice will feel disenfranchised. A child denied consequences will feel repressed.

As childrearing has become unmoored to the ties that traditionally bound it to extended families, schools, neighborhoods, and towns, parents have placed increasing importance on how they appear to be. What is left is impersonal. What is left is doing the right thing because it's supposed to be the right thing. What is left is psychological correctness.

When PC dads discover that their wife is expecting a baby, they say, "*We're* pregnant," and they create solidarity with their spouse by picking up their infants and carrying them from the cradle to bed for nighttime nursing. PC moms boast of their husbands' prowess as labor coaches. When grocery shopping, PC parents frequently ask for their child's input: "Do you want peaches or bananas? White bread or whole wheat?" As you might expect, PC kids tell them to buy the latest sugary breakfast cereal advertised on TV.

Political correctness thrives on self-consciousness and fear of failure. Remember metaparenting, the habit of fretting about our performance? Not only does metaparenting make us feel guilty and insecure, but it also makes us feel that other parents are watching to see how we're doing. (And often, we're right. They are.)

PC parenthood is not only a symptom of our lack of confidence but also of our distance from each other. When those around us know us well, they also know we are well-intentioned. If we lose our temper with our kids, friends and family will not suspect us of child abuse. But in a world dominated by impartial expert opinion, our actions are more likely to be scrutinized for improprieties. We are judged for how we appear to be as parents rather than how we actually are.

I'm not suggesting we bring up kids Archie Bunker style. But by being so resolutely correct in everything we say we risk becoming bland, homogenized mothers and fathers, every one of us the same. We never raise our voices. We always use the disciplinary phrase of the moment. PC'ness makes it difficult to be ourselves.

A Spoiling Story

I've noticed the creeping PC'ness of parenthood for years but when it came time to write this chapter, I wondered if maybe I shouldn't change the focus because PC'ness was becoming passé. The more I thought about it, though, the more I realized that politically correct attitudes are too much a part of parenthood to ignore, and if I pretended they didn't exist when in fact they do, I would be silent because of political correctness myself.

One of the first times I noticed there were certain parenting ideas you could and couldn't express was when I wrote an article on spoiling. It was in 1989, earlier in my freelance magazine-writing career, and I interviewed, among other people, a mother who was a cashier at our local supermarket. We had recently moved to Virginia and I didn't know many people here yet, but this woman was friendly and we had struck up an acquaintance. In her line of work she saw a lot of strung-out parents and rowdy kids, and this, among other things, had convinced her to be firm with her own children. She came across as no-nonsense and sure of herself.

Ah, the innocence of youth, or at least of youthful inexperience! I would never include her views on controlling behavior with a swat on the bottom anymore. I would include more anguished mothers, ones who had tried the old ways and found them lacking. But this was my first article on a topic as sensitive as spoiling, so I went with my gut.

Something else was different, too. This was one of the first major stories I'd written since having a child. Suzanne was a baby still, but an increasingly demanding one. I was beginning to think about my subject from a parent's rather than just a journalist's point of view. The spoiling article reflected that additional perspective.

My editors were not pleased with the story I turned in, especially the cashier's comments. Her words were too strong. In fact, the entire story reflected a point of view that was far too strict, they said. Soon I was embarked upon a major revision that not only changed my story, but changed my life a little, too.

After I rewrote that spoiling article, I started to think that maybe I *was* being too strict with Suzanne. It was silly of me, I realize now, but I bent to the weight of expert opinion. I began giving our baby girl more choices and thinking that some of the instinctive ways I was doing things were harmful. Was I demanding her respect at too young an age? Did I expect our daughter to obey me too well too soon?

I can't put all the blame on that story. I wrote many other stories and read many other books that made me ignore that faint voice of reason inside, straining so hard to be heard. But it wasn't long before we had a young toddler who ran away from me in stores and talked back to me at home. I had become an "okay" parent. That's "okay" as in, "Suzanne, come with me. Okay? We're going to go now. Okay?"

The spoiling story taught me some important lessons. It showed me that I had to watch what I wrote, that some subjects are sensitive enough that I needed to carefully weigh my words. It also showed me how much writing these articles would influence the way I was raising our own daughter.

The PC Police

To have psychological correctness, you need someone to enforce it. And do we ever. We have each other, for one thing, the parents we meet at play groups or while waiting for our kids to finish gymnastics class. We don't know each other very well so we want to make a good impression. Whether it's at the company picnic or with a couple other parents down the block, we live in fear that our childrearing methods will be taken to task.

When I listen to the voices of parents, I hear, over and over again, this need for approval and notice. We're always wondering what other parents will say about the way we're raising our kids. Nancy, a woman in my STEP parenting class, says she's mortified that her two-year-old son keeps telling his dolls to "sit down" and "be quiet" because anyone who listens would realize that she says these words to him! "Well, things could be worse," the STEP instructor chimed in. "Some neighbor children where we used to live would say to each other, 'Do you want a spanking?'"

Whether or not the judgment is there, we feel that other parents are watching to see how we'll handle a situation. "We pretend like we're not judging each other," Chris Anderson says. "But we are." Perhaps it's not as much a climate of judgment as a climate of notice that we interpret as judgment. We are, all of us, casting about for a new way to raise kids, and we're looking to other parents for guidance. But what may be observation can feel a lot like judgment if we don't know what's behind the long stare.

You might argue that parents have always watched other parents, have always compared children to see who's more well-behaved. But we have something parents of the past didn't have—the standards imposed on us by books, articles, and classes. The discussion group guidelines of the STEP class I took included this ominous warning: "Don't suggest physical punishment as a solution. There are other, more effective ways to handle discipline problems. And, your facilitator is expected to report any suspected incidence of child abuse." This goes beyond the PC police into the realm of real police.

When I questioned this rule the first day of class, Mary, my instructor (or, to use the politically correct term, my "facilitator"), said she understood my concern. She pointed out that she was not an expert in child development, but merely a trained parent volunteer and that she would not feel confident making a diagnosis of potential abuse based on parents' comments in her class. Anyway, I offered, a little flippantly, it seemed unlikely that child abusers would sign up for a parenting class. Not necessarily, she said. Some mothers and fathers attended the class by court order. Hmmm. We all eyed each other. Were there any court-ordered cases in our class? It was strange to think of us jumbled together, parents who think too much and parents who spank too much. All of us trying to learn another way.

But as I would discover in this class and other classes, it doesn't take a rule to make us watch our words. A lot can be said with lowered eyes and forced smiles. On the night we talked about letting our children express their true feelings, I couldn't keep *my* true feelings to myself anymore: "I would never allow a child to say 'I hate you!' to me," I blurted out, fully aware of how retrograde it sounded to this mellow crowd. Up to that point we had been discussing how best to communicate "I messages," but I doubt that saying "I won't let you say you hate me" was the kind of "I message" the facilitator had in mind.

Mary's face scrunched up a little in disappointment when I made this confession. Up to that point, I think I had seemed a relatively well-informed and sensitive parent, but from now on I would be the token authoritarian. "We must guide children to develop their own motivation for being good rather than making them obey us. Doing something just because Mommy wants them to won't stand them in good stead when they're in their teens and have to make decisions about sex and drugs." I might have assumed that Mary was trying to scare me with such talk. But she wasn't. She really believes this stuff. Later, she would tell me that I must have had strict parents, because "I seem to have this tape of how I should behave running through my head."

Once you start looking for them, you can find many examples of psychologically correct parenting, the special words and phrases we use in order to appear sensitive and aware. It's especially prevalent, I think, when we feel conflicted about something. For instance, there's the careful way we ask one another what we do. "So do you work . . . outside the home?"—the last part of the question ever so tentatively attached, so as not to offend.

Some politically correct terms become part of the way we define our lives. Take such a carefully calibrated phrase as "quality time." It has become such a crucial concept for millions of American parents that *Newsweek* magazine did a cover story on it, discussing how the term originated in research which showed that the more actively mothers engaged with their babies the better they learned and developed.[19] But it quickly became an excuse by which working parents could convince themselves that it isn't how much time they spend with their child but how much they can pack into that time. As the concept spun further and further away from its original meaning, parents crammed more "meaningful" activities into the evening and weekend hours. Yet because the term was part of the politically correct currency of working and parenting, they could convince themselves it was okay. The myth of quality time may be beginning to crumble. But there are many more myths still ruling our thoughts, myths made possible by the PC proneness of our times.

"I Can See You Worked Hard on That"

The most chilling use of politically correct dialogue is the way we use it with our kids, how we've memorized the pre-fab conversations we learn from books or parenting classes. If your four-year-old shows you a picture he drew, you're not supposed to say, "What is it?" or, worse yet, "I like your horse." (What if it's a barn?) Instead, you're supposed to utter a diplomatic, "I like the way you used red in this picture." Or, when all else fails, "I can see you worked hard on that." It's bad enough that we should watch what we say when we're talking to other parents. But that we should tiptoe around our children is truly frightening. Yes, they have feelings. But they also have phoniness detectors that must be blinking away madly at our lack of sincerity.

Take the big deal made about praise versus encouragement. I mentioned it briefly earlier in the book and you've probably read about it in magazines. The current wisdom would have us believe that praise is dangerous for kids because it doesn't motivate them and makes them overly reliant on our judgment.

The night we spoke about the dangers of praise in our STEP class, Mary stepped out of her "facilitator" role (which she did often and to the class's benefit) and admitted: "This one is hard for me. It took me a long time to stop saying, 'Good job' or 'wonderful' to my kids." But her admission was short-lived. It was as if she caught herself and realized she was supposed to be preaching the "STEP" message. So she drew herself up and said, quite assuredly, "The real point here is that praise is judgmental. And after all, we want to make sure our children aren't still trying to please us twenty or thirty years down the road." Well, why not? I think to myself. Of course we want our children to live their own lives, but don't we try to please everyone we love? No one lifts an eyebrow when we talk about pleasing our spouse or friends. And as for pleasing our kids, well, there's no length to which we would not go to please them. But for kids to please their parents is shocking and dangerous. Anyway, this horrifying thought apparently pushed Mary to avoid pat phrases of praise, and she urged us to do the same.

We talk about all the ways we can encourage children without praising them. We can say, "You can do it" or (if she hasn't quite done it), "Look at the progress you've made." We can acknowledge effort in specific ways rather than heaping on unjustified accolades. One mother says that when she's tucking her children into bed in the evening, she always concludes the evening ritual with, "Thank you for a wonderful day." Other class members murmur in delight. To me it sounds like what you'd say to a tour guide after a bus trip around Washington, D.C.: "Thank you for a wonderful day." This mother says it even when the day is not so wonderful, by the way. She is an equal opportunity encourager. And in fact, that's the point of encouragement. That you give it just as much when your child isn't making progress as when he is.

It is quite natural for us to praise our kids. It feels right and—it seems to me—it *is* right, as long as we don't overdo it. Yes, there are subtle differences between praise and encouragement. Yes, kids know when we're putting them off with a shallow compliment, and if we always say "good job," those words won't have any meaning for them. But I think kids can sense false encouragement, too. If we reserved praise *and* encouragement for those times when children truly deserve it, if we weren't supplying them with a steady stream of parental feedback, then they would know that when they win recognition from us, it's the Real Thing. Praise is criticized in parenting books and classes because it's a reward for performance, but what could be more of a "performance" than the way parents are trained to encourage their kids? Perhaps it was just a coincidence, but three of the parents in my STEP class dropped out after our lesson on praise and encouragement.

Fooling Ourselves

There's another way that psychological correctness affects us. It lets us fool ourselves. If our two-year-old is throwing a tantrum because he didn't get to climb into the car seat without our help, we pull off the road, stop the car, and let him climb in by himself. This is called "empowering our child." Or when we say to our three-year-old, "You must be very angry with Mommy" when she's screaming in the checkout line, this is called "validating her feelings." The psychologically correct language of modern childrearing techniques allows us to put a glossy spin on our failures of courage and resolve. It allows us to wimp out and feel good about it.

Sometimes, though, this dialogue becomes an impossible standard we can never meet. One night at STEP class, Nancy, the woman who was embarrassed that her two-year-old told his dolls to "sit down" and "be quiet," told us another problem. She felt she would never master the new dialogue she was learning in the class. She could be "encouraging" for a little while, but then the old ways began to assert themselves.

"I hear my daughter using my own voice, I hear the impatience there. I've really been trying to be better. But it's just so hard. And I'm afraid I've blown it with her. She's already six. The things I'm using now I should have used with her a long time ago. It makes me so sad to think I've blown it." By the time she finished her testimonial, Nancy was racing over to the paper towel dispenser in the daycare classroom where we met to dab away her tears. Everyone was aching for her, but what made Nancy's tears even more poignant to me is that they weren't necessary.

Nancy may never be the kind of mother she is striving to be, a perfect parent with the right word for every situation. She's trying to take every natural reaction she has and replace it with an artificial, learned one. She could have spared herself this anguish simply by staying clear of the parenting class.

We've all had moments when we've thought what we're doing is wrong, that we've made horrible mistakes with our children. But the lexicon of psychologically correct parenting makes us have these feelings far more often than we need to. There's a template now that we must use, a prescribed way we're supposed to handle our children. We overlay our real thoughts and feelings with the veneer of expert-certified lines and phrases. In fact, many of the books and classes tell us to assume that what naturally wells up in us must be wrong. It's PC'ness to self and PC'ness to children. I can imagine no greater block between parent and child than constantly watching the words we use together. When we concentrate so much on what's "right" and "wrong," how can we let our true selves emerge? The answer to that one, of course, is that we're not supposed to.

PC Kids

It's not hard to see how we might inflict political correctness on our kids. We have a good example of this at our children's preschool, which was until recently an island of old-fashioned values in a modern suburban sea. Two years ago, we had to purge all the sexist language from the handbook. Last year the PC Police seized upon the Indian Pow Wow the children put on each year. It was changed to a bland "Thanksgiving celebration." It's not that the teachers were perpetrating untruths, but as soon as they talked about Indians (even if they called them Native Americans) the kids would erupt in war whoops. Our kids must be watching the politically incorrect Disney's *Peter Pan* more often than the politically correct Disney's *Pocahontas*. As it was, these changes were good preparation for the politically correct world of public school, with its awards for everyone, its frequent references to self-esteem, and its cautious avoidance of such politically incorrect words as "Christmas."

We are padding our children's world with the right kind of thought and language. The movie *Pocahontas* is a good example of what happens when ethnic sensitivity meets Hollywood, and how our children pay the price. Disney creators took great pains to make sure this film would be politically correct, unlike some of their others. (Arab Americans were so incensed by their portrayal in the movie *Aladdin*, that Disney cut offensive lyrics from the opening song when they released the video version of the movie.) Disney consulted with American Indian organizations as well as historians, academics, and even descendents of Pocahontas. But when it was released, Disney was once again criticized, not only because ten years and tons of sex appeal significantly changed the character of Pocahontas, but also because the film was trying *too* hard to be politically correct.[20]

When we took our children to Jamestown the summer after they saw the film, they asked where the greedy Englishmen had dug for gold. I realized then that they did not want to hear about the courage it took to cross an ocean and start a new life in an unknown land. I tried to give the story a little balance, but my approach could not compete with the politically correct one, which was the first version they heard and would always remain with them.

The summer after *Pocahontas,* Disney released *The Hunchback of Notre Dame.* Once again, the entertainment company weathered protests. One editorial said that the movie insulted people with disabilities, depicting Quasimodo as unable to have a romantic relationship and friendless except for stone gargoyles. But at least Disney was spared the embarrassment that plagued Mattel. Only a couple weeks after the toy company introduced its new doll, Barbie's friend "Share a Smile Becky," who sits in a wheelchair, it was discovered that Becky's wheelchair couldn't fit through the door of some Barbie dollhouses. Maybe the big companies will decide that PC'ness is more trouble than it's worth.

What the politically correct movies and toys tell me is that we want our children to be caring, sensitive human beings. But can we do it by rewriting history, changing literature? Can we do it by making the world perfectly bland? And don't we mislead our kids when we try to? We want our children to grow up free and unbiased. But is that what we do by making the world so politically correct for them? By thinking so much about our own presentation, we are leaving our children a hollow legacy, a legacy of appearances.

Some parents poke fun at the PC rules and thereby loosen

their power. When Chris Anderson encounters parents who boast of their children's intellectual achievements, she imagines herself saying, "My daughter reads Britannica every evening. Doesn't yours?" It seems to me that humor is the weapon of choice against those who would tell us what is right or wrong to say and do because political correctness is, above all, humorless. It takes parenting Very Seriously. Being able to laugh at ourselves or being able to admit our frustration and say, "My kids are driving me crazy," helps us put PC'ness in perspective. It means we can hold two notions in our head at the same time: childhood the way we envision it, and the world in which our kids are growing up.

If you're not the kind of person who can do this in a crowd, maybe at least you can provide a sort of running commentary to your child, can give him some sense of how things were before. I tell our children to respect all people, but I make sure they know that names for peoples change, that before there were Native Americans there were Indians. I don't want them to narrow their world with stereotypes, but neither do I want them to wallow in political correctness. I want them to know there was injustice in the past—there still is—and we're trying to correct it. But I want them to have values that are deeper than the latest superficial trends. I try to give our children the "other side" from the one they hear about in school. I try to give them my opinion, not someone else's.

Living in a politically correct world makes it more challenging to teach our children true kindness, I think, for to be kind means to reach beyond the borders of what is prescribed, to take a chance and touch the core of someone, not just their outer shell.

Digging Deep

In this chapter we've talked about the connection between buying advice and buying products, and that our need for approval makes us susceptible to political and psychological correctness—a PC'ness we then pass along to our children in toys, movies, and attitudes. In other words, the complex constellation of habits that I call thinking too much has been noted, studied, and used to entice us into a consumer culture, in much the same way that children's play preferences are noted, studied, and passed back to them in eye-popping array on toy-store shelves. And the more we think of ourselves as consumers rather than creators of childrearing ideas, the easier it is to fall for the PC lines.

How do we keep ourselves and our kids from being absorbed into the maw of commercialism? "If parents are not to feel defeated by the media and pop culture, they must get over their reluctance to make choices that are based on clear assertions of moral values," said author and critic David Denby in *The New Yorker*. He describes parents he knows who, in the face of this onslaught, choose to strictly limit or ban most movies and television. They are locked "in an unwinnable struggle to shut out pop culture and the life of the streets," he says. "I don't want to be like them, but I understand their absolutism."[21] The rest of Denby's article is an engaging discussion and debate (with himself, most of all, it seems) over just how much control well-educated, thinking parents can or should wrest from this dragon. He doesn't leave us with a lot of hope, but he certainly pinpoints the problem.

I don't necessarily agree with Denby's conclusion—I'm more optimistic than he that we can triumph over consumerism—but I mention his article and the others I quote in this chapter to prove that the culture of consumerism is being noticed. Notice is a big step from eradication. But it's a beginning.

And noticing can be a beginning for us, too. When we understand just how much advice we consume, for instance, we can start to limit it. The same holds true for buying things for our kids or because our kids beg us to buy it for them. The way I see it, we have to be squares. And we have to be willing to make our kids squares, too, which is much harder. We have to be willing to send them to school with the wrong brand of sneakers. We have to dry their tears when they come home saying that everyone else saw the latest dinosaur disaster movie and why can't they?

I'm one to talk about consumerism, with a house full of toys, but I am trying to keep our kids money-free for a while and to limit their television viewing and to buy them clothes that don't have cartoon characters emblazoned on them. I've also counteracted consumerism by trying to find my own parental voice, digging deep through the detritus of other people's advice and coming up with thoughts which are my own. For me, finding my voice has been renewing the principles I was brought up with—moral standards, a belief in something beyond myself—perhaps a little more militantly than my parents because they never felt themselves in opposition to the culture as much as I do.

I don't think you have to drop out of society to do this, by the way. We live a normal suburban life. The battles we fight are small ones, best revealed in what we demand of our children and ourselves. If we lose one day, we win another. It's not always easy, but I try not to worry about what other parents will think, or what the latest good doctor said in his latest good book.

For all its promise of cultural diversity, a world dominated by consumerism and political correctness is a world where everyone is the same, where difference is suspect. Don't we want our kids to inherit a world full of twists and turns and interesting places? We always say we want our kids to be their own unique selves. Well, this is where it all begins—with us being our own unique selves. What we're striving for is the confidence to raise *our* children *our* way. We're the only ones who can.

8

Kidcentricity
It Isn't Easy Being a Grown-up

"Between the dark and the daylight
When the night is beginning to lower,
Comes a pause in the day's occupations,
That is known as the children's hour."
—*Henry Wadsworth Longfellow*

By now, the story has become frayed from the retelling, but it fascinates us still. When 18-year-old Melissa Drexler arrived at her high school prom, she quickly went to the bathroom, locked herself in a stall, and within a half hour delivered a six-pound six-ounce baby boy. She apparently cut the umbilical cord with the jagged edge of a small metal trash receptacle, put the baby in a plastic bag, and threw him in the garbage can. Then she went back to the party. The girl had told no one about her pregnancy, not her parents, boyfriend, or classmates. If someone hadn't noticed the blood in the bathroom, which led to the discovery of the baby and a futile attempt to revive him, Melissa Drexler might have kept her secret.

Understandably, the story lingered in the media and the public consciousness, with much speculation about whether Drexler killed the child before putting him in the plastic bag.

One thing is certain: She did not want the baby and she pretended as if he didn't exist.

She is not alone. Although infanticide is as old as time, within the last year there has been a well-publicized rash of teenagers killing infants. These are tales of affluent, conscienceless children grown old too fast, of parents who wonder where they've gone wrong, and of a society that can't stop thinking about its youngest members. These are all hallmarks of what I call kidcentricity.

Kidcentricity is what happens when thinking too much becomes institutionalized, when it spills out of the home and into society at large, when it permeates business, entertainment, and popular culture. There doesn't have to be a tragedy for us to obsess about kids. Newspapers are full of articles about schools, daycare, spanking, smoking, drugs, sexual activity, you name it. I clip a couple dozen articles a week from the two daily papers I read. I'm looking for material about children, but the articles would be there even if I wasn't.

In a kidcentric society, the lines between childhood and adulthood are blurred almost beyond recognition. Kids grow up fast, and adults don't seem to grow up at all. We dress in jeans and sneakers while babies wear designer dresses. There are almost as many adult activities at Disney World as there are kids' activities in Las Vegas.

We need to recognize kidcentricity because it plays a large role in why we think too much and makes a big difference in how we live. Enter many houses and you will discover the living room has disappeared; instead there is a family room and another room which seems designed to have been a living room but is now full of Little Tykes climbing equipment. Come to those houses long after 9 P.M. and you will find its youngest inhabitants still awake. Perhaps they'll be channel surfing Nickelodeon, the Cartoon Network, the Family Channel, or other kiddie cable stations. One night last year they could have watched an all-kids' version of the *Tonight Show*. Parents take their babies everywhere, at any hour—from joint sessions of Congress to fancy French restaurants. When I reach a home answering machine, I often hear a child's voice delivering the message. These are details, and I know I must seem grumpy carping about them, but to me they are telling evidence of how kids rule our lives, of kidcentricity at work.

A National Malaise

Every year around the beginning of June, I again come to terms with the kidcentricity of our suburban world. As you may have guessed from my earlier rhapsody on summer, I always want an old-fashioned one for our children, with ample time for them to contemplate sunlight on leaves, eat Popsicles, read books, and run around with other kids in the neighborhood. But I always forget that their friends will be busy: two weeks daycamp, two weeks intensive ballet, two weeks art classes, two weeks family vacation and one free week at the end of summer—or some such schedule. Our kids, with their unscheduled lives, seem out of place.

It's easy to rebel against modern parenting practices in the abstract. But when it comes to depriving my own kids of company and activities, it's a lot tougher. I end up depriving them anyway, but I feel guilty about it. And no wonder. Experts tell us we hold the key to our children's intellectual, emotional, and social development. We're encouraged to defer to little feelings, to put our instincts on hold, to study childhood as if it were a prep course for the SAT. At some point we look up from our private contemplations to realize that a lot of other parents have been doing the same thing, and our child is not the only one with attention excess disorder. It has become a sort of national malaise.

I'm not pretending that the way we read, study, and talk about kids is the only reason our world has become child-centered. There are other forces at work: fewer kids, older and more affluent parents, many of whom work and want to focus intently on their kids the little time they're with them. Certainly the consumerism we talked about in the last chapter makes us kidcentric, too.

When I talk about kidcentricity, I also realize there are families in America which have no center, kid or otherwise. The over-advantaged lives we create for our kids look all the more extravagant when compared with the lives led by the poorest and most disadvantaged children. However, there are plenty of well-off families in which children's true needs are also ignored. You've probably heard that average parents spend only a few minutes a day in substantive conversation with each child. One study showed that parents spent ten to 12 hours *less* a week with children in 1986 than they did in 1960.[1] One could certainly argue that kidcentricity is as much a guilty second best as it is anything else.

Of course, children are precious to us as individuals and as a group. They are dear to us simply because they exist. But there are social and economic reasons for their heightened importance. Children are no longer assets who will work in the family business and support us in our old age; they are liabilities who require four-figure nursery schools, a six-figure college education—and everything in between. Because we are giving up so much to have them, we must appear (again, that's a key word) to be giving them our all.

Maybe we take pride in our devotion because it sets us apart from parents of the past. "I remember when my older daughter was born and we were filling out the insurance forms and they asked what my occupation was, and I said, 'Kate's mom,' " said Mary Scott. "The insurance agent said, 'Oh, so you're a housewife,' and I said, 'No. I'm Kate's mom. I'm not married to this house. You should see this house. I would not be staying at home if it were not for this child. I am not Donna Reed.' " I'm not suggesting that women who stay home should go back to calling themselves housewives, but our choice of words reveals much about our state of mind. Our mothers described themselves as "homemakers," which implies an obligation to family and home. We describe ourselves as "stay-at-home moms," which implies a duty only to children.

This is not to say that child-centeredness has no advantages. It's easier to swallow hard choices in our political life when we reframe issues around our children's future. And now that Hollywood has discovered family films score big at the box office, high-quality adaptations of children's classics are making blood-and-guts fare scarcer than it used to be. But after a while, even the most well-intentioned kidcentricity becomes tiresome: There should be more to talk about than the local school board elections and our kid's soccer game. But often there isn't.

Babies on Board

It's difficult to pinpoint the genesis of kidcentricity; it's been creeping up on us for many years. Did it begin with those distinctive yellow signs plastered on the back windows of cars and vans? I can remember being mystified about "Baby on Board" notices when they became popular. Why did parents feel it necessary to announce to the driving public that there were children in their cars? Did they think it would make everyone else a safer driver?

One of the first times I remember seeing kidcentricity in action was when I visited my friend Kathleen, who'd recently had a baby. I shared several restaurant meals with Kathleen, her friends, and her baby. I had no children yet, Kathleen was one of my first friends to become a mother, and I was startled to see how her daughter went everywhere with her. Kathleen was raising her daughter alone—that helped explain the inseparability—but I would later meet many two-parent families where mothers and fathers took their children to art museums, formal evening weddings, cocktail parties, and other adults-only affairs. These parents had a sense of entitlement backed by the culture of kidcentricity, and adults who craved grown-up conversation were often bullied into going along.

Taking kids with you has become such a trend that it received front-page coverage in *The New York Times* "Home" section recently. "A Night on the Town (Bring the Stroller)" teased the headline. Inside was an anecdote about a seven-year-old and 13-year-old who attended a Broadway play about prostitutes and hustlers, then had dinner at Joe Allen's, a quintessential after-theater eaterie. Another anecdote chronicled the change of heart fatherhood worked on an art gallery owner who a decade ago worried that strollers would hurt the finish of his floor but today hardly flinched when a toddler left a handprint on a $20,000 painting. "It's the baby boom generation moving through their social life with children in tow," Gina Bria of the Institute on Family Development said in the article. "Baby-boomer parents don't want to give up their fun. They're trying to find a new way to swing and still have their kids along."[2]

One of the defining moments of early parenthood for Tom and me occurred at a solemn ceremony of lessons and carols in a Gothic chapel near the little village in Massachusetts where our daughter Suzanne was born. This was the famous Groton School Christmas program and we had gone there with our friends Kip and Kim and their son, Owen, 11 months old. Owen began to fuss before the program began, and Kim nonchalantly pulled up her shirt and began to nurse him. I was still new at nursing, and it was hard to imagine unbuttoning my blouse in a Gothic chapel. To make matters worse, we were sandwiched into some seats from which there was no easy escape, and when the choirboys filed in and stopped right by our pew, blocking even the narrow exit there once was, I saw, with horror, that they would be making their way down the aisle very, very slowly, that they would pause every few pews to sing another lilting carol in their high sopranos, in a chapel so still that I could hear my heart pounding. Our baby was only two months old and she had colic. She would cry inconsolably for hours—commencing usually at this very time of night—and although she had fallen into a fitful sleep in the car on the way over, we had little hope she would nap through the entire concert. In fact, we were convinced she would scream during the quietest moment. Why did we bring her? I asked myself. How careless we were! Now we would spoil this ceremony for everyone else.

Miraculously, Suzanne slept through the whole concert. And though we've acted like modern parents in many other ways since then, we don't take kids to grown-up events. We either stay home or get a baby-sitter. I wish I could say we've avoided other aspects of kidcentricity as well as that one.

Organized Play

Whenever parents gather these days, there is one topic sure to engage them—their kids' activities. In my book group we often drift away from our literary topic to discuss the relative merits of various swim teams, the Marlins versus the Mini-Marlins, or the difference between male and female T-ball coaches. Always we chatter about the Byzantine complexity of the activities, signing kids up for them, getting kids to and from them, which becomes especially complicated when there are two or three children each with their own set of interests. I always come away from these conversations amazed at the extent to which parents involve themselves in kids' activities.

As I mentioned in Chapter Five, the stimulation must begin early, so we sign babies up for Gymboree, and toddlers go to Kindermusic or karate. We push play dates so tots can learn "social skills." One man who directs a T-ball league for five- to eight-year-olds had a mother call and ask him what he had for her daughter, who just turned three. "Try a daycare center," he said.[3]

Kids get used to going out of the house for their fun, and we find ourselves on a treadmill (not our own, of course, that one is gathering dust down in the basement while we work out in a "strollercise" class). Scouts or soccer or Little League fill our afternoons and weekends. Swim practice gets us up before dawn. Ice-skating or gymnastics take every weekday and some weekends. Children involved in music have weekly lessons, and when they're older, orchestra, band, or chorus rehearsals on top of that. One soccer league near us holds their tournaments Thanksgiving weekend.

Friends tell me they never really needed appointment books until they had children. Now each day is an obstacle course of drop-offs and pick-ups. Parents plan vacations around camp schedules because camps are harder to book than a week at the lake.

"Our daughter Rachel was on a basketball team that always used to hold tournaments on Sunday mornings," Ron Lord told me. "We always missed church for that. And nobody on the team even raised the subject that games were on Sunday mornings."

It goes without saying that adult-organized activities mean that kids play with grown-up supervision. So instead of spontaneous games with kid referees and rules, there are planned games with adult referees and rules. "Sports are great for kids," Ron says. "But I liked it better the way it was when we were kids and there were no parents around. Kids had to work things out on their own. I mean, parents might get involved eventually, but not very much. We were forced to get along."

Most kiddie activities have two price tags, the one measured in dollars and cents and the one measured in parental involvement. Your five-year-old wants to join a swim team? In many parts of the country you'll have to join a pool or a country club to get him in one and then wake up before dawn to drive him to practice. Your daughter wants to attend Girl Scout camp? The best way to get her into the crowded one in my area is to become a leader and take the adult training course, which guarantees her admission. There is such a shortage of soccer fields here that parents camp out to snag places for their kids to practice. When that doesn't work, they must raise as much as a million dollars to buy the space.

Of course, we often enroll kids in sports or other activities because we're at work and we want them to have safe, planned fun until we get home. In many neighborhoods, if they want to see other kids after school, they'll have to participate in organized activities because that's where other kids are. But that doesn't explain the extent of our involvement. Sometimes I wonder if we don't get involved in kids' activities because more of us live away from our extended families, move often, and quite frankly, use kids' activities to forge adult contacts. We moved to our house when our oldest was a baby, and when I complained about not having made any new friends, people told me, "Just wait till your children get in school. Then you will." They were right, of course; we have. But I like making friends on my own, too.

Not only do our children absorb more of our waking hours,

but there seem to be more waking hours to fill. Kids' bedtimes are getting later and later. On an average night, about 3½ million children ages two to 11 (more than nine percent of youngsters that age) are watching television shows between 11 P.M. and midnight.[4]

Oftentimes, kids are kept up to see one or both of their working parents. Eleanore and John Keenan often don't put their sons to bed until 10 P.M. or later. John doesn't get home from the office until late evening and he wants to see his children at least a little while. "But it seems like there isn't a minute when the boys aren't with us," Eleanore sighs.

Children also stay up because they are more and more integrated into the adult world. They are so much a part of the action that it's hard to pry them away from it. And because we think we must be constantly available to our children, we feel little sense of entitlement to our own time and pursuits.

Make Rooms for Kids

With smaller families and larger houses, it's almost a given that each child will have her own room. But our homes are oriented to children in other ways, too. For instance, new house designs use up much of their ample square footage in the family room or great room, and although most builders still feel obliged to include living rooms, they're much smaller than they used to be. Some architects predict that twenty-first-century houses will be built without living rooms. Formal dining rooms are heading toward extinction, too.

True, these changes have something to do with the informality of our times, but I think it's worth noting that as we have become more child-centered, we have dropped the rooms that used to be reserved for adult pursuits, for reading, quiet conversation, and grown-up entertaining. Maybe we're still a little bit sore about being excluded from the living rooms of our childhood and are determined to right old wrongs by getting rid of ours entirely. I know I'm making a leap here, but perhaps the living room we couldn't enter is like the anger we had to repress. The great rooms of the '90s signal acceptance and equality. You can let your feelings out in them; they're big enough to take it. Banishing the old-style living room, where our parents might have sipped cocktails or displayed porcelain figurines, means one less thing for us to say "no" to, also. Modern living rooms have new functions. They serve as playrooms or jail cells, perfect for time outs.

The deck is another feature of modern homes that might not seem at first to be child-centered. But decks are safer for kids than front porches. They are private and less accessible. Kids playing on them are less likely to wander off or be snatched.

We are drawing up our bridges, filling our moats, and making our castles even more impregnable to the forces we think are threatening the family. But maybe we're missing one. For all the attention we pay to kids, kidcentricity does little to heighten togetherness. Many families I know scarcely have an evening a week to call their own, time simply to be together and do nothing else. It's become a cliché of modern American life that families no longer share the evening meal. Perhaps we're so busy we miss the irony, that in paying so much attention to kids, we're neglecting the family. We talk a lot about family friendliness. The family friendly workplace, family friendly politics. Perhaps family friendliness is like charity. It best begins at home.

Let Us Entertain Them

Kidcentricity is painfully obvious when we go to the mall. There's the baby store with its mind-boggling array of expensive gadgets; the kiddie clothing boutique, which has a hole cut in the front of the store so kids can climb in and out; the toy emporium with its mechanized stuffed animals enticing young visitors inside; the candy store with its vats of chocolates and lollipops and jujubes; and, finally, one of those ubiquitous preteen magnets, the jewelry and ear-piercing store. In between there's a Victoria's Secret, an elegant paper store, and a couple other adult havens. But we never enter those, of course. Instead, we dodge the strollers and the lolling teens and try our best to reach the relative sanity of our own automobile.

Shopping has been revamped for kids. In the middle of our

mall there is a lounge area with step seating and a sort of stage at one end. Through the years the place has become more and more kidcentric, climaxing last year with the addition of a half-dozen pieces of indoor climbing equipment made in the shape of breakfast foods. Kids could climb up the banana slices into the bowl of cereal. Or slide down the bacon onto the fried egg. The climbable breakfast foods were one of those things that probably seemed a good idea at the time, but which, when introduced, made squabbles and shoving matches much more common. A friend of mine wrote mall officials to express her frustration that this one-time sanctuary for kids, which offered nothing except space, had now become a potential liability for both management and parents. She received in reply a terse note instructing her in the need for parental supervision. The mall management missed the point, but not long afterward they got rid of the breakfast foods. Now kids can play on their own again.

Many stores have set up play areas with Lego tables and computers for little customers. Others supply pint-sized shopping carts, perhaps so kids can feel "empowered" pushing their own. In one store I visited recently, these little carts bore signs that read "Customer in Training." Some stores have movie theaters with the latest animated films and so many high-end, hands-on toys to play with that "look don't touch" no longer has meaning.

It seems to me as if the individual fears of "Will my children like me if I don't entertain them?" are being writ large in our kidcentric culture. We want to make things easy and accessible and comfortable so kids won't be bored. You can see this in family restaurants. At many places, your restless young diner will be handed a box of crayons, a toy, or even a lump of pizza dough to knead while he waits for his food. The newest trend is the theme restaurant with dining and entertainment wrapped into one. At the Rain Forest Cafe, for instance, kids can dine amidst faux rain showers and tropical plants and birds. Our local paper reviews restaurants not for their service or their cuisine, but for their family friendliness.

Sometimes kidcentricity bespeaks a concern for our children, an appreciation of their emotional fragility, if you will. A few months ago, I heard a radio report about how the Cook County, Illinois, Child Protection Division now has a children's room with soft music and nature videos, plants, and stuffed animals. The theory: Children who must endure court visits will be soothed by the kid-friendly environment.

We also seem to believe that children can't sit still without staring at some sort of tube. "We put a TV and VCR at every hair-cutting station. Your child is certain to be entertained," boasts a kids' salon called Kool Klips. I've taken our kids to one of these salons, and it's difficult to get them to look down so the stylist can trim the back of their heads they're so mesmerized by the screens in front of them.

Kidcentricity is most awesomely present in establishments that are geared to kids anyway, which explains the existence of Kids' World, a Toys"R"Us production billed as "the only superstore just for kids." Kids' World has toys, a learning center, bike shop, clothing store, pizza parlor, salon, portrait studio, carousel, shoe store, and candy factory. "Kids' World . . . It's what the World is coming to!" boasts the ad. All the more reason to explore another galaxy.

Kid Culture

If trips to the restaurant, hairdresser, and mall have become "events," imagine the burden placed on the entertainment industry. Movies, television, and music must woo the hyperstimulated, well-esteemed youth of today in ever more elaborate fashion. It's little surprise that many of the greatest strides in the entertainment world are virtual ones. Let's forget about improving the real world and just spiff up the one on screen.

In addition to rebuilding Times Square in its own image, Disney cranks out several children's movies a year, at least one of which is an animated event complete with fancy New York City premiere. The rock music industry is aimed almost exclusively at teenagers. Most summer movies are assumed to be mindless kid-oriented fare. Children's network television has been the focus of much attention lately, if only because of its poor quality. The hit kids' cable network Nickelodeon credits much of its success to the fact that it listened to what children want from the beginning. Although many parents complain about the sex and violence on television, as proven by enthusiasm for the V chip, the content matter of many shows seems more and more juvenile, and the children portrayed on them more and more wisecracking. In other words, entertainment is dumbed down, way down, to satisfy young appetites.

Those popular movie columns for parents that rate films for sex and violence are barometers of both kidcentricity and our need for expert assistance. It's true that family movie reviews help parents make informed decisions about films they have not seen and which they cannot figure out from the title and advertisement. But do we really need to be told to keep our kids away from a film about a group of convicts who take over an airplane? Before the television premiere of *Schindler's List,* director Steven Spielberg made a cameo appearance to tell parents that the film they were about to see was a violent one and he wouldn't even let his own grade-school children see it. Could we not have figured out on our own that a film about the Holocaust is not for young children? Kidcentricity is in part made possible by this urgent need for expert confirmation of what we *must* already know is right or wrong.

In the last chapter I talked about the extent to which advertisers pitch their products to children. Commercials often use kids to tell us what to buy. An advertisement encouraging businesses to relocate to the Washington, D.C., metro area used the picture of a superbaby with a laptop in his crib and this headline: "They say that children are products of their environment. Meet the average Washington area toddler." It's enough to make me want to move *out* of the Washington area.

"In one evening's viewing I counted nine different products for which a child served as a pitchman. These included sausages, real estate, toothpaste, insurance, a detergent, and a restaurant chain," wrote Neil Postman in *The Disappearance of Childhood.* "American television viewers apparently do not think it either unusual or disagreeable that children should instruct them in the glories of corporate America, perhaps because as children are admitted to more and more aspects of adult life it would seem arbitrary to exclude them from one of the most important: selling. In any case, we have here a new meaning to the prophecy that a child shall lead them."[5]

Kidcentric Vacations

Working parents don't want to vacation apart from their children, yet they want to pursue adult activities, too, so resorts and vacation spots now cater shamelessly to the affluent tourist with child. One way to do that is to create fake worlds which sanitize the real thing. If you want to visit New York City, for instance, you can either go to New York City or you can visit Las Vegas, which has a replica of the Manhattan skyline. Atlantic City has the Taj Mahal and Disney World has Europe as well as an old-fashioned Main Street. Why take kids to real places when the make-believe ones are so much easier?

For parents who want a little authenticity, a cruise presents an entertaining and self-contained way to travel. Carnival Cruise Lines hosted 100,000 kids aboard ten ships in 1996, according to *Travel Agent Magazine*. The cruise line features all-day programmed activities for children ages two to 17. Many of the programs have a distinctively adult character, such as aerobic classes and karaoke parties. But there's plenty of kids' stuff, too. Premier Cruise Line, also known as The Big Red Boat, has Bugs Bunny, Daffy Duck, and other cartoon characters on board and available for everything from autographs to tucking kiddies into bed at night (for an additional charge). Even the prestigious Holland America Cruise Line is doing a booming juvenile business. It estimates the number of kids sailing with them has tripled since 1991.[6]

Children's museums are now prevalent throughout the country. These are generally "hands-on" places, where kids can learn by doing rather than, as I suppose we must have done, by looking. The Children's Museum of Indianapolis, one of the oldest and best in the country, bills itself as a place "Where children grow up . . . and adults don't have to." Perhaps to compete with these places, historic sites give themselves a kidcentric spin, too. "There's fun for children of all ages at the Hands-on History Tent, where you'll play colonial games, crawl into a Revolutionary War tent full of soldier's gear, explore Martha Washington's travel trunk and more!" says a brochure from George Washington's home, Mount Vernon. It sounds as if the residence of our first president is on its way to becoming a popular birthday party destination.

The epitome of kidcentric vacationing is, of course, Disney World and the rest of the kid-entertainment megalopolis in Florida. This area is such a popular tourist destination that there are numerous guidebooks to help us navigate it. Ever mindful of public relations and demographic trends, Disney is trying to woo parents there for more "adult" pursuits with the Disney Institute, a Chautauqua-style adult education center where grown-ups can take classes in cooking or gardening, listen to lectures by James Earl Jones and Martin Scorsese, and hear jazz music concerts. But the Institute seems as much like a college campus as it does anything else, a place for grown-ups to play at being a television news anchor or learn to draw an animated cartoon. A place for grown-ups to stay children while pretending to be adults.

Playing the Kid Card

The most amazing aspect of kidcentricity is how subtly and effectively it has insinuated itself into every fiber of our lives. It's difficult to find an institution kidcentricity hasn't permeated. Orchestras rely on child prodigies to help boost ticket and recording sales. Libraries are no longer still and silent; they ring with the sound of little voices at a story hour.

Political discourse is filled with references to children. The first bill President Clinton signed into law was the Family and Medical Leave Act, which allows workers to take unpaid time off to care for newborns. The president has made education the cornerstone of his second term and, unable to pass a national healthcare plan for all Americans, is concentrating instead on guaranteeing health insurance coverage for the youngest citizens. One of the most active anti-tobacco groups—in fact, the only health group that was present at the original tobacco settlement talks—is the Campaign for Tobacco-Free Kids, a sign of how much anti-tobacco muscle is now aimed at cutting off the supply of young smokers.

The attention paid to children, as one writer notes, is much more than politicians kissing babies. "Government efforts on behalf of children today—initiatives that strike responsive chords with baby boomers still rearing their own children—go far beyond such gestures," says Robert Pear. He points out that children are the reason behind heightened food safety and environmental safety standards. Kid-centered policy making is a skill perfected by liberals such as Children's Defense Fund's Marian Wright Edelman, who has focused on children to draw attention to the plight of poverty, a tactic that's also been adapted by conservative organizations such as the Family Research Council, Pear says.[7]

In fact, Marian Wright Edelman organized the first "Stand for Children" rally, which drew more than a quarter-million people to Washington, D.C., in 1996. This show of support for youngsters was the catalyst for scores of other rallies across the country, a "Virtual Stand for Children" on the Internet in 1997 and what organizers hope will be "a national movement for children."

It's difficult to argue against children, which is just what politicians and others are counting on. Still, all this attention is puzzling. Does a society that is truly "standing for its children" need a rally to encourage people to do so? Announcing that you're "for" children is chic. But being "for" children seems like being "for" air. Children make possible the continuation of the human race. Do we really need to announce that we are "for" them?

Apparently, though, being *there* for children is harder than merely being *for* them. The "Stand for Children" literature tells us that every day 16 children die from gunfire, 466 babies are born to mothers who received little or no prenatal care, and almost 8,500 children are reported abused or neglected. Again, kidcentricity does not mean better lives for all kids. Politicians may be using children for good ends, but they are using them just the same. They're not using them in a vacuum, though, but in a kidcentric climate in which using them seems perfectly natural.

Fewer Kids, More Kidcentricity

Sometimes I wonder if kidcentricity is giving childrearing such a bad name that it's helping lower the birth rate. In one generation the average number of kids per family has dropped from three to about two. Although fertility has been more or less declining since the country was founded, the baby boom years were a notable blip on the scale. Many of us who are now parents were reared in larger families. In our bigger, emptier houses there are shades of what used to be and what might have been. We have traded in kids for kidcentricity. And in doing so we have changed the shape and the focus of the modern family.

Rather than blaming declining birth rates on kidcentricity, the reverse makes much more sense. It's easier to dote on kids when there are fewer of them. A few years ago, I wrote a magazine story about why working mothers stop at two children. At first glance, the reasons were predictable: because they could not afford or didn't have time for more, because two children were all they could handle given their careers and their husband's. But when pressed to go deeper, many of the women I interviewed said that they could have no more than two because they had to keep a one-to-one ratio, because each child needs an adult's undivided attention to flourish.

As I hinted in Chapter Three, thinking too much may be one of our greatest undiscovered birth control methods. Because we hold ourselves responsible for our children's happiness and believe we must lavish incredible amounts of time on each child, we can only have one or two. A kid-centered society has a lot to do with this, I think, because the time and attention we feel each child deserves is culturally dictated. Parents of the past did not feel that two kids wore them out.

What will our society be like with so many more of its inhabitants raised in one- or two-child families? Here's one possibility: "The children of boomers will display an interesting mix of birth-order traits as they grow into adulthood in the next century. Because today's families average less than two kids, the proportion of firstborns among today's children was 43 percent in 1994—a record level. These children ought to conform to the standards and values set by their parents. . . . The one piece that could make the transition rougher than in the past is today's comparative lack of middleborns. Many baby boomers are middleborns, who play the role of mediator and ease the passage from one era to the next. In a world of two-child families, middleborns have disappeared. In the future, the contrast between firstborns and lastborns could become stark indeed."[8]

Little Big People

A few months ago on the radio I heard an interview with a young boy who started a group that lobbies to stop child labor. When one embarrassed adult caller awkwardly brought up the enforced prostitution of children in Asia, the prepubescent and carefully polished young leader smoothly intervened: "You mean, 'sex trade,' " he said, confidently. "Oh yes, that *is* a problem." Were it not for the high pitch of his voice, the child would have sounded exactly like an adult. He may be saving the children, but he has lost his own childhood. Kidcentricity is a force that sucks children into the vortex of adulthood. By making kids a part of almost all we do, we have turned them into little big people.

Even when they're tiny babies, we dress them to look like little adults. "When I brought our babies home from the hospital they looked like babies. Now they come home from the hospital in baseball suits and jeans. People say, 'He looks like a little man.' But he's got the rest of his life to look like a little man. I've always been big on babies looking like babies," said Kathy Friedlander, who's a grandmother several times over.

The photographer Lauren Greenfield spent four years taking pictures and interviewing children in Los Angeles for her book *Fast Forward: Growing Up in the Shadow of Hollywood*. She includes photos of a 13-year-old dancing with a stripper at his friend's bar mitzvah party, a ten-year old preening by the pool of the hotel where she lives, and a five-year-old virtual surfer. One teenager told Greenfield, "In L.A. . . . it's not cool to be a kid."

Of course, L.A. is not Des Moines or Mobile or Tulsa. And yet kids everywhere seem a little wiser, a little more knowing. A Denver mother quoted in the Public Agenda survey, said, "My daughter is wild. She is seven going on 21."

Those of us who try to keep our children innocent feel like we're doing them a disservice. "I remember the innocence I had as a child. I've encouraged it in my children. But I've watched other children be disrespectful to mine because they don't seem as 'grown up,'" says Heather Babiarz.

It seems to me that we're getting what we've asked for, independent children who are in touch with their feelings and accustomed to telling adults what to do. I know seven-year-olds who quite earnestly ask their parents, "How do you feel about that?" mimicking the urgency with which we dissect their emotions, keeping tabs on their parents' psyches just as we always have on theirs. If there's anything that will age you quickly it's trying to figure out what someone else is feeling.

As I mentioned in the beginning of this chapter, the news is filled with adult-like children: Jessica Dubroff, the seven-year-old aviatrix, died when her plane crashed as she attempted to set a record for youngest "solo" cross-country flight. JonBenet Ramsey, the murdered six-year-old beauty queen from Boulder, Colorado, wore lipstick and mascara and pouted for the camera in come-hither costumes. "If I were writing my book now the lead would be that case in Colorado," Neil Postman, author of *The Disappearance of Childhood*, told me in an interview. "Not so much her murder but what she was made to do."

In our area recently, nine fourth-graders (four girls and five boys) were caught in a classroom playing a sex game. An investigation concluded that the sex was "consensual," although parents wondered how fourth-graders could know enough to consent. A 1995 Centers for Disease Control and Prevention survey found that one in 11 high-school students reported having sexual intercourse before age 13.[9] Incidents and statistics such as these make it less amazing that sexual harassment charges were leveled against a second-grader who kissed a girl in class.

The line between adults and children is also being blurred by computer technology, especially the Internet, which as Postman points out, "makes available the same information to everyone in the culture. So the whole content of the adult world is as available to the young as to anyone else."

Unfortunately, adult-like kids also seem to have adult-like problems. By the early 1980s, David Elkind was already pointing out signs of kids' stress in his book *The Hurried Child:* the 50-percent increase in obesity in children and adolescents over the last 20 years; the highest teen pregnancy rates for any Western society; suicide and homicide rates for teens triple what they were 20 years earlier; plummeting SAT scores; and millions of children on medications, a several-hundredfold increase over the previous five years.[10]

These conditions have intensified since he noticed them. Take children on medications, for instance. In 1996, prescriptions for the antidepressant Prozac increased 47 percent for 13- to 18-year-olds and almost 300 percent for children six to 12. Although many physicians obviously believe that Prozac is a safe drug for kids, it does not have FDA approval for use on children and many doctors question its effect on the growing brain.[11]

Young offenders are often tried as adults, and juvenile crime is exploding. The number of delinquency cases handled by juvenile court has almost quadrupled since 1960, and child abuse and neglect cases, which also fall into the juvenile court jurisdiction, have increased five times faster than juvenile crime. In fact, many judges, probation officers, and others believe that having a separate justice system for children is outdated. "The very notion that has been its cornerstone, that children are different from adults and therefore need to be treated differently, is in question," Bart Lubow of the Annie E. Casey Foundation said.[12]

Many parenting books portray children as victims of "stress" and "burnout" and offer ways to "inoculate" kids against stress. In fact, you might say that kids' stress has itself become an industry. The number of psychiatrists nationwide specializing in kids (which is only a subset of the many professionals counseling children) has more than doubled in the last decade, from 3,000 in the mid-1980s to 7,000 today. Even so, there are countless children who need help and don't get it. In fact, one report estimates that our country will need 32,000 child and adolescent psychiatrists by the year 2010.[13]

Elementary school principal Sharon Davis-Holmes worries about some of the children in her care. They are burdened with so many extracurricular activities that they often don't do their homework. "We had a game last night," they'll say. Their parents are tense, too, Davis-Holmes says. "They're very driven themselves and so they drive their children." One of the things that worries her most about her students is when "they won't answer questions because they don't want to get a C. 'My mom doesn't want me to make mistakes,' they will say. These kids aren't risk takers," Davis-Holmes says. They want to be perfect. "This is a great school. I have great parental support. But sometimes the parents don't let kids be kids."

Boundary Problems

There are many explanations for why children seem so adult-like today. To a certain extent, I think we want our kids to grow up fast; we think it's good for them, it gives them an edge. The world is competitive, and we don't want our kids left behind. Many of them have been in organized group daycare since they were infants and have learned to roll with the punches in a way that makes them seem less childlike. It's also easy to blame our children's early adulthood on the high divorce rate and the legions of single parents struggling to raise kids on their own. Undoubtedly, these psychological and sociological causes are responsible for some of the acceleration. And then there's the cuteness factor. Babies look precious wearing adult-style clothes. And kids sound adorable when they're urging us to buy cameras or cereal.

There's little we can do about competition and the high divorce rate. But since this is a consciousness-raising book, let's at least look at our own lives. One reason we may be treating kids like adults is that experts tell us to. For example, parents expecting a second child are told never to explain the new arrival to their first child by saying they love him so much that they decided to have another baby. The reason: Imagine how your husband or wife would respond if you said, "Honey, I love you so much I've decided to get another spouse." This equates siblings with spouses and presupposes that children and adults think the same. A similar assumption explains our habit of giving toddlers frequent choices (albeit often phony ones), and of ending almost every command with "okay."

I know I've talked about the "okay-ing" of American parents before and don't want to beat this subject to death, but it seems relevant to mention it again here.

"I used to end my sentences with 'okay,' " said Maggie Mulqueen. "And my husband said, 'You have to stop saying that because you're not asking for their approval. They don't have a choice.' And he was right. What I really meant by the 'okay' was, 'Have I been heard?' " Maggie's explanation is the clearest I've heard for why we say "okay." But for those of us who can't kick the habit, adding "okay" to the end of our requests not only creates discipline problems, but also makes us defer to our children in matters on which they have absolutely no judgment or taste. We've gotten so used to soliciting our children's opinions that we ask them whether they should go to summer camp or stay home or whether we should put chestnuts or sausage in the stuffing. The day after heavyweight boxing champ Mike Tyson bit the ear of his opponent during a championship fight, the *Dallas Morning News* asked children what they thought his punishment should be. Kids are the true biting experts, the article explained, a little tongue in cheek.

In our house, the more often we treat our children as adults, the less often we succeed as parents. Sometimes when our two-year-old is cranky and I ask her, "Do you want to take a nap now?" I think to myself, "I must be crazy." Even if she was well-rested and in a good mood she shouldn't be the one to make this decision. When we give kids too many choices or even a few ill-timed ones, they do not handle them well, and we all suffer as a result. A child's mind is not an adult's mind. And when we pretend that it is and aspire to the culture of modern childrearing (my child will thrive if I respect his needs), we subvert our own instincts (I am the parent; I ought to know what's best).

If a term usually applied to people can be equally applied to a society then we might say that a kidcentric world has "boundary problems." We don't know how to keep ourselves out of our children's lives, and in the process of insinuating ourselves into them we re-create children in our own, adult, image. Don't get me wrong. It's not as if we're all stage mothers. We are infinitely more subtle than that. And we have lots of reinforcement from a culture that thinks no price too high if it makes kids happy.

If You Can't Beat Them . . .

What I've described so far must sound like a sort of family systems domino effect. We focus overly much on kids, which in turn makes kids overly more like adults. The final domino, then, is this one: The more children act like adults, the more adults act like kids. Only the whole thing is not so much a bunch of tumbling dominoes as it is one big interconnected loop. All three are happening at once; they emanate from the same ideas about childrearing. For instance, you could argue that our tendency to let young children determine their own punishments makes them seem more like adults, while our habit of turning to experts makes us seem more like children.

But there are other, funnier, ways we act like kids. A mother in Massachusetts took a sandbox dispute to court. Apparently, her three-year-old had been assaulted several times by a toddler bully, and she wanted to do something about it. Or, I suppose I should say she wanted someone *else* to do something about it. So a Boston judge issued a restraining order to keep the three-year-olds apart. The case attracted much media attention because it seemed to point out the flaws of both modern child-rearing and the justice system. Parents unable to help their children solve petty problems seek help from a legal system that actually tackles such an absurd case. The incident is also an example of adults who act like children forcing children to act like adults.

And then there's our fondness for exercise and play. As we've gotten "into" sports, our children have become increasingly flabbier. In our suburban neighborhood, you're far more likely to see an adult running or pedaling a bicycle along the street than you are a child. Adults have also usurped kids' holidays. Eighty percent of Halloween costume rentals and 65 percent of sales are for adults now.[14]

Advertisements celebrate the kid-like abandonment with which we would like to live out our lives. "Why Grow Up?" tempts an advertisement for a Delta Dream Vacation. A Starbucks ad queries, "Is the coffee break the adult version of recess?" One of my favorite television commercials features "Oh, Lord, won't you buy me a Mercedes-Benz?" in which a song written to mock the consumer culture of our parents is now used to peddle the car it once satirized. Along the way, it's also making fun of our selling out. We're a self-conscious bunch. We think the country is always watching (which because of our sheer size and buying power, it often is) and so we have to justify our longing for a luxury car. It's hard to admit we might want it because we're grown-ups now.

As I mentioned earlier, and many others have noted, we baby boomers have enshrined our wonder years. Thanks to the miracle of television, our childhoods are still with us in the form of *I Love Lucy, The Andy Griffith Show,* and *Bewitched.* When we tire of those we can watch movie remakes of *The Brady Bunch* or *The Addams Family,* read *Growing Up with Dick and Jane,* or access the Chatty Cathy Web site. It's easy to stay childlike with these props. We experienced one of the most comfortable childhoods in history, we adored college so much that there are a growing number of us who want to be buried on our former campuses, so why *should* we want to give it up entirely?

The answer, of course, is that it's hard to be a suitable parent if we don't grow up. Perhaps the most telling evidence of our reluctance are the over 3 million children who live in the care of their grandparents—a 40 percent increase in the last ten years. In fact, grandparents as parents have their own support group, newsletter, and books. If we don't feel like raising our children, why not let our parents do it?

We want it both ways, I think. We want our children to be old before their time and we want to stay young past our time. We want our "childrearing style" to be based more on friendship than authority. We want to become expert parents—and quickly—by reading a book or taking a class rather than learning the old-fashioned way, on the job. This split between what we want and what we are willing to pay for is creating an increasingly more dichotomous world for our children.

I am certainly not the first writer to note the great extent to which adults are acting like kids and kids acting like adults. And I guess the point is not so much who's become who as the fact that the distinctions are gone and, some say, childhood along with them. When I talked with Neil Postman, author of *The Disappearance of Childhood,* I asked him if he thought childhood has disappeared completely.

"I don't think it will completely disappear for generations. But it is moving very rapidly in the direction of invisibility. I think it's gotten worse," he said. Postman is heartened, however, by what he sees as a greater awareness of the commercialism of childhood. "There are a lot of people who are asking questions, 'What are some of the effects of television and violence and commercials and computer games?' I must say I've been a little encouraged in the past three or four years at the attention that people generally, including parents, have been giving to these issues. When I was talking about all of this 25 years ago, you could draw a bigger audience for a lecture on how to improve your backhand in tennis." In the introduction to the revised edition of his book, Postman quotes letters children have written him. At least children seem to want childhood, even if their parents don't, he concludes.

I know some parents who find that having three or four kids restores childhood to their families. There are more of "them" than "us." In a larger family there simply isn't time to be overly solicitous of each child. You're forced to make simple declarative statements (also known as orders). There's less time to ponder every move and you must act on instinct, at least occasionally. But of course, larger families aren't for everyone and there are plenty of other ways to restore adult time and family balance.

I'm not sure I can define what motivates them, or even if *they* can, but some parents I know persist in believing that adults are different from kids. Our friends Barbara and Bryan de Boinville, who I mentioned in Chapter Six, have adults-only cocktail parties and no childrearing manuals in their home. Perhaps they are simply more idealistic than most people I know, or less likely to let go of the way they were raised. Whatever the reason, it's always refreshing to hear their unique, nonkidcentric views.

What Are Children For?

A couple of years ago, *The Washington Post* ran a feature article entitled "What Are Children For?" It was a two-part series. The first part explained the changing roles of children through the centuries, how kids were once prized for their economic value and now they are not, thus raising the question, "What are they for?" The newspaper invited readers to write and explain what they thought children were for. The second part of the series contained the reader responses. Their answers were heartfelt and illuminating. Most mentioned some way in which children were teaching them the meaning of life, or acting as a bridge to the future. But the most amazing part is that the question needed to be asked at all.

The other night I settled down and read to our eight-year-old daughter. This is not something I do very often since she reads to herself now. But it was a good chance to learn about Jack

Pumpkinhead, the Scarecrow, Nick Chopper the Tin Woodman, and other characters in *The Land of Oz,* by L. Frank Baum. In the last six months Suzanne has lived more in Oz than in Virginia, I think. She has read and reread the eight or so Oz books that we own and we have searched libraries and issued an all-points bulletin to family members to secure the few we haven't yet found.

As I read to Suzanne, I asked questions. "Why is he called H. M. Woggle Bug?" She couldn't believe I didn't know. "Mommy," she giggled. "The H. M. is for 'highly magnified.' " She also cracked me up pronouncing "conquered" as "conquired." What was most enjoyable was the true childishness of it all. The Land of Oz, as interpreted by Suzanne, is a funny, earnest place, where battles are waged, evil is done and good prevails, although not without a fight. It is not a simplistic world; in fact, it is quite complex. The themes are mature, in the best sense of that word. It is an engagingly naive world. A child's world.

As Suzanne and I read together about Oz, I felt a sudden pride in her, in the delicious fact that she still is a child. And at that moment, at least, I knew exactly what children are for. I hope I can express it now without sounding hopelessly kidcentric. We need children for their fresh and endearing logic, their ability to suspend disbelief, then suspend it over and over again. We need their ability to forgive. We need them because they say what they think without censoring themselves. We need them because we can sing old Beatles songs at the top of our lungs with them.

Now having said these things, I must qualify them. I don't want to sound like a pair of touchy-feely parenting conference leaders I once had, who portrayed children as all sunshine and rainbows. We all know it isn't that way. It is easy to love babies, with their cuddles and coos, and, when they're not throwing a tantrum, it is easy to appreciate toddlers, too, with their jaunty independence and first lisping words. Preschoolers delight us with their full-hearted love of life.

But about eight or nine, kids get gangly. They start telling bad jokes. Adolescence looms large. Not only that, but at eight or nine many kids are no longer children but small adults, fully integrated into the culture. They are smart, sassy, and computer-literate. They are over-enrolled and under-chored. They have lost whatever vestiges of childishness they might once have had. Perhaps the question, then, is not, "What are children for?" but rather, "Why do children need to be children?"

Now I'll admit that this is a rather adultcentric question, so before I answer it, I should probably tackle another one: Why do adults need to be adults? Given the way we are encouraged to dress and behave, what good does it do us to assume the responsibilities of adulthood—other than the fact that sooner or later most of us have to? What do we, and our children, gain from our being adults? You might think this a simple, self-evident query. But I think it's worth some thought.

One of the times I've felt most "adult-like" recently occurred when we were at the end of our rope with our five-year-old daughter Claire. She is a passionate little person. She has "difficulty with transitions," as they say. But even knowing this we were unprepared for her tumultuous entry into kindergarten. Nothing pleased her, she frequently screamed at us and her sisters. No article of clothing fit her comfortably. I took the class for parents of spirited children that I've mentioned earlier, and yes, there were some techniques that made life easier. I would respond to her requests twice and then no more, which cut down on badgering. We let her play with birdseed or Play-Doh, tactile occupations which soothed her temporarily.

But none of these strategies cracked the spiral of misbehavior and shame that was threatening our family's peace and Claire's sense of herself. She was starting to say, "I'm bad, Mommy," which was not something we said to her but something she deduced from her frequent transgressions and punishments. I thought and thought about how to reach her. And then it came to me. It was an image really, a way to explain something to her about herself.

"Claire," I said one day in the car. I can remember exactly

where we were when I said it, a four-way stop near a wooded path. "Do you know what you have?"

"No, Mommy," she replied, looking at me warily.

"You have a big heart. That's why you're a big hugger, and that's why you're a big screamer sometimes, too. Everything you do you do in a big way, and that's because you have a big heart."

She looked at me with moist eyes and utter relief. I knew I had reached her. I won't say she never screamed again. She will always be hot-blooded. But I often allude to her "big heart." It has become a sort of code phrase.

I think parents need to be adults because it is as adults that we can best know what our children need—not because of anything we've heard in a class or read in a book, but because of something we have learned from living and from getting to know our children deeply and well. Adulthood is when we gain wisdom, when we can recognize our place in the scheme of things. This is not a guarantee, of course. We can let opportunities for self-knowledge pass us by. But if we're not stuffed full of other people's theories, our own will come to us. We will find meaning that is piercing in its fullness.

Though people often talk about children making them feel young again—and they certainly do that at times—it seems to me that children really ought to make us feel old. They ought to make us feel wise. The more often that we are fully, unabashedly adults, the better we'll be as parents, I think. Not because we've invented a magic formula, but because we've realized there isn't one.

To go back to my original question, then, why do we need children to be children? I often think it's because this earth is meant to have variety. There is supposed to be a difference between children and adults just as there's supposed to be a difference between male and female. These differences, though not ironclad, give life a zest and a richness that homogeneity and androgyny do not. We need children because they are constantly growing, and we no longer are. We need them because they remind us that a year is still a considerable chunk of time.

But children do all these things best—in fact, I would say that they do these things only—when they remain children. It may help us live our lives more efficiently to conceive of our children as miniature adults, but it won't help us live more deeply.

If you think there is some purpose to life, that all is not chaos, that we're meant to do something with our lives, then think of what grown-ups and children can mean to each other. We with our wisdom can guide children, can help them become the best people they can be. Children with their freshness can remind us what the world was like when we were just coming alive to it. And those, I think, are gifts worth fighting for.

9

I Am a Parenting Class Dropout
In Search of Instinct

"The pleasures of instinct are more real than I
would ever have known."
—*Mary Gordon*

"If only they came with instructions," reads the caption on the picture poster of the little child. The poster is the first thing I see when I walk in the door of the Parent Encouragement Project in Kensington, Maryland. This is a place I've heard about for years. Friends have told me of classes they've taken here, of revelations they've experienced within these four walls. So I've arranged to attend a sample class tonight to see if what happened for my friends can happen for me, to see if there are "instructions" and if this is the place to find them.

We talk about "instructions" as if they were a joke, but they are actually a sort of Holy Grail for modern parents. Though we laugh about needing an "owner's manual," our constant quest for help and information is proof we think we need one. The parents here seem especially desperate for instructions. Many of them have two or three young children who know where their buttons are and have learned to push them—kids who are perfect products of modern childrearing methods. So they're seeking advice from . . . a modern childrearing class. Hmm. Well, I'll give it a try.

The Parent Encouragement Project (fondly known as PEP) is probably one of the best programs around, I reassure myself. It's based on the work of Rudolph Dreikurs, the Austrian-born psychiatrist who translated Adlerian psychology into childrearing theory. Dreikurs's books were considered progressive a generation ago and still attract thinking parents who want some discipline in their home. We get homework right away, to read the first chapters of Dreikurs's book, *Children: The Challenge.*

We talk about discipline and why it has such bad press. No one wants to be a police officer. We want to be friends with our kids. We do some role playing and take turns acting as mother or child. The premise: a mother has cleaned the carpet and doesn't want her child walking on it till it dries. In one scene she scolds, in another she shames, in still another she bribes. In the final scene she presents her case ahead of time in a family council, in which mom, dad, and kids all come up with ways to stay off the wet carpet. This is the "correct" scenario. Our leader stresses how important it is to cultivate the right tone of voice—friendly and matter-of-fact. Raising one's voice is very un-PEP.

Better than the information are the stories, tales of modern family life that make me feel less alone in my struggles. Stories like Carol's, who described a battle with her three-year-old son, Jason. Carol was late to class tonight because she'd had trouble with Jason. He wouldn't get out of the car. She had to lift him out still strapped in his car seat. He wouldn't eat his dinner, either. She practiced techniques she'd already learned—reflective listening, walking away when she got too angry. She "refused to let him engage her in a power struggle," she said, although it sounded as if she'd had nothing but a power struggle for the last few weeks.

A father of two, Glenn, tells how he and his wife, Sheila, did not take their children out to a pizza restaurant because they had misbehaved. "What did you do? Did you give the kids dinner at home?" asked another parent. "No, we got them takeout

chicken from Roy Rogers,'' Glenn admits sheepishly. The instructor tries to make him feel noble; after all, he didn't take
them out for *pizza*. But trading chicken for pizza hardly seems a
punishment to me. No one else in the class mentions this, and
no one uses the word punishment. It is very un-PEP, too.

When I get home, I try to practice what I've learned, but the
reflective listening seems false, the explanations tiring, and I
cannot let our kindergartner miss school just because she refuses to put her socks on. I am tired of sitting in a circle on a
metal chair and saying, ''My name is Anne. I have three children: Suzanne, Claire, and Celia. My husband's name is Tom.''
So I never go back to the Parent Encouragement Project. I will
have to encourage myself, I suppose. Whenever I think about
enrolling in another class, I remember what our oldest daughter said: ''You're taking a parenting class, Mommy? But you
already are a parent!''

By now you have probably heard more than you want to
know about my adventures in parenting, how in the beginning I
fell for the expert theories, how I've written articles which furthered those theories and further confused me. You know I've
taken plenty of parenting classes, too, admittedly to find out
more about what other parents were learning and thinking, but
also because some of the topics tempted me. I eagerly enrolled
in a ''Spirited Child'' class and I took a seven-week STEP class
and a three-part seminar on how to improve your child's schoolwork. Everywhere I went I found parents anxious to improve
their childrearing skills and teachers dedicated to making the
world a better place by sharing their knowledge with others.
Sometimes I asked questions. Most of the time I just sat quietly
and took notes and tried to understand what was going on
around me. Though each class was different, they had two
things in common: They made bringing up children sound
easier than it really is, and they took me further away from the
parent I want to be.

So I became a parenting class dropout. I wanted some time
to ponder what I'd learned and what I hadn't. I wanted to go
''off class'' just as I'd gone ''off book.'' Off-book parenting is a

bit like off-road cycling. It requires a different sort of propulsion, less air in the tires, more self-sufficiency. I feel as if I'm on a long road trip away from familiar scenes, down a rutted, abandoned highway. I want to clear my head of the shoulds and oughts I've been imbibing for years. I'm in search of a more instinctive way to raise our children. The further down the road I go the fewer signs there are to mark my way, and yet the more confident I am that I'm heading in the right direction. I have a feeling that when I come to the end of this road, I'll see a bay with shining water and mountains in the distance—the heady view from instinct's perch. I'm not there yet, but I can taste the promise of it, just as you know when you're near an ocean by the salty tang of the air you breathe.

A Clean, Quiet Place

To help me on the last leg of this metaphorical journey I have the literal calm of a week without children. My good-natured husband has trundled them off to visit their grandparents, and I have time to ponder parental instinct alone. The first thing I do, of course, is cry. As the packed station wagon inches out of the driveway, and the cheery, if slightly teary, faces look out at me and all the hands wave good-bye, I wave back at them with both my hands until they round a curve, then I run in the house and out again to wave from the backyard as they drive down the street behind us.

And then, they are gone. It is just me and the cat. I trip over toys, I weep into breakfast bowls as I clear the table. How can I be parted from my family for a week? Nothing is more important than they are! I believe this when they are here, too, but when they are gone I feel it so much it almost takes my breath away. This is why we think too much. Because we love so much. But if we love enough, that much, then can't we figure out a way to think less?

I throw myself into writing. It is hot outside and the air conditioner is broken. But I discover with a thrill that I can open windows from the bottom—something I don't do when the kids are here, for safety's sake, of course. This week I can dispense with that precaution. I have a breeze and can see much better, too. The outside world swings into view.

I know I can't force instinct. It will only surface if I have the quiet and time to let it. I cannot make it happen, just as I cannot force a child to eat or drink or go to sleep on command. But this week I try to create an environment in which instinct will flourish. I talk to my children on the phone, but the ten-minute chat is a far cry from their presence. With them gone, I have few appointments to keep. No one needs to be driven to a birthday party or to a friend's house to play. The only time I leave is to take a walk in the summer evening.

The quiet overtakes me, and I begin to revel in the silence. There are no sounds in the house but those of my own creation. Without this pause I don't think I'd notice how much we fill up our days with other people's words and thoughts. For what is all this information if not so many voices, urging us in many directions. We have junk e-mail, ubiquitous cell phones, beepers, advertisements everywhere, round-the-clock news. We need never be alone with our own impressions. The voices of parenting class instructors are just part of it. There is the voice of the announcer on the radio that I absentmindedly flick on while driving the children to their sitter's house. The voice tells me about the latest study on gestational diabetes or oppositional behavior disorder. For parents who think too much, this information can take our day and turn it upside down.

"It's really a sad thing that everything can be fine and all it takes is one critical word to make me think there must be something wrong," Barbara Bailey, a television news anchor in Lexington, Kentucky, told me. "When I read one of those articles, even a columnist that appears in the paper every day, when I read someone who's saying the opposite of what my instincts tell me to do, it does make me feel like, 'Gee, I must be doing something wrong. I must be a bad mom.' It does shake me to the core."

I feel the same disquiet in my own life. It often seems I am at the mercy of the next bit of information that comes my way. It's no wonder that the voluntary simplicity movement gains more converts weekly, why a blizzard we had a few years ago was met with such glee. We all want to stop the world and get off.

"Parents are information management systems for children," Neil Postman said to me when we talked. We reveal information kids ought to know when we feel they need to know it. And we conceal information a child would misunderstand or couldn't handle. But what happens when the information management systems (parents) are themselves deluged with information? Can we manage the information, can we manage the children, when we can't even manage ourselves?

Though I certainly miss my children and get sad every time I walk past their rooms, I realize how healthy it is to be apart from them for a week. In the past, when extended family lived and worked and raised children together, there was often a mother or father or aunt or sister or other relative to diffuse the responsibility a little. Now many of us live hundreds of miles from our families, and there is no easy respite or occasional distance from the cares of raising young children. To make it worse, today's expectations of perfect parenthood are that we be constantly available to our children, that we be more fully "with" them than parents of the past. The result is that we have little time to put them into perspective, to muse on them, to gain the vision we can only gain by having a bit of space between us.

I begin to think of quiet as a state of being. And it is not just the quiet of an empty house, but the stillness of an open mind. I am trying my best to clean house, not literally, of course— there's never time for that—but metaphorically. I want to empty myself of the old confusion so a new surety can take its place.

I've touched on the frantic pace of modern family life in other chapters, so I won't belabor it here, except to say that although we're constantly deploring how busy we are most of us don't take steps to end it. We don't cut back our hours at work (perhaps we can't) and we worry that if our child isn't enrolled in activities she will miss out on friendship. We wear busyness like a badge of honor. The busier we are, the more successful, well-intentioned, well-informed.

Busyness blocks instinct. "Sometimes I'll get to the end of the day and think I've never had enough time just to have a clear thought," said Barbara Bailey. She is in search of instinct, too, but realizes that juggling career, family, and house is not conducive to it.

Have we simply grown too busy for instinct? Is it yet another quaint remnant of a bygone era? One thing I've thought about lately is the extent to which modern time-saving appliances have taken away the rote tasks during which our minds could wander and we could muse on any number of things—a favorite book, a laundry list, a troubled friend, an upcoming party, or of course, our children. Parents of the past might have done a lot more "mindless" tasks than we do—ironing or sewing, planting or plowing, chopping wood or washing dishes. But while their hands were busy they were ruminating. Their minds were not idle, they had time to let impressions sink in. Now we have dishwashers, permanent-press clothes, forced air heat, take-out foods. The time we save we work hard to pay for and the leisure left over is filled with noise from a television, radio, or other electronic device. We have no quiet time to ponder our children's natures slowly and meditatively—not to think about them as much as to digest them. There is not only an information overload, but a quiet-time shortfall. I hope the silence of these days will fill me with peace. I am *almost* tempted to do some ironing to test my theory. But not quite.

We cannot always have literal quiet, but we can cultivate a sort of inner stillness to reach the clean, quiet spot where instinct lies. How to do that? Some parents I know have deliberately cultivated simplicity. They've learned to live with less, on one income, for example. They scale back on goods and activities. That's a start. But the simplicity I'm after means getting by with less information, too. It means the willful cultivation of ignorance: turning off the radio when I'm in the car. "Ignorance was bliss," said one mother who raised her children a generation ago.

What fills my emptiness may be a type of ignorance, but it feels much richer than what it replaces. Without the clutter of other people's thoughts, my own theories have room to wiggle their toes. I begin to ponder what I really want for our kids. My sleep program. My pacifier-removal program. No one else's but mine. No more excuses if they don't work out. The failures will be my own, too. But that's okay. It's gotten far too easy to blame our mistakes on other people's advice.

As I grow accustomed to the silence and the emptiness, I realize that I've had a clue to their importance all along. The days I feel most natural and comfortable as a parent are inevitably the days I've arisen early and had maybe an hour alone to write, read, sip tea, and turn a few thoughts over in my mind. Part of the difference is that I get some work accomplished before the kids have awakened, and so I'm in a better mood. But these are also days when I've given my instinct a chance to surface. Those few morning moments allow me to collect myself, to become myself, if you will, before being cast to the lions of daily routine.

Instinct as Harmony

What is instinct? How do we raise our kids "by heart" when it's become so very difficult to know what is our heart's desire? Will I know instinct when I feel it?

There's a family of baby birds in our backyard. They are twittering away madly now, and their "tweet-tweets" crescendo whenever mom or dad flies in with a worm or grub or some other treat. Here is instinct at its most basic: Parents caring for their young with nary a thought. I wish I could be those birds for a moment to see what pure instinct feels like. But my rational mind, the part that cuts me off from instinct in the first place, stands in the way. Is this what we strive for, to shut off that part of us that constantly seeks to intervene, to rationalize, to fit the ragtag ends of our own experience into the mold of someone else's thoughts? I know I think too much. But I'm not willing to stop thinking entirely.

I look up the word "instinct" in the dictionary. It's defined as a "natural or inherent aptitude"; a "largely inheritable and unalterable tendency by an organism to make a complex and specific response to environmental stimuli without involving reason and for the purpose of removing somatic tension''; a "behavior that is mediated by reactions below the conscious level.''

Some of these definitions seem more fitting for birds than for people, especially the second one. If human instinct is "largely inheritable and unalterable" then I think the parenting gurus would go out of business. And if we think of instinct as a "complex and specific response to environmental stimuli . . . for the purpose of removing somatic tension" then it's only physical; there's no spirit in it. This may be true some of the time, but it ignores something we have that birds don't have—free will. How can we live with a definition of instinct that gives us no second chances?

When I asked Tiff Wimberly about instinct, she focused on the third definition, "behavior that is mediated by reactions below the conscious level.'' "If it's below the conscious level then how do I know if what I'm doing is instinct?'' she pondered. "Maybe our instinct is becoming extinct.''

You can see the problem of pitching instinct to parents who think too much. We'd like to remove what Shakespeare described as the "pale cast of thought,'' which threatens our "native hue of resolution.'' But we've got to get our minds in there somewhere. Perhaps we might be better off sticking with the first definition of instinct, "natural or inherent aptitude.'' It doesn't rule out our heads, but still makes clear that feeling comfortable with our actions is part of the package. It's a definition of instinct that implies there must be a harmony of mind and heart.

I looked up a passage from Anne Morrow Lindbergh's book *Gift from the Sea,* in which she talks about living "in grace.'' "By grace I mean an inner harmony, essentially spiritual, which can be translated into outward harmony. I am seeking perhaps what Socrates asked for in the prayer from the *Phaedrus* when he said, 'May the outward and inward man be at one.' '' When one is in a state of grace, Lindbergh says, "One seems to carry all one's tasks before one lightly, as if borne along on a great tide.''

Instinct in Stages

If instinct is "natural or inherent aptitude," though, many of us might say we have no aptitude for mothering or fathering. It is true that some of us take to the job more readily than others. I saw this only a few hours after our oldest was born. Some new moms in the maternity ward were holding their babies as if they'd held them all their lives, casually flipping them back and forth with accomplished ease. I was holding Suzanne as if she might break. Each time I had to move her from one arm to another, I took a little breath in anticipation.

How easy it is to be fooled by this early sense of caution, to think that unless the juices of motherhood or fatherhood flow swiftly and immediately that we need help. How easy it is to think, when we're exhausted and overwhelmed, that this new life is too precious to trust to our own inexperienced hands.

For it is in pregnancy and the early months that we begin to think of ourselves as parents. And it is in pregnancy and the early months that we are drawn to the books and classes like moths to the flame. I can't imagine a new parent not at least peeping into some of the many books on childrearing. I certainly did. And we can handle a few suggestions. But if we lack confidence and time in the beginning and get wrapped up early in expert recommendations, there will be that many more layers of other people's advice on top of our own instinct. And it will be that much harder to find our way when we look for it later.

Of course, raising children requires different aptitudes at different ages, so it makes sense that we feel more at ease in some stages than others. Some of us love the baby days, the smell of a newborn's head is a tonic to us, and we would nurse our kid till kindergarten if he'd let us. Others come alive to a child once she can talk and we glimpse the workings of a new mind. I've spoken with parents who are most confident in the "family fun" years, when kids are old enough to go places and do things but not so old that they no longer want to be seen with the old folks.

But some parents never take to parenthood at all. They may

go back to work six weeks after the baby is born and never get to know their child inside out. Many of us have no choice but to go quickly back to the office. But this early return may wreak havoc with our instinct. Whereas late-blooming parents of the past would have had a chance to grow into their roles or at least come to terms with the fact that they never would, today it's easy for seedlings of instinct to be so buried by information that we forget they're even there.

In Sickness More Than Health

When I ask other parents when they feel most instinctive, they often mention a time they took their child to the doctor or stood up to a teacher even though their more rational side said they shouldn't. Something didn't "feel right," so they follow their hunches only to find out that yes, indeed, there is a case of blood poisoning, or that their son does need tutoring, that something isn't quite right after all. This happened to us just the other day. Our youngest daughter fell off a low couch onto a soft carpet. We didn't see the accident happen, but it didn't seem to have been a dangerous fall. When the crying went on longer than usual, and when she began to hold her arm in an odd way, we thought she might need an examination. It was complicated, though. We were away from home and there was the usual insurance hassle. So we hesitated some more. But we finally trusted our instincts and took her to the emergency room. She had a broken collarbone.

I know some parents who've fought for months to get their child's illness or a school problem taken seriously. We love to read stories like this in magazines. Parents as David up against the Goliath of the medical or educational establishment. Instinct appears like a prince on a white horse. It is our salvation. That little voice inside leads us to the truth.

There is a clarity of intention that we feel when our children are troubled that allows instinct to emerge. Suddenly we are not conflicted anymore. We are not broken up into tiny pieces— one bit for the job, another for home, and other bits for children and family. It may not be a matter of life and death, but nothing else matters until our little one is back to normal. We can put aside our work if we have to, we can stop worrying about our dual roles as parent and breadwinner. There is a unity of purpose in our actions.

But must we have a crisis in order to have instinct? Surely it's possible to summon up this feeling without a frightening cue? It's confidence that makes the difference, to feel strongly enough about our hunch that we'll go to bat for it. It's similar to the way we behave when our child runs out into the street. Our reaction is swift and certain then, too: "No. You can't do that. Get back here right now." We feel sure of ourselves because we don't question whether we're right or wrong. Instinct, then, need not always be coaxed to the fore. Sometimes it leaps out at us like a caged lion suddenly freed.

Just as we cannot live our lives in monk-like silence, neither can we live comfortably in the whirl of constant catastrophe. But we can notice the times when instinct emerges. It appears not only when we're quiet but also when an outside threat makes the unimportant things drop away. So it is not only simplicity we must seek but also unity. We must be willing to let some things slide, to focus on what's most important. Tuning out the "gotta haves" from the outside can help us notice the "must haves" from the inside. Each time I trust my gut, I recognize the feeling I get when I do. It's the way you feel when you swing into a ball with a tennis racket or a bat and you know, even before you connect, that you've swung true and strong. We must be willing to let instinct lead us. And that means we stop thinking, for a change.

Family Stories

Around our house there is one surefire way to snag our daughters' attention, and that's to tell them a story, especially a family story. They love to hear about the pranks their daddy played when he was young or about the time on a boring Sunday drive several decades ago, when my brother Phillip and I told our then three-year-old sister, Ellen, that we were going to a wonderful motel with a pool called Lakewood Lodge. We kept up this ruse for hours, regaling her with details about a magical place that existed only in our teasing imaginations. When we pulled up in front of our regular old house late that afternoon, it was the maddest I'd ever seen her, and almost the maddest I'd ever seen my parents.

You cannot talk about instinct without talking about family stories, the lore and legends that become a part of us as we grow. My grandmother on my mother's side was a prodigious storyteller. She loved nothing as well as talking, and we whiled away many afternoons sitting in the rocking chairs on her front porch while she told me the tale of a little girl who put her eye out with a scissors (gruesome, yes, but effective as a cautionary tale) or the funny things my mother and aunts and uncle did when they were kids.

The more we feel we must follow some prescribed path, the less we have the time or inclination to tell family stories. They're crowded out by the activities and the book-sanctioned dialogue. And yet, family stories can lead us back to instinct. They can rekindle in us some of the deepest truths about ourselves as people and as parents. Our children are hungry for them, and we, too, can gain sustenance from their words.

Family stories take on much more meaning, however, when they're backed up with family contact. And that's where modern parents grow skittish. Over and over again I hear parents who tremble in fear lest anything they do resemble their own parents. I can't count the number of times parents have said, "I opened my mouth, and I sounded just like my mother," as if that were the worst thing that could befall them.

The more I ponder instinct, the more our attitude toward our own upbringing seems to play in it. We distrust instinct because our deepest thoughts about parenthood are the ones we pick up in childhood. In the worst cases we see our families as monsters with tentacles that seek to capture and absorb us. In the best cases, being a parent ourselves gives us a better idea of what our own parents went through. When Anne Wolf says or does something with her own two children that reminds her of her mother, "I wind up realizing there's a reason why she did it that way. And that gives me a better appreciation of my parents, that they did a really good job.''

Of course, some families are tyrannical, and you must escape them to keep your sanity. But these days it seems as if all families are dysfunctional; they're guilty unless proven innocent. And if you're close to your family, you're suspect, too, perhaps a victim of "emotional incest."

In her book *The Shelter of Each Other*, Mary Pipher, a psychologist in private practice, criticizes her own profession. She cites ten mistakes therapists make, and the first, she says, is giving people the impression that "family is the cause of all problems. . . . It's a common American belief that to be free of one's family is to be mentally healthy. Many tribes from all over the world believe that to be without family is to be without identity, to be dead. They are not far from wrong. An absolutely free self is an empty self."[1]

Our studied desire to "get beyond" our families fuels the modern advice industry, which is built on the foundation that there is a Better Way to raise our children than we were raised. Purer. More scientific. Purged of "negative patterns." Through my years of writing magazine articles, I've had numerous experts tell me, with thinly veiled disdain, that some idea or another is the kind of thing you'd hear from a grandmother, as if that made it the most ignorant approach of all. Parents I've interviewed say they don't ask their own parents for advice because they'll receive "old wives' tales" in reply. I've heard of grandparents chastised for putting babies to sleep on their tummies, grandparents afraid to offer even passing comments to their children. It's no surprise that there are now classes telling grandparents how to behave. Our local hospital offers a class on "grandparents in the '90s": "Hear what today's experts say about childbirth, breast-feeding, and parenting. Learn how you can help the new family while you settle in to your new role."

But for every grandmother who recommends outdated remedies like paregoric for babies' gas pains, there are grandmothers like the ones I've been talking with recently, who say things like this: "There are two secrets to raising children. One is common sense and the other is anticipation. You have to anticipate what your children will do before they do it. You have to be one step ahead of them." This comment came from Barbara Cowden, who raised four sons and lived across the street from us for years. Betty Griffin, another mother I knew as a child, intuited the title of this book without my ever having told her: "Anne, you think too much," she said. "You need to feel more."

If there is any viewpoint I seek now it's the voice of experience. But when I embarked upon parenthood I had steeled myself against advice my parents gave us. When our oldest daughter was born, my mother flew out right away, before my father, to meet her first grandchild, who was named for her. The visit was less than idyllic. Not only was I miserable because our colicky infant wouldn't stop crying, but I was also rattled because my mother seemed upset. A few months later her reasons gradually emerged: She thought Tom and I were making our daughter's crying spells worse by making such a fuss over them. She worried we were setting ourselves up for years of frustration by making ourselves totally child-centered. Maybe she went a little overboard inferring so much from a first visit, but actually, she was right. We did center our lives too thoroughly around our kids, especially our oldest. It is the tendency of our times. And many of the changes I've made draw on her insight.

I don't expect my mother to have read the latest studies linking tummy-sleeping with SIDS and to know that babies are now supposed to sleep on their backs, nor have I much sought her advice on feeding or toilet training. I save her wisdom for the big questions: How to help children be good, how to keep them children in a society that seems determined to make them little adults. We've talked more about discipline than anything else. Once I realized the modern ways were a dismal failure with our kids, once I began to feel they were getting away from me, I asked my mother how she kept us in line. It is from her that I've learned the importance of letting children know early on that you, the parent, are in charge, and that they, the children, are not.

Do I value my mother's and father's advice? Certainly. Do I always take it? Certainly not. But there is no one else like them, no one else who knows me in the same way that they do. I appreciate their perspective, their way of helping me make sense of childrearing. They have been an essential counterpoint to the modern ways I've imbibed from books, friends, doctors, television, seemingly the very air we breathe. They aren't preaching generalities or teaching techniques, but offering their view of particular children, our own. They know how things used to be and they have the wisdom that comes from seeing kids through not only the terrible two's but the trying twenties as well. One woman said the best advice her mother ever gave her was "stop reading advice books." Sometimes it only takes one comment to head us in the right direction.

Andrea Johnson says she often relies on instinctive feelings with her two boys, three years and 18 months. And she feels comfortable doing things the way her mother did. "I don't call my mother up and say, 'Oh my God, tell me what to do,' " she says. "But if I'm having a problem I rely on the way things were done with me. So many of the things I do with our children I do because they are the way things were done with me. It's the important foundation that you can't get from a magazine or a book."

Andrea says she often feels different from other parents she meets. For one thing, she is a young mother by today's standards. She was only 23 when she had her first child. She once mentioned at a support group that she recovered quickly after the birth of her second child because her mother was there to help her. "The women in my group said, 'Oh, I could never have my mother there so long.' And then it turned into a mother complaint session. My mother lives in Pennsylvania, and up until a few years ago [when I moved to Virginia] we'd talk to each other every day."

Families are more than just nuclear. They are grandparents, aunts, uncles, and cousins. They are the link from one generation to the next. They are continuity, sentiment, and strength. If you read much about the history of childrearing, you will see that a new generation often thought the old one didn't know what it was talking about. The difference is, we have alterna tives. We can put distance, both psychic and geographical, between ourselves and our families. We can replace them with hundreds of theories, studies, and expert opinions. But it's too bad when we do.

It would be amusing, were it not so sad, that the very parents who crave rituals and traditions in their lives and seek them out in artificial ways are the very parents who turn their backs on the instincts and traditions they were born with.

I realize that not everyone wants or needs to ask their own parents for advice. I do so increasingly less as our children grow older. But I'm thankful to have their wise presence in my life, these people I love who know and love our children, who have their best interests at heart and who understand my vision. All grandparents aren't like that, I know. Some parents feel the only way they can survive is by building a wall between themselves and their past. What I'm suggesting is that we recognize the power of our own families in our lives. We may disagree with some parts of our upbringing but agree with others. Most of all we can celebrate the connection and pass it along to our own children.

Role Models?

This is what Mary, a college friend of mine who lives in Ohio, told me one day: "No parents are perfect. None of us has perfect childhoods. When you see where there are holes in your upbringing, you look for a role model to find what to do on your own. And if you can't find one you read what some of the experts have to say. I don't feel I have a natural instinct. Parenting has not come naturally to me. I never baby-sat as a child. I have one sister who's three years younger but I was never put in charge of her. I hadn't changed a diaper before I had Molly [who's now five]. Not a single diaper. So I guess I approach parenting in an intellectual way because I have no instinct."

I want to stop right here to point out how excessive thought can be traced to insufficient instinct. Only a few have stated as directly as Mary that it's lack of instinct that drives them to intellectualize. Though in Mary's case, it's perceived lack of instinct.

"I have this vision inside, but executing it and getting it real tangible is where I need help," she says. So Mary turns to books that she feels will strengthen values buried inside her and which fly in the face of modern childrearing theory. She reads James Dobson and John Rosemond, conservative fellows who fit perfectly with her conservative philosophy. And she concentrates, she says, "not on specific topics such as how to raise an only child," but on values. "The books give me confidence to go against the prevailing climate," Mary says. "They reinforce something inside me. They bring it to the surface and solidify it for me." For all her insistence that she has feeble instincts, I think Mary knows how to get the help she needs. But for every Mary there is a Deirdre.

Deirdre, a professional working mother of two children, ages ten and six, told me she had no role models and so has sought to find a better way to raise her kids through reading and therapy.[2] But the books she's read and the counseling she's received seem to be eroding her instincts rather than bolstering them. When I asked her if she made parenting decisions based on the way she was brought up, she told me, "Actually, my bad parenting decisions I make that way. I've received more advice from my family than I ever hoped to have." Earlier in our conversation she said, "I just finished reading *Toxic Parents*. It's a fabulous book." *Toxic Parents,* by Susan Forward, is subtitled *Overcoming Their Hurtful Legacy and Reclaiming Your Life.*

Reading books and seeking professional help have led Deirdre to believe she has no natural role models. She discovered, for instance, that her parents expected more mature and adult-like behavior from her when she was a child than was realistic to expect. So now, she says, "I have problems when my kids get crazy and fight with each other." Her therapist has told her that if she denies her children the freedom to act out now, they'll act out more when they're older. While Deirdre admits she has problems accepting this advice—"Sometimes I think, 'It's extreme' "—she's also trying hard not to repeat the "pattern" of her upbringing and is allowing her children "to get more into themselves and really experience what it's like to be a child."

At the end of our conversation I asked Deirdre if she ever wondered why she was uncomfortable with her children's misbehavior and why they were misbehaving so much in the first place. I was hoping this might prompt more discussion of instinct. But instead she quoted more of her therapist's advice: "As my therapist says, my children are misbehaving because they're being kids and it's okay, they're exploring. And why it bothers me is because I wasn't allowed to be like that when I was a child and I have no ability to cope with it. I have to learn how to now. But it's hard for me. I have no experience, no intuition, so I'm reading *Toxic Parents, Dance with Anger,* those kind of books."

Throughout our conversation, there were signs that Deirdre isn't totally comfortable with all the advice she's receiving. But like many parents, Deirdre seems to fear her instincts. She doesn't want to be her own parents, but she hasn't figured out who she wants to be instead.

"Strong at the Broken Places"

Who can criticize the need to make a better life for our children? This is what has driven generations of mothers and fathers to leave their homes and families and strike out for friendlier shores, to work long hours, to seek an education—all this so they could give their children a better life than the one they had.

But the impression I get after talking with parents is that the "better life" we want to give our children is not so much materially better as it is psychologically better. It is, to use the words of one conference leader, "clean." We want to give our kids openness and self-awareness and, above all, no hang-ups. But trying to give our kids a psychological edge is an entirely different notion than trying to give them a material advantage. It is more controlling, even as it pays lip service to liberation. The message beneath the message we give our children is, "Live for yourself, not for others."

Before there were experts and pop psychologists, there were plenty of parents who had bad role models growing up, people who were abused and neglected. Yes, some of them kept the cycle going. They beat or ignored their children because they were beaten or ignored. But some became, to use Hemingway's words, "strong at the broken places." They found someone to help them, a teacher or a friend, a minister, priest, or rabbi. Or maybe they searched down deep in themselves, deeper than memory, and came up with a set of precepts by which they would raise their own children. They did not beat them. They did not ignore them. Neither did they disparage their own up-bringing or lament their "toxic parents."

The power we have as parents is to such a great extent un-conscious power. I know people who have survived incredible difficulties—alcoholism, abandonment, divorce, or the death of their own parents at an early age—and have gone on to be wonderful parents. They have done it without classes or books. They have probably done a better job than they would have had they endured a life without hardship. Their strength springs from deep within them. It's a part of who they are. If they always agonized over their upbringing or analyzed every move they made, then the flow of power and strength from them to their children would have been interrupted, snapped from its source. I don't think they've thought a lot about their instincts. But they've certainly followed them.

A Small Boat on High Seas

When we were kids we hung out in our neighborhoods, went downtown by ourselves on the bus, entered high schools with-out fear. Today kids are carted around to activities. There are few city buses and even fewer downtowns, and school violence has become increasingly commonplace. Can an old-fashioned, instinctive way of childrearing keep pace with modern prob-lems, or is it like a small boat on high seas? A common excuse for abandoning instinct these days is that the unique challenges of bringing up children now require expert assistance, or at the very least, expert confirmation of what we think is best. Is it more difficult to raise a child in the latter years of the twentieth century than it was in the last few centuries?

I've danced around this question in previous chapters and don't pretend I can conclusively answer it. Earlier in the book I put our childrearing into some historical perspective to show that when it comes to basics like infant and child mortality, medical care, educational resources, and standard of living, we are lucky mothers and fathers indeed. Yet four out of five of the parents surveyed by Public Agenda say it's much harder now for parents to do their jobs. And most parents I interviewed agreed:

"Before if kids made a mistake and experimented with something they weren't supposed to it wasn't a life-threatening situation," said Barbara Bailey. "But the dangers are so much bigger out there now. One mistake could cost a child a life. That scares me to death. It makes me think that diapers and the toddler years and all the stuff I'm going through now are nothing compared to what's ahead."

"We have all these modern conveniences that should make our lives more relaxed, but they're more hectic than ever," said Colleen Sullivan. "Maybe it's because years ago people stayed home, because they had so much to take care of, like washing diapers the old-fashioned way. If I need something I don't wait until I need something else. I hop in the car and I go get it. I think we're pulled so many directions." Not just our activities but our decisions are more complicated. We have more choices for our kids—medical, social, educational—which complicate our lives.

In the Public Agenda survey, four out of ten children 12 to 17 years of age say they see people their age using drugs or alcohol every day or almost every day. Our children are exposed to more violence, more consumerism. Of course, we must protect them. But don't we protect them best by knowing them well? And don't we know them best when we trust our instincts?

When I was visiting my hometown recently, I ran into Anne, a friend I hadn't seen in several years. Her children are 14 and 16, and she's raising them alone. They sound like good kids, but she's having the usual teenage problems and is finding herself increasingly disenchanted with the modern ways. "Kids these days have parents in their pockets," she said. Her 16-year-old daughter, for instance, went downstairs to do her laundry one day and didn't come back up. She was grounded for a previous infraction and had slipped out the back door to meet some friends at a nearby coffee house. When Anne figured out what had happened, she wanted to talk to another adult—but not a parent—about how to handle her daughter. She didn't want someone who would give her the party line. "I wanted someone pure," she said. So she called a friend of hers who has no children. "Don't humiliate her by going down to the coffee house and confronting her. Talk to her later," the friend suggested. Anne tried to play it firm but cool, but that night she sat upright in bed. Her instinct clicked in. Of course she should have gone down to the coffee house and retrieved her daughter. Humiliation or no humiliation. Later on, when she was imposing a restriction on her daughter, the girl said, "Mom, everyone else has parents who are like their friends and you're not." Anne breathed a sigh of relief, knowing that she was finally on the right track, then replied: "That's because I'm *not* your friend. I'm your mother." What Anne and so many other parents have found is that the firm expectations with which we were raised (that parents are in charge and kids are not, for example) have crumbled beneath our feet. Now each new situation calls for a new response. Instinct can give us a firm footing again.

Above all, I think raising a child is more difficult than it used to be because we've been handed an impossible set of goals by the modern advice industry. We are constantly trying to keep up with the perfect parents we've read about or to incorporate the latest bit of research into our childrearing repertoire. Experts have convinced us that we must never raise our voices, that we must ask our children permission before we discipline them. No wonder it's harder.

So will the high seas dwarf the small boat? Not if we trust the boat. Yes, we have problems—the high divorce rates, the lack of time, the juvenile violence—but instinct is a seaworthy craft, because it is genuine, it is our own. I've tried it both ways, with instinct and without, and it seems to me that the best way to face modern problems is not with modern advice, but with inner strength. And that flows from following our own "natural and inherent aptitude."

The Expert Within

Perhaps the greatest threat to instinct is that we have developed a sort of "expert" mentality. This is different from feeling we know best about our own individual child. It means we don't trust something unless it's proven to us with hard data. We can't accept what we see in front of us but must seek confirmation of it from other sources. It's like the parent who doesn't believe her child has a disease until he fits all the Merck manual definitions of it. There's nothing wrong with thinking like a reseach scientist if you are one. But to think like one when you're a parent is something else entirely. It represents a vast change in the way we raise children. I can get rid of the books and the classes, but can I get rid of the experts in my head? Can I stop being a parent who thinks too much?

I recently attended a breast-feeding support group. Even though breast-feeding is more encouraged and accepted than it was a generation ago, many mothers receive no support from their families, employers, or even doctors when they decide to nurse their babies. They do it anyway because they think it best. On the surface, at least, gatherings like this one should help instinct flourish. But at the meeting, women referred to studies they had read: breast-fed babies have higher IQs, the average age of weaning in the world is over four years of age, and the World Health Organization has come out in favor of nursing children up to age two. Yes, there was some instinct in evidence at this meeting, but I couldn't help but notice how often the mothers referred to scientific research.

I don't think we have adapted this expert-like tone consciously. It's just that we've read enough books and magazine articles that it has seeped into our language and, I fear, into our heads. Even if we go "off book," the books are still in our minds.

The irony, though, is that to such a great extent our power as a parent is unknown and unknowable. We exercise it unwittingly. The child doesn't hear the fancy dialogue we lift from the page of our latest favorite book. Instead he hears the uncertainty in our voice as we deliver the words of strangers. When parents say things that they don't really mean, children can see right through them. "It's like saying to your kids that the sky is green," says Maggie Mulqueen. It is not in studying and learning that we act best as parents, but in the thousands of unconscious ways that traditions, visions, and goals are handed down.

When we believe in the force of these invisible messages, perhaps we won't fight against ourselves and our own instincts. We will have a little more faith in the inherent goodness of our own hearts. We won't feel a need to beat ourselves over the head as much as we have in the past. In short, we will relax.

Here's Where It Gets Complicated

I'm looking at a full-page public service announcement paid for by the Partnership for a Drug Free America. A very large, hairy gorilla holds a smooth, blond baby. The headline reads: "If he were her child she'd make sure he never tries marijuana." Underneath the headline is this message: "Every animal instinctively teaches its young how to survive the dangers of a hostile world. We humans are the smartest animal on earth. So why is it so difficult to talk to our children about the real danger of marijuana? Trust your instincts. Talk to your children. It's perfectly natural."

All discussion of marijuana aside, this ad conveys interesting messages about instinct. First, it implies that instinct should be easy. After all, if a gorilla can do it, why can't we? I'll take up that point in a minute. Second, it proves that instinct is in vogue.

That we crave deeper thoughts about childrearing is obvious. The books give it away. If you live in my area and want to read *Everyday Blessings: The Inner Work of Mindful Parenting*, by Jon and Myrna Kabat-Zinn, a book about meditation and parenting, you'll either have to buy it in hardcover or wait on a very long reserve list at the library. I found *Our Share of Night, Our Share of Morning: Parenting as a Spiritual Journey*, by Nancy Fuchs, right on the shelf. It's not as well-known, but just as affecting. The presence and popularity of these and other books show that we're tired of the formulas and the pat suggestions. Seen in one way they are an encouraging sign, a trend away from shallow techniques and a quest for something more profound. Seen another way, it's frightening to think of books gnawing closer and closer to our core, to the spiritual underpinnings that underlie our most fundamental decisions as parents.

As further illustration of the direction in which we're heading, let me take you to a parenting conference I attended one rainy Saturday a few months ago—before I had become a parenting class dropout but after I'd learned to approach these events with a critical eye. It was entitled "The Heart of Parenting" and combined spirituality and psychology with childrearing, a good combination, I thought, trying to make myself feel better about the $150 fee.

The conference was more touchy-feely than practical, although it covered such chestnuts as discipline and self-esteem. I'd describe its tone as New Age meets PEP. We could attend seminars called "The Sacred Mother," "Becoming the Parent You Want to Be," and "Spiritual Dimensions of Family Life." One session opened with a sweet story about how when God wanted to send a great idea into the world, he didn't do it with bells and whistles or writing in the sky. He did it with a little baby and the warmth in a mother's heart.

As with any self-respecting conference, we were encouraged to mingle and participate. In one session we took turns drawing pictures of our kids. Many people drew pictograms with sunshine and rainbows and shooting stars. We talked about the ideas we wanted to pass along to our children and how we thought they could best serve the world. These are important topics, big picture topics, and I'm glad we discussed them.

It was also at this conference that I ran across the word "clean." One of the leaders used it over and over again. "Clean" was the way he felt after he apologized to his child because he "laid" his bad mood on her. "Clean" was how he felt when he realized he was disciplining his daughter for himself rather than for her. When I asked him what "clean" meant, he said that clean means "admitting you own it."

Later on in the session we broke up into small groups to discuss critical questions. Ours was, "In the post-spanking age, what is the ultimate 'stick,' how do we get our children to obey us?" The question was my suggestion because I thought it might lead to a frank and lively suggestion of modern discipline. Apparently, I was almost the only one who thought so. The 40 or so participants in our session could choose which of the four critical questions they wished to discuss. At first I didn't think anyone would come to my corner. My friend Linda came, out of loyalty, I think, though she said she was truly interested; and a pleasant though bewildered young father; and a thin woman in a green skirt and a yellow crocheted vest who said her first-choice group was too crowded. As a matter of fact, other small groups were bursting at the seams, especially the one that was discussing the critical question, "What is the makeup of the filament that attaches us to our children?" (As I said, this was a touchy-feely crowd.)

The woman in the yellow crocheted vest assumed the lead of our small group. She was a daycare teacher seeking professional enrichment and accustomed to taking charge. Her children were grown. As we explained our various discipline problems, she told us how we should give choices and provide consequences—the standard stuff—and then she said, with great joy, almost pride, that her own son was just out of jail on probation. "He was just in for teeny-bopper stuff," she explained. "But now that he's over 21, it's a felony." I stopped dead still. Her comment was a turning point for me, the beginning of the end. It's not that I have anything against mothers of felons. But I'd rather not take parenting advice from them. It was not long after this episode that I became a parenting class dropout.

The conference day ended with a keynote speaker exhorting mothers and fathers to "become the parents you want to be." Maybe it has something to do with the turn of the millennium, but it seems that a pilgrim in search of instinct will find plenty of people these days willing to give it to him. "Instinctive parenting" has a nice, New Age ring to it, and conferences such as this one are increasingly more common. Some of the participants found this kind of gushy approach reassuring, but I left the conference feeling as if I'd eaten too much cotton candy. The "instinctive parenting" that was packaged and sold at this conference and is peddled in books, newsletters, and the gorilla ad, make it seem easy to follow our instincts, make it seem like a "letting go." But my instincts often tell me to do hard things.

We learn from the beginning to read our child's cues, to decipher a hungry cry from a tired cry, to understand toddler willfulness, six-year-old stubbornness, and the hormonal mood swings of the teenager. In fact, we become much more adept at reading our children's feelings than our own. It's hard to be principled when your child's little lip is quivering. It's easy to say, "Okay, you can have your birthday party at the Discovery Zone." We are afraid to make mistakes. We are scared that one miscue will send our child to the therapist's couch.

One of the comfortable but dangerous notions about instinct is that our children's interests and our own usually coincide. That has certainly not been the case in our family. It's not that we're in a constant state of battle. But we have our share of conflicts: Children who would like to stay up until 10 P.M., and parents who would like an hour or two to themselves before bed; children who would gladly live in a room buried in books, socks, and paper scraps, and parents who insist on occasional order. It makes sense that the instincts of rational, farsighted adults would differ from the instincts of irrational, shortsighted children.

It sounds nice to say we must lead with the heart, but the heart is a sentimental fool which cons us into ending the time out before it's done or sneaking our child dessert after we've told her she must go without. The head is mercifully just, too much so at times, and frequently confused, too. The head and the heart must work together in this business. When they do, I think we will have a much better shot at instinct. What we are after, I think, is ourselves. We are no exalted creatures, but we are who we are, and in the long run, we want our children to reflect us, our dreams and traditions.

The Backlash Trap

If New Age parenting is one way "instinctive childrearing" is portrayed, then another, somewhat related, style is attachment parenting. As I mentioned earlier, attachment parenting refers to nursing, wearing baby in a sling, co-sleeping, and other practices which offer themselves as a romantic and primitive response to the more rationalized world of mainstream expert advice. I wonder sometimes if conservative parents fear instinctive parenting because they feel it has become a synonym for attachment parenting, which is to them another way of saying capitulation, as in, "It's easier to pick him up when he's crying. It just feels right," or, "Bringing her to bed felt very natural." But trusting your instinct doesn't mean being a doormat.

On the surface, attachment parenting is anti-expert; its emphasis on the primacy of feeling, on going with baby's flow, would seem to put it solidly in instinct's camp. Yet it comes with its own set of instructions, its own books, journals, and gurus to show the way. It is entirely possible to be an attachment parent who thinks too much, for example. You simply trade one set of experts for another. I don't want to disparage parents who have sincerely chosen these ways of raising their children; in fact, I've chosen some of these ways myself. But once again, I think we can be fooled into thinking we're trusting our instincts when really we're following another party line.

Parents at the other end of the spectrum, like Deirdre, shy away from instinct because they think it means authoritarian childrearing. Deirdre says she was hit with a belt as a child and doesn't want to whip her children. She fears her instincts because she thinks they will lead her toward spanking.

Fears of being either too strong or too weak are proof to me that backlash thinking is in the air. It's easy to say that instinctive parenting is whatever you're *not* doing. Some parents, pushed till they'll be pushed no more, tired of all the advice in the air, much of which they can never live up to, truly do become backlash parents. It's that inevitable pendulum swinging back and forth between extremes. Diana Baumrind, the researcher who has written widely on authoritative, authoritarian, and permissive parenting styles, has noticed the phenomenon of lax parents who lash out in anger against the dictators their children have become.

And then there are parents who make a sudden course correction. It feels right, it feels instinctive, yet often it's triggered by a book or a motivational speaker. Lucrecia Crimmins and her husband, Chuck, who live in Perryville, Arkansas, have dramatically changed the way they're raising their children since their third daughter was born five months ago. Before, Lucrecia said, "I was reading all these magazines and learning all these tricks to get our children to behave, but what was I doing but spending countless time on these little tricks? We were just so scared to damage their spirit, their inner child." Then one day, she said, "I had loads of laundry to hang up and the older girls were out there fighting . . . and it hit me, this is not going to work." Lucrecia is a religious person and she began to pray about how to better handle her children. Within a week, she says, a friend came over with a tape called "For Mothers Only," by Elizabeth Elliot. The tape, and books she later read, instructed her in "how to establish a peaceful home" centered around Biblical principles of obedience and submission. She began to spank her older children, who arc two and five, and has noticed a big improvement in their behavior. "I don't feel we'll be spanking them when they're eight or nine. We're going to work with them in other ways then. But now we're setting a precedent, that you don't get away with things. I'd say out of all our friends, we're probably the most conservative in some ways."

That conservative childrearing practices are more in vogue now than they were a few years ago is proven by the many Christian parenting books in the bookstores, by the Family Life conferences now held in 85 cities and 15 countries every year. I wandered around one of these conference sites last spring and visited their bookstore, where there were scores of titles on building a Christian home and marriage, on chastity and celibacy, on sparing the rod and spoiling the child.

The Christian parenting movement is not the only sign of a return to traditionalism. At the 15th annual La Leche League conference you could attend a session on "Reclaiming the Lost Art of Homemaking." A different brand of traditionalism is served up in the regular newspaper and magazine columns of John Rosemond, a psychologist who dropped out of modern parenting himself. In his columns and books Rosemond encourages parents to center their families around their marriages rather than their children, to realize that we must sometimes hurt children's feelings to make them behave, and other prescriptions that have earned him such epithets as "the anti-Spock."

And then there are developments that could truly be called backlash. For instance, many states have laws that punish parents of minors for crimes their children have committed. In a closely watched test of these laws, a Michigan couple was convicted of a criminal misdemeanor and fined for failing to control their teenager, who served a one-year prison term for burglary and drug offenses. The parents said they didn't know much about their son's activities—including the stolen handgun and the marijuana plant in his room. They just wanted to give him "space."

The frightening thing about this backlash is that it springs from a collective, societal disgruntlement and may spread soon, whether we like it or not. If you cannot control your children, these new laws say, we will help you. From time to time I hear stories of states trying to pass laws requiring a "parenting license." There was a rumor like this circulating on the Internet recently. When about half the states in this country have some sort of laws holding parents' feet to the fire you get the feeling there's broad dissatisfaction with the way we're rearing our young. Backlash thinking should be a clue that unless we listen to our own instincts soon, we may have to answer to someone else's later.

Burnout and Support

About a year ago, after the members of my book group spent the requisite hour or so on *A Thousand Acres* or whatever novel we were reading, we began to talk, as we often do, about our children. Why, we wondered, were we so tired of parenting classes, advice books, the whole gig? It's not because we'd reached some pinnacle of perfection, we quickly agreed. No one could put her finger on why, but we were worn out sooner than we thought we'd be. None of us had children in high school yet. As I sat back and looked at us, so well-intentioned and earnest, I knew what the answer was. We were burned out. We started off as sprinters instead of long-distance runners. We were wound tight.

My children have no major problems. But you wouldn't know that by the way I toss and turn at night. No wonder I get more than my share of headaches and sore throats. And I am not alone. One estimate says that at least half of parents have symptoms of burnout. And burnout is a big impediment to instinct. You get to a place where you don't care anymore. And the view from there is not that idyllic bay with shining waves I described in the beginning of this chapter. It's more like the view I used to see from studio apartments in Manhattan—the solid brick wall of the building next door.

If backlash is one roadblock on the way to instinct, burnout is another. Not that burnout is imaginary; it's real, all right. But now it's become chic. Now seminars are offered to help us deal with it. Remember Vince, who led the parenting class I described in Chapter Four? I found out that the same week he was spreading the gospel of consequences at an elementary school, he appeared at a nearby preschool to talk about, of all things, "Preventing Parental Burnout." At that meeting, he encouraged parents to take a burnout quiz and to have a "prevention plan" to avoid burnout. I had a chuckle when I discovered that he was telling one group of parents to "let things go" even as he was making another group uptight. I've found a similarly ironic progression in the books of a child psychiatrist who has always encouraged parents to pay close attention to their children, to play with them frequently on the floor, and who has now come out with a book to help parents deal with the "challenging" child. And what, pray tell, has made the child so challenging? First, the experts lead us away from our best intentions, and then, when our children are out of control, they tell us we must relax to regain them. If we could just relax in the first place we'd be much better off.

Our parents were nervous and anxious; we are stressed and burned out. The '90s words suggest both an overload and an extinguishing. Like a 120-volt circuit with 220 volts of energy surging through it, we flame up then blow out. One frequently offered explanation for our exhaustion is that parents who work outside the home have more to do and less time to do it in. Go a step further, though, examine why we have more to do, and at least part of the reason is that we think too much. We strive to be the best possible parents and want our kids to be the best, too.

Burnout can be a spiral down into darkness and depression. But it can also be a signal to change course. Some burned-out parents heed the message and lighten up. They work fewer hours. They limit their children to one activity a week so they will have more downtime, too. Or they move to a smaller town where they cut their commutes and their expectations.

In the year since we had this discussion, some wonderful things have happened for members of my book group. One has given birth to a long-awaited second child, another has completed a successful but exhausting tenure as PTA president, still another has bought a house in the country and is moving out of the rat race. I've had the chance to write this book, of course.

And another group member, a lapsed PEP student, says she no longer takes classes and workshops because what she really needs is a sense of community, and she gets that from other sources now. On the whole, we seem less burned out than we did this time last year.

Many of us (and where I live, most of us) are raising our kids away from family and old friends. In that sense, it is harder to raise a child now than it used to be because we are not supported in our instincts. Many times I think parents take classes as much for the friends they hope to make in them as anything else. I made a friend in my "Spirited Child" class, as our conversations led us to discover we were compatible in other ways besides being the parents of rabble-rousing little girls. I think friendship is possible whenever parents open up with one another. And the confessional nature of the "Spirited Child" class made us open up with each other quickly. We felt free to talk in apocalyptic ways, to use phrases like "crash and burn" (what a spirited child does at the end of the day), or "bail out" (what a spirited child's parents do at the end of the day). This was not intellectualizing. It was rolling our eyes and saying, "Can you believe it?" It was commiseration.

Parenting support groups range from working parents meeting on their lunch hours to nursing mothers gathering in a church hall to Internet chat groups in which parents from all over the world come together to discuss teething, willfulness, and anything else that's on their minds. I think the best support groups are the informal ones, and their presence is pure serendipity. They may grow out of a mother-and-child exercise class or a birthing class or a play group. But what they share is a respect for viewpoint and, often, longevity. The advice you receive in them is not nearly as important as the relationships you build in them. After six years together, my book group buddies and I have what most quick-fix parenting groups lack, which is history.

My husband and I have found like-minded parents in our children's cooperative preschool, which has given us a community in the suburbs. But what makes the most difference in finding other parents to talk to is being willing to admit my failings as a parent. Nothing opens up a conversation like a little shared guilt. The parents who don't take the bait are probably still reading a parenting manual a week and are best avoided.

Having other parents to talk to makes us less dependent upon the experts and less inclined to be competitive with each other. I must add a caveat, though. Many of us live where there is no sense of community, so we try to purchase it by joining a preformed support group or taking a class. As Andrea Johnson discovered, a support group does not always support your instincts because many times participants spout off the same old expert theories you find in books or magazines. When I called Andrea a couple months after our first conversation, she told me she had stopped going to her group. "I realized it wasn't for me. You have to pretend that you're *on* all the time with your kids. When I said I like playing with my kids, one woman actually asked me, 'How many hours do you spend playing with your kids?' I said, 'I don't know.' " (I later visited this group, by the way, and met a woman who has yet to leave her six-year-old son with a baby-sitter and another mother who said she and her husband have discovered that the secret to childrearing is letting their 27-month-old daughter lead the way. I think I know why Andrea dropped out.)

What strikes me about all these organized support groups is that they are at best a catalyst and at worst a substitute for what must well up inside us. For many parents, mothers especially, individual support can ease the transition to off-book parenting, in much the same way that nicotine-laced gum helps smokers stop smoking. We are eased off our addiction by the support of others—not just any others, though, but parents like us. As antidotes to experts, support groups serve as humble and helpful way stations between addiction and recovery. And, if we are lucky enough to find a group that feels right, it can lead to the kind of true community for which so many of us long.

Where to Go Next

I've been thinking about instinct for a while. Long enough. Now it's time to practice it. I'm making progress. I no longer care as much what people think. I'm willing to be politically incorrect if need be. I'll change my mind and my plans at a moment's notice if that little voice inside tells me I should. I am willing, to put it bluntly, to fly by the seat of my pants. In my own struggle to shuck the modern ways I've adapted the motto of addicts everywhere: One day at a time. I wish I could say I've made a single dramatic change and then my struggles were over. But the messages bombard me daily, so resolving to be my own kind of parent must be a daily act, too. I don't make excuses for my behavior. I accept responsibility. But for me the transformation has not been as much a "Eureka!" experience as an "Oh, yeah, I'm beginning to understand."

I'm glad I've changed, but my instinct seems like a pale copy of the instinctive parenting of people who've never done it any other way. Janice and Steve Hughes of Spokane, Washington, had their children when they were young. Though Janice and Steve are only in their mid-40s, their five children range in age from 23 to 13. Here's Janice on breast-feeding: "When I had my first child I just knew I wanted to do it because that's the way it's supposed to be. My girlfriends read every book about breast-feeding, how much water you should drink, and none of them actually ended up breast-feeding because they got real nervous and dried up. I just did it, you know." Here's Janice on Lamaze: "I wasn't a big believer in it. I didn't want to go to the classes. I mean, people have babies all the time." On discipline: "We were pretty strict with them when they were little but I don't think we had to spank any of them after three. And now that they're grown up they're so nice to each other and they like each other." And here's what she has to say about adolescence: "As they grow older they don't always agree with us. They have different views. But we've always held firm to our certain beliefs. Kids like the security of knowing where you stand." What is her secret? "I never got into the books. I just never did. I don't know why. I think it's just natural instinct. I think people get confused reading stuff about how to raise kids."

People like the Hugheses are an inspiration to me because I still struggle with overanalysis. I give myself headaches and heartaches when I shouldn't. Far too often I shun the present for the future—should I start her in preschool this year or next? Or the past—how could I have better handled that tantrum in the shoe store? I know I'm happiest as a parent when I'm just enjoying the girls—being silly with them, baking a cake with them, driving around in the car and singing "This Old Man." In other words, when I'm fully "with" them the way the mindfulness experts tell me to be. But I'm realistic enough to know those moments are rare. After all, we're not living in a cotton commercial. To be an adult means we have to live in two dimensions: the world of the child, fantastical, soft-edged, and often irrational, and the world of the adult, where the mortgage must be paid, and children must be fed, clothed, and disciplined, as well as nurtured and enjoyed.

But I have left behind the prescribed formulas of a hundred parenting books. I have put them down like a heavy suitcase I carried much longer than I'd planned to. It's not as if I've always been seeking out a new way; I've seldom had the single-mindedness of a pilgrim. My awakening was more a matter of chafing at the modern constraints, of feeling at first bewildered, then enraged, and finally amused by all the fuss and bother.

If there is anything I seek now, it is inspiration. I'd rather be inspired than instructed. I'd rather read a poem or a novel or a book of essays that makes me think in a new way about life and childhood's place in it. I would rather find excitement and ardor in a piece of good music, or in a particularly touching film.

Inspiration is what we need as parents, I think. Raising children requires supple adjustments of the sort that makes any preformed theory dismally inadequate. What better way to tackle such a job than with instinct. Like mother's milk, there will always be enough of it and it will always be the strength and consistency we need. Many parents have told me how they rely more and more on their instincts as their children grow older and they grow more comfortable with themselves as parents.

Sometimes I think there's a collective unconscious of child-rearing, a mother lode and a father lode, a repository of wisdom that is buried deep inside every new parent. It is composed of common sense, patience, humor, idealism, persistence. I'm talking about the place where Parentese resides, that high, lilting tone of voice that we instinctively use with babies. Parentese appears in the beginning of our lives as parents, of course, before we've been corrupted. What other instinctive responses might there be that are drowned out by the general din of expert opinion? Perhaps there's an instinctive commandingness, a style of telling children you mean business. I sat next to a young mother on an airplane recently. When her 11-month-old daughter threw a bag of peanuts one too many times the mother uttered a sharp "no." The child, unhappy to have displeased her mother, began to cry. The mother comforted her baby and rocked her in her arms till she was asleep. How natural it seemed. The mother had set clear limits based on common sense. There was no waffling in her voice. It was a definite rebuke. And yet she was very sensitive to the child and what she needed. I would be willing to bet this mother hasn't read many modern parenting manuals.

Perhaps, too, there is within us an inherent style of parenting based on our sex. One of the questions that has needled me as I've written this book is whether to address it solely to mothers or to all parents. I've chosen the latter. Yet I've found myself interviewing many more mothers than fathers, partially because I am a mother, but also because mothers are more likely to have their fingers on the pulse of the family. Many of the women with whom I spoke say they buy the books, read them, and then pass along the tidbits of information and advice they think their husbands might like. Even Karen Hastings, who's a patent attorney in Washington, while her husband, Steve Hazelton, stays home with the kids, is the book reader in their family. Still, I address all parents in this book because I believe that thinking too much affects—and afflicts—us all.

I mention this now because I believe that instincts have more gender to them than I originally thought they did. Frequently, I've found myself writing "intuition" when I meant to write "instinct." I think most women tend to operate on hunches a little more than men do, and so we may find it a little easier to discover our instincts. Fathers have a different problem, I think. They are caught in the "sensitive dad" trap. Among parents who think too much, it is not fashionable for fathers to be strong disciplinarians. They are supposed to be as "into feelings" as moms are. But their instincts might give them a different message—if they'd listen.

After hesitating for almost a decade, I have finally shed my inhibitions and become more like my own parents than I used to be. I'm letting myself use expressions I'd almost forgotten, like the phrase "elbow grease," for instance. Whenever I was cleaning as a child, scrubbing a pot or helping wash down the woodwork, my dad always told me to put a little more "elbow grease" into it. My parents have always been full of little sayings like that: "Don't make a mountain out of a molehill." Or, when I couldn't find a pair of shoes or a hairbrush, "If it was a snake, it would have bitten you." It seems that with the rise of uniform parenting practices, and the reluctance many of us feel to call upon our own upbringing, we aren't teaching our children the little sayings that warm up our speech, make it friendlier and more poetic. So it's not just the old-fashioned morals and values many of us have forsaken, but the little things that make up the big picture, even colloquial expressions, which, as it turns out, also have a way of fixing a worldview within us.

Chris Anderson recently lamented to me that she wasn't playing her daughters the old-fashioned songs from musicals that had been such a staple of her growing up years. She hopes it's not too late, but she's starting now. The last time I was at her house, music from *My Fair Lady* was blaring from the stereo.

I can't describe what instinct will feel like for you. But I have tried to describe my search for it, my ongoing pursuit of it. It isn't always as simple as we'd like it to be. But it's worth it. I've never been sorry that I dropped out of modern childrearing.

Only sorry that I didn't drop out sooner. I like myself better as a parent who thinks a little less and feels a little more.

Dropping out gives us more time for ourselves, too. Another friend of mine is an avid bird watcher. She sneaks out before daylight in a quest for rare raptors. "I know the owls are out there, waiting for me," she said once. And I thought: There's something out there waiting for all of us. But we have to break woofree to claim it. The activity doesn't matter, as long as it's nourishing. I feel better about everything (especially the children) when I read, write, take walks, or play the piano.

I'm glad to cultivate the lost art of parental daydreaming, to be a woolgatherer instead of a manual reader. I pick up clues from a thousand sources, like birds build a nest of countless bits of string, brush, grass, and twigs. The material comes from many places, but the finished product is my own. It is not based on anyone else's philosophy, is not adapted from the tribes of South America, nor pushed by well-meaning academics. It comes from the same places as my daydreams as a child, those big glorious concoctions in which I discover the ruins of an ancient civilization, dance the waltz at a Viennese ball, or climb to the top of Mount Kilimanjaro. It's the "why nots?" of child-rearing I've tried to put back into my life. These are not firm expectations, mind you. They are not plans. They are our fond hopes and dreams for our children, what we can imagine them being in the future.

A few years ago, before our youngest daughter was born, when our dear friends Debbie and Jim would come to dinner, we would chat about the children after they went to sleep. Debbie and Jim had no children and took a special interest in our own. I realized once with some dismay that our friends were daydreaming more about our kids than we were. We were too caught up in the daily grind to speculate whether Claire would channel her fabulous persistence into a law career or Suzanne would become a dancer or an artist. I would always think after these dinners that we, the parents, were missing out. The little time I had for daydreams I wasted, worrying and thinking too much. But that was several years ago, and I'd like to think I've changed a little.

I don't know anyone who wouldn't like a wise, benign presence in their life, someone who holds the key to understanding their children. Some of us seek this counsel in each other, others look for it in a hundred books or more. But why not seek it in ourselves? I hope that this chapter will inspire you to listen to your own instincts. They may be buried down deep. But they are there. And if you give them a chance, they will nag you until you listen to them. Once you do, you will become a parenting class dropout, too.

10

An Old-fashioned Childhood

*"We could never have loved the earth so well if we had
had no childhood in it."*
—*George Eliot*

Our children live in many mansions: in air-conditioned houses where screens light up their faces with a flickering blue gleam and the summer sun is just a glare on the blinds; in classrooms where they learn to feel good about themselves before and above all else. The mansions are enticing but imprisoning: long on activities, short on dreams; cushioned for comfort, but lacking in challenge. These are the nests we have built for our young, we who've had fewer children and read more about them than any generation before us, who measure our words and actions so as not to stunt egos or squash spirits.

Every day, it seems, I struggle to build a different kind of life for our children. I try to stop thinking so much and listen to my own heart and hunches. We've made a few simple hard choices: very little television and lots of good books; few structured activities and ample time to play alone; part-time childcare rather than full-time; responsibilities as well as privileges. These may not be the best choices for everyone, but they've helped give our children what seems more endangered than the rain forests—an old-fashioned childhood.

When I say old-fashioned childhood, I don't mean bloomers and Victoriana or Howdy-Doody and Hula-Hoops. I mean one where play is deliciously unorganized and seemingly without end; where children are left alone to make their own fun; where parents talk with and shape their children instead of analyzing and scheduling them; where parents seek guidance from relatives and friends rather than only from books; where children are members of the family, not prized possessions.

Sorry, No Tips

This is the part of the book that begs for solutions. I've described the problem, tried to understand it, and now it's time for the boldface tips and the four-week plan to stop thinking too much. But I've lost faith in boldface tips. I have no plan. I don't want to add to the clamor of voices telling you what to do. All I have is a vision, and it's just my vision, I don't pretend that it should be yours.

I want to raise children who are children, first of all, who are delightfully different from adults, who believe in fairy tales and magic, and who see the world in that crazily skewed way that kids do. I realize that I risk being thought indulgent and nostalgic, and I'm willing to take that gamble. I know that the 1950s and '60s, against which I and many parents measure our children's youth, was perhaps the golden age of childhood. Our parents, or I suppose I should say my parents and other parents I knew, were child-centered enough to give us paradise but not so child-centered as to spoil us with its fruit. I have no use for the pat and sentimental solutions of *Father Knows Best* or *Leave It to Beaver*. We need something infinitely more practical and hard-edged. After all, our families are smaller, leaner, more efficient. Many have just one parent at the helm instead of two, and two parents who work outside the home instead of one. Surely an old-fashioned childhood cannot work for our children. And yet . . . I see no reason why we can't hold on to many of the time-tested ways. In fact, I *know* we can—as long as we have faith in ourselves and trust our impulses. We may have to dig deep to remember the old songs and sayings. If our parents raised us wrong, then we must do better. But we don't have to second-guess every gut feeling we have.

Some critics of modern childhood decry the lack of social and cultural support available to parents. How are we supposed to do a good job when our role is weakened by politicians in Washington? How are we going to believe in ourselves when we aren't backed up by schools, the workplace, and the pulpit? If I read one more article about how modern parents are powerless I think I'll scream. We are the voters who put the politicians in office. We are the taxpayers who finance the schools, and the parents who operate the PTAs. We are the churchgoers and the Sunday school teachers. More to the point, we are the ones to whom our children's young lives are entrusted. If the revolution is to begin anywhere, it must begin with us.

I began my own revolution by trying to keep the big picture in mind, the overall plan of how we want our children to be. It's the broad brushstrokes, the morals and values. Without being a fanatic, I try to stick with it. For instance, our children must respect us. They must be honest and tell the truth, even when it's difficult to. They must be kind, even to each other. They must entertain themselves and pitch in around the house. I don't think there's anything remarkable in these expectations. But holding on to them means devaluing the other stuff—the play dates, the soccer teams, the gifted and talented classes.

I need not tell you how hard this can be. I've read enough books and written enough articles that I often second-guess myself. I try to be a buddy instead of a mother, and I ask our children for their approval. I wrote an article recently about giving chores to five- and six-year-olds. The angle was that chores are good for kids, that being responsible for little jobs around the house gives children a sense of accomplishment and independence, but that parents must introduce chores gently and gradually. I was to downplay the fact that delegating chores lightens our load, too. This was beside the point. So I reported what the experts told me—the fun ways to involve a child in picking up toys or making the bed, and how we shouldn't expect too much of our little ones in the beginning. Don't correct them; this would squash their budding sense of helpfulness. I even told a story on myself. (I do that a lot, as you may have noticed.) I confessed how I barked out orders to our daughter Claire: "Set the table," I would command, in the midst of my own hurry to prepare the evening meal. Shame on me! I should be coaxing her, cajoling her, setting the table *with* her. And after I wrote the story, that's exactly what I started to do. I began to think, "Well, maybe I am asking too much of Claire. She's only five, after all." Never mind that I'd seen her set the table beautifully many times before. I bought the advice I was selling.

Well, I'm not buying it anymore. Instead, I'm trying to distill what works from the past—my own past and further back, if it's relevant—and apply it to our family. We cannot give our kids the kind of upbringing we had, when there were children in almost every house on the block, and we moved from backyard to backyard like a herd of buffalo. Our children's childhood will always seem limited to me. But there are certain basics that Tom and I expect: That our kids approach this world with humility rather than arrogance, for example, and that they earn self-esteem the old-fashioned way—by meeting the challenges that will inevitably come their way.

Since I began to write this book and share my confusion with other parents I have been amazed at our collective bewilderment. We really don't know where to go next. We have tried books, classes, and support groups, and still we're bamboozled by our children. Some months ago a friend told me about her eight-year-old son, who refuses to wear underwear. Each day it's a battle just to get him into his sweatsuit (the only clothes he will wear) and off to school. Most parents I know are so worn down by entertaining and negotiating with their kids that they no longer see their children as people-in-the-making and themselves as people-shapers. We've become bystanders in what could be our greatest creative endeavor—helping our children grow up to be the best people they can be. We've lost something our grandparents took for granted—the conviction that we know instinctively what's best for our kids.

Giving our children an old-fashioned childhood is a radically new idea because it means resisting the commercial and psychological pressure to be like everyone else. It means helping children wait for things—until they're older, wiser, grown up. It means paying as much attention to our children's dreams, to their moral and fantasy lives, as to their intellectual growth. It doesn't mean we shelter our children; in fact, we make them a part of the family in good times and bad. And then, when it's their turn to grow up, they will want to become strong adults, too. They will be people with minds of their own who can listen to our advice and take it or not, as they see fit.

"To be the best parent you can be you must walk against the wind," an expert once told me during an interview. Of all the advice I've heard from psychologists, psychiatrists, pediatricians, and teachers, I remember this the best. It's so important and so difficult—especially for parents who think too much, since we take to heart whatever we hear. Yet we must believe enough in ourselves that we're willing to take unpopular stands.

Between the Packs

I'm driving down the Beltway, the sometimes six-, sometimes eight-, sometimes ten-lane ring around Washington, D.C. I avoid it whenever possible. I can't forget news accounts of famous Beltway accidents: the time a motorist happened upon a queen-size sofa in the left lane, swerved to avoid it, and had a fatal collision. Odd sorts of accidents seem to happen on the Beltway and just your normal everyday crashes happen there, too. So I've developed a strategy. I've seen how the traffic seems to move in packs or waves. Since the cars in the pack usually go much faster than the speed limit, I can, if I drive 55 or 60, stay between the packs. This helps me stay calm as other drivers zip in and out around me. It is, I think, akin to raising old-fashioned children in the modern world. I keep my eye on the goal ahead of me, bringing up our daughters as we see fit, even though other families are moving ahead of us in possessions, activities, and other achievements. A glance in the rearview mirror tells me that another pack is gaining on me, but I keep my speed. I'm glad to let the traffic pass us by.

The first way I stay between the packs is tuning out the advice industry. No surprises there. I still turn to manuals for health problems—I'm especially fond of looking up symptoms in children's medical encyclopedias and then tossing and turning all night because I've imagined one of our kids has a disease! I still flip through magazine articles, read the newspaper, and watch television specials on childhood. The information is still all around me, but I'm on top of it most of the time. I guess you could say I've become a discerning consumer. When I come across a fact or a theory, I run it through my own filter first. I take ideas and digest them rather than swallowing them whole. I question what I hear. A few months ago on television I caught the teaser of an upcoming news show: "Babies have their own language. And you need to learn it." I can remember a time when I would have stayed to watch, would have thought, "Maybe I'm wrong to be encouraging our baby to speak my language. Maybe I should try to speak *her* language." Instead, I just turned off the television.

And speaking of turning off the television, another way we stay between the packs is by leaving our set off most of the time. We're not purists. Our kids watch the occasional video. But our television is usually out of sight in a cabinet; we've never signed up for cable; and about the only time we allow significant viewing is when a child is ill and doesn't feel up to her regular activities. Once when Suzanne was four and quite healthy, I rented her a movie for a treat. As we were leaving the video store, she looked up at me, all worried, and said, "Mommy, am I sick?"

I don't make a big deal out of our low-TV policy because it seems self-righteous. But I'll risk that label here to point out that turning off the television has encouraged our kids to use their imaginations, to be active rather than passive, to play, sing, read, and build forts. It gives us all more time to talk and be with each other. Our kids aren't exposed to as much violence, nor are they being sucked quite as quickly into commercials and the consumer culture. Our kids seldom ask for a toy they've seen on TV and when they do, it's usually one that isn't available anymore because it's from a movie we taped three years ago. If Neil Postman is correct in his belief that television is eroding childhood (and I think he is), then abstaining from this electronic medium is keeping our children childlike longer than they would otherwise be. Not coincidentally, bringing up children without television is, in itself, an old-fashioned approach.

Another between-the-pack strategy is working part-time. (My husband works full-time.) You might think that full-time motherhood would be the logical way to raise old-fashioned children because that's what many of our mothers did. But staying home with three children (two of whom are in school)—and a dishwasher, microwave, washer and dryer, and other labor-saving appliances—doesn't give me enough to do. Frankly, it didn't give me enough to do even when the children were younger. It's a recipe for thinking too much. With time on my hands, it's easier to over-involve our kids in activities and over-involve myself with them. I'm neurotic enough as it is. So working part-time makes it easier for me to raise old-fashioned children.

As for both parents working full-time, this doesn't allow for enough talking and listening to suit me or for enough time to be gently unraveled together every day, rather than spending our hours in perpetual fast-forward. Since I began this book, I've crossed a line I hadn't intended to cross, and our youngest is now with someone else more days a week than she's with us. Never mind that the someone else is Eva, who's wise and witty and who takes such tender care of her. I miss Celia, I miss having her around me, and I think she's missing out on something, too. Although it's only the chaos of a mother working at home, there are lessons to be learned from it, lessons in self-reliance and deferring to others. So I'm going back to a three-day week soon.

I know a part-time schedule is not possible for everyone. Work and family decisions are hemmed in on every side by personal choices: the income you need, the profession you've chosen, and deeply felt expectations of family life. Many families do fine with both parents working and others thrive with one parent at home. I'm fortunate that my career lends itself to part-time work, and I wish it were possible for more families.

Purpose

I don't want to give you the impression that I always know what I'm doing. I usually don't. But that's the point. There's no formula for raising old-fashioned children. I'm after something elusive, and sometimes in the busyness of modern living, I almost forget what it is. But then I'll read a passage from a favorite novel, or one of the girls will say something to me, and I'll remember what I'm after. I do know this: It matters how we introduce children to this world, with what degree of passion or delicacy we open their hearts to the world beyond. We need to give them purpose. But first we have to have some purpose ourselves.

I read recently about a Vietnamese couple who came to this country with their six children 22 years ago and left everything else behind. The father, who'd been a journalist, got a job parking cars and later became a technician. The mother, a teacher in her native land, began as a baby-sitter and eventually landed a position with a small computer firm. For 13 years one parent worked a day-shift and the other a night-shift so that one of them would always be with the children. Last spring their youngest child graduated from the University of Virginia, the sixth and last child in the family to earn a diploma from this prestigious institution. Older brothers and sisters have entered professions such as teaching, acting, and law.

Theirs is a modern success story built on old-fashioned virtues: hard work, ambition, a belief in the future. What they have going for them, I think, is the struggle and the yearning. These are conditions that have all but vanished from the well-off suburban American families I know. It's not that we don't have high expectations for our children, but we aren't all making sacrifices to reach a common goal. Most of us cannot replicate the conditions that infuse immigrant families with a sense of purpose and drive. But because we believe that families should revolve around children's happiness, I think it's easy to miss the chances we do have to forsake immediate pleasures for long-term gains.

When I think back to what's responsible for the best qualities my brothers and sister and I share, it's not the easy times, but the hard ones that come to mind. A friend once told me that what helped her and her husband raise four sons (and I know them; they are respectful and unspoiled) in an affluent suburb was being at the low end of the economic scale. That made it easier to say no to a new bike or a new car. Our daughters often hear that we can't afford this or we'll have to wait for that. These minor deprivations are nothing compared with what some children must bear, but at least they are small lessons in making do.

One thing that even affluent children of the past had going for them was that living wasn't as easy as it is now. Go back to our grandparents' time, for instance, and children had to walk more, to be hotter and colder, and, when they got sick, to be sicker. Don't get me wrong, I'm thankful for antibiotics and pain relievers. I don't deprive our kids of those. I'm not forcing them to live through a Depression of our own creation. But I recoil against climate-controlled comfort and the tyranny of the automobile.

There aren't many places our kids can walk, but if you cut through a backyard and a wooded path, you'll hit a gravel road that leads to the elementary school. They're still too young to walk there on their own because they'd have to cross a busy road (and they usually ride a bus), but sometimes I pick them up on foot from summer and afternoon activities. Walking back gives them a taste of what it's like to get somewhere on their own feet instead of being driven. When they're a little older, they'll be able to walk to their friends' houses in other parts of our neighborhood.

I wouldn't say we've burdened our older daughters with chores, but at least they are expected to make their beds, vacuum, set and clear the table, pick up after themselves, and watch their younger sister—and they are not paid for their work. We give our girls these jobs not to bolster their self-esteem but to improve our sense of sanity. We need their help.

Homeschooling of the Heart

One of our dreams—and I admit it's not a very practical one—is that our family might someday live out in the country, where the girls would absorb the rhythms of the day and seasons, where they would have real chores, not just a little housework, but feeding and caring for animals who would die without their attention. But this isn't possible now, so we make do by picking green beans and blackberries in a friend's several-acre garden and driving down the road to a little farm park where they can see baby pigs and lambs. They also have a cat, fish, and turtles to care for.

I keep reminding myself that to a child a vacant lot is a dream come true, a patch of purple clover a fairy meadow. Maybe it's just false hopefulness on my part, but I think that if our girls do some work inside and some play outside, they will come to love the world in the way that George Eliot describes in *The Mill on the Floss*. "Our delight in the sunshine on the deep-bladed grass today might be no more than the faint perception of wearied souls, if it were not for the sunshine and the grass in the far-off years, which still live in us, and transform our perception into love."[1]

Sometimes I feel like I'm homeschooling all right, but not in reading and writing and arithmetic. I suppose you could call it "homeschooling of the heart." I teach our children that we expect better behavior of them than the prevailing model. To do that I provide a sort of running critique of popular culture. For example, I recently read the girls *Stephanie's Ponytail,* by Robert Munsch, a children's story with the worthy message, "Be yourself." Just as I was about to point out that the heroine, though quite good at being herself, is not very nice to those around her, our oldest daughter, Suzanne, rolled her eyes and said to me, "We couldn't talk that way to you, could we, Mom?"

Is Suzanne indoctrinated? You bet. There are ways in which I do not want our kids to think for themselves yet. That we expect them to defer to us because we're their parents may sound retrograde. It certainly doesn't put their feelings above all else. But it's teaching them self-discipline, to soften their voices and hold their tongues. They know how to let their feelings fly; in this they need no instruction. But when it comes to restraint, they can still use help.

So many of the problems we face as parents are problems of affluence. We think too much, we spend too much, we worry too much. Our children also suffer from too much too soon. So that's why we insist that our kids wait for ballet lessons, sleep-overs, pierced ears, even bubble gum. One day when our oldest was three or four, she asked me if she could chew gum. I imagined for a second what it would be like to clean bubble gum from the carpet, to cut bubble gum out of her hair, and then I said, rather arbitrarily, "You can have it when you're six." Now it's a big deal at our house to turn six—starting first grade is just part of it, the rest of it is going to the store and buying a big bag of bubble gum. I'm glad we've made waiting part of growing up. For when society conspires to give children everything at once, it is up to parents to say, "Not now, not yet."

Perhaps the ultimate in delayed gratification is a belief in God. Religion is another way I give our daughters an old-fashioned childhood, although that is not the only reason I do so. It's a source of strength and meaning for me, too. A couple years ago, I wrote an article on teaching children about God. It took a developmental approach, citing experts to explain the spiritual concepts kids can understand at various ages. It was an interesting story to write, but I remember thinking at the time that I was building a case for religion, much as I'd built a case for why toddlers need to say "no." It confirmed what I already believed: that for many parents spirituality is something they've added to their lives because they have children, sort of like a Brio train set. It's religion by-the-book, "let's do it for the kids." I do it because I believe we were put on earth for a purpose and that it is our duty to carry it out; we are responsible for each other. If a hundred other hopes and dreams for our children come to nothing, I hope these few remain—that they be good people, strong people, that their lives be infused with conscience and moral wholeness.

Nonchalance

Our kids are not pampered, but they are more like yesterday's children and that makes them an oddity. They don't see all the latest movies or buy the newest gadgets and clothes. So I wonder, are we giving them the edge they need in a competitive world?

"I know I am burdening my children by parenting against the mainstream values," says Maggie Mulqueen. Her three children watch only the occasional video and no televised sporting events, so when her seven-year-old son, Colin, plays on his T-ball team, "he doesn't know any of the professional sports stuff, like why all the other kids are high-fiving. He's clueless. There's a way in which he's socially ostracized because of how we're raising him," she says.

Over time I've beaten back my own worries on this front by trusting that the warmth and strength our kids receive at home will help them deal with whatever the world throws their way. Maggie says that when she makes a stand against the prevailing culture, "I don't feel like I'm depriving our children of something, I feel like I'm giving them something. I'm giving them a childhood." That's a good way to think about it, too.

But I continue to wonder how much we can or should isolate our children from the culture at large. Where do we draw the line? I want to cultivate an old-fashioned garden, not raise a crop of hothouse roses. Of course, we steer our kids clear of drugs and gangs and guns, but what about a PG-13 movie for an 11-year-old? Should we be the lone holdouts on this one? I have this image of the parent I don't want to become, a humorless one, always fretting about racy language on television and congratulating myself on how unspoiled we've managed to keep our kids. I know I sound contradictory, but to avoid this pose, I often strive for nonchalance. There's a difference between trying to stay out of the rat race and making a fetish out of staying out of the rat race. One of the things I like best about having three kids instead of two, for instance, is that our family has a little more friendly chaos to it. We don't have time to dot all the i's and cross all the t's of our children's upbringing. I think kids thrive in this looser loam. It's a balancing act, this need to keep kids both out of the fray and happily occupied. I don't pretend it's easy to balance protectiveness with nonchalance, but that's what we have to do.

The Big Picture

Besides, in our quest to give our kids the perfect childhood, don't we lose sight of the silly and endearing ways that kids play havoc with our best intentions? We may be the directors and producers of their young lives, but the performance is theirs. They write their own lines and claim their own memories: the smell of grass on a summer morning, the acrid taste of snow on the tongue, the time the door slammed on their fingers. They'll remember these—and forget all about that perfect birthday party.

I recall a trip we took to Colorado when I was five. We saw Pikes Peak, the Garden of the Gods, all the splendor of the Rocky Mountains, and what I remember most is my father stepping outside our ordinary motel room one morning, looking up, and saying, "There's not a cloud in the sky." He said it with eagerness and delight, and I can't look up at a cloudless blue sky now that I don't hear his words.

We don't—and we shouldn't—raise kids for the history books. As citizens we have great disdain for leaders who govern with one eye toward the future and the other constantly scanning for reaction, wondering how this decision or that law will be interpreted, trying to purchase greatness with efficiency rather than passion. Doesn't true greatness mean believing enough in what you're doing that you don't worry what grade you receive? Perhaps we should raise kids the same way: Keep the big picture in mind. Believe in our vision. To a certain extent what our children make of it is up to them. This is not to downplay our role. Childhood matters. A good one helps kids love the world the rest of their lives.

On days when there have been no answers and few easy moments, I put pen to paper and describe what I see in front of me. I ask myself questions: How true is temperament? How lasting is rage? Can I change our children? Can I change myself? I scribble my thoughts on stray sheets of paper or write them down in my journal. These ramblings remain for me one true way of reaching some truth about these little beings who wrench my heart and fill my life with purpose. They are, in fact, my own observations, right or wrong, and they have come to me after much time and reflection upon the real subjects themselves.

It is 11 P.M. and Tom and I make our final rounds. In the small bedroom, Celia is snuggled down in the blankets with her bottom up in that unique way that babies and toddlers have. She must have just turned her head because one of her cheeks is red from resting it against her pillow. In the next bedroom, Suzanne and Claire are finally asleep. Suzanne, in the top bunk, has covers pulled up to her chin, and there are books and papers spread all around her. In the bottom bunk, Claire is twisted up in a tangle of sheets and covers, which is better than usual, since she's often on the floor or curled up at the foot of our bed.

All of us have our challenges, our graces and blessings and burdens. All of us have plenty to think about—without thinking too much. But at the end of the day when we, like most parents, check on the children before we go to bed, I am always struck by how simple it is when they're asleep. That it should be simple at night and not during the day is hardly news to any mother or father. In nine hours I'll be in an all-out battle with one of them about school work or breakfast cereal. But they're safe now, well-removed from the morning's rigors. And we are safe, too, from the voices that tell us we must do more, think more. These end-of-the-day reveries let us imagine the world we want for our children. For one seamless instant we are sure of ourselves as parents.

Family Reunion

I was not supposed to come here. There wasn't time. I had parceled out the hours I needed to write and there was not a weekend, not even a day, that I could spare. But I came anyway, drawn by a cousin's wedding, a family reunion, and something more. I knew I could not finish this book without returning to my hometown, to the people and places that shaped me. Most of my family would be at the wedding: My parents, brothers and sister and their families, my aunts and uncles and cousins. Lots of cousins. It was something to celebrate. So I came home, to Kentucky. I hadn't been here in a year, a year spent attending classes and reading books that preached how we must get beyond family. And here I was in its very bosom. The irony was palpable.

The wedding was fun. The reception was held in a Knights of Columbus hall, a couple miles down the road from where my parents live. It was dark and hot inside. The beer flowed freely. It seemed as if I'd stepped back in time. The dance floor had one of those multifaceted silver balls that pick up reflected light and sprinkle it across the walls and ceiling. At first no one danced, but then the song "YMCA" came on and everyone hit the floor. I danced with my brother Drew, who flew in from Oklahoma for the wedding and who got into the spirit by making a Y, an M, a C and an A with his arms. My cousin Kathleen, the bride, danced with her new husband, Terry. My cousin Julie, from California, danced with my brother Phillip, from New York. My sister, Ellen, and her husband, Eric, from Philadelphia, danced with their kids. Other family had come here from Illinois and Michigan and Belgium. We are a large family, an accomplished family. There are lawyers, doctors, engineers, accountants, musicians, writers, and artists among us. At a big round table sat my parents and aunts and uncle, surveying the crowd, wondering what the lyrics said, waiting for the bride and groom to cut the cake. I flashed forward to the day when those of us on the dance floor would be sitting at the table. And our children, the ones who now spun like tops in front of us in the blinking lights, would be dancing with their children. It was life itself I felt there in the Knights of Columbus hall. And it was glorious.

At one point it occurred to me that the last time we were all this happy together was when my grandfather took me and my cousins on a train trip to Cincinnati sometime in the mid-1960s. I think we went to see *Babes in Toyland,* although my cousin Pat thinks the train trip was to see the Reds play baseball. It doesn't matter. What's important is that now I can ask Pat if he remembers. Because shortly after the train trip, there was a major fight in my family, a split that to this day bisects my childhood: the years before the fight are fixed as a sort of Eden in my mind, and the years after it as a time of exile. The squabble itself was silly, as squabbles usually are, but it was the tip of decades of resentment. Sides were taken, barricades erected. For years we did not speak to my aunts and uncles and cousins. Both my maternal grandparents died during this feud. We had to sneak over to see them during their last years. It was a sad time for my mother and for all of us. I can remember feeling so vulnerable during those years. What if something happened to my parents? Who would look after us? My father's relatives had never been particularly close. We were a family without a family.

But after ten or 15 years, things began to thaw. There was a wedding invitation. There was another funeral. There were more weddings. We began to see each other again. Things were not the same, of course. We had all grown up during those years. But each time I visit with my relatives, it becomes a little easier to think of them as blood kin. And at gatherings like this jolly wedding, it strikes me with a sudden clarity how deep is the pull of family within us. It provides us with our earliest and most enduring sense of belonging. We are drawn back to it over and over again, for the sad times and the happy times and even just the boring times. This is what our children miss back in suburban Virginia. This is what old-fashioned children had.

Whenever we bring our girls to Kentucky, I always show them the three houses where I grew up: the first small one close to the park, the second one, with its secret passageway in the attic (which they must imagine since they can't go inside), and the last one on the cul-de-sac. I've lived in many places since I went away to college, but the streets and smells and vistas of my hometown are engraved so deeply on me that they can't be erased. That's why I want our kids to know this place, where roots run deep and generations rest beneath the soil. They're getting to know their father's roots, too, also deep, a state away in Indiana.

We feel especially compelled to give the children our past because we're not raising them in what I'd call a hometown. We've lived in the same house since our oldest was a baby. We have many good friends here, including one we've had since college days who treats the girls as if they were her own. But it's vast and centerless where we live. I know that northern Virginia is the place where our children are coming alive to the world, and because of this it is blessed to me. But our girls are not growing up with family all around them, so we're trying to give them a hometown of the spirit, a family that stands up to the disparateness of modern times, that shouts down all the windy spaces and says, "We are here for you."

Children feel safest and most free to be themselves when they know they're surrounded and supported by many layers of family, so we do a lot of driving, a lot of calling, and it's the odd month that passes without some relative sleeping on the pull-out sofa in our living room. Despite the distance, we want our girls to feel part of a large clan—not just a group of strangers who gather on holidays.

When we teach our children that family counts—not in a superficial way but down deep—we're giving them an old-fashioned childhood, a sense of the whole fabric of human life, the closeness, the jealousy, the old hatchets, some buried and some not. Families, as we all know, are messy. But think of the lessons they teach our children, of love and tolerance, of loyalty and forgiveness. It is certainly no coincidence that the rise of the parenting expert directly coincides with the breakdown of multi-generational family living. Instead of pretending our family doesn't exist or trivializing it to the point of sideshow, I teach our children that there is strength in unity, that there is a bond between us that cannot be broken. You can take the shallow self-esteem exercises in any modern parenting manual and they will pale next to the lessons that families teach. So as our daughters grow older, I want them to taste the things we tasted, to hear the sounds we heard. I want to give them, to graft onto their souls if I can, some slips of childhoods past.

An Old-Fashioned Childhood

How do we stop thinking too much? We were analytical over-achievers when we became parents and we'll probably be analytical overachievers till the end. But if we're as interested in our children's futures as we say we are, we will *rethink* how we're *thinking*. As you can probably tell, I haven't stopped thinking entirely. But I no longer seek information, I seek inspiration; I don't want knowledge, I hope for wisdom.

Many of us lament the lack of creativity in our lives, that our jobs or modern life in general keep us from acting out our deepest dreams and impulses. Yet aren't we artists of the spirit? Parenthood certainly demands creative solutions—our freshest, truest thoughts. Why not think of it as our ultimate creative act, our best chance to put a stamp on the world? Let the experts debate nature and nurture, time outs versus spankings. While they're doing that, we'll raise our own children as we think best.

If you've learned anything from this book, I hope it's to recognize when you're thinking too much, thinking too shallowly, allowing yourself to be tied in knots by books, magazines, classes, the ideas of others. This is not the kind of parenting book to which you must continually sneak a peek to remind yourself of the words you should use when talking to your child. If you remember anything, remember to be yourself. After all, this child of yours is unique in all the world. She has never been before and will never be again. She is your chance to reinvent the world. Sure, she has been born with her own set of muses, her own talents and tempests. She is not totally yours to shape. But you can make a difference. You can and you do. The question is, what kind of difference do you want to make?

By the time our third child was born almost three years ago, I had become painfully aware of the perils of thinking too much. As I held Celia in my arms, I thought to myself, here is a person unblemished by the world and our own clumsiness. Here is another chance. Not for this child the flickering blue screen, the comfortable life, the overabundance of shallow self-esteem. I vowed to give her an old-fashioned childhood from the beginning. I hope we're giving her and Suzanne and Claire the kind of childhood they, and all children, deserve.

There isn't much more I can tell you about the old-fashioned childhood of my own children. They are, after all, their own little people, and I have told too many stories about them already. But sometimes in them, or in their friends, or in the children at the bus stop, I glimpse a little face that peers out at me with such sweetness and guilelessness that I keep that face in my mind the rest of the day. It's as if I've seen the universal face of childhood, an "Everychild," and that face makes me vow to keep my wonder alive. It's hard to appreciate children when you're constantly charting, comparing, and analyzing them. But what could be more marvelous than watching a baby become a person. Maybe if we could marvel a little more, we would obsess a little less.

So parents everywhere, put down your books. Get rid of your baby development charts, your safety consultants, your anxieties. Instead of following someone else's philosophy, live out your own. You're not only saving your child, but childhood—and parenthood—itself.

Endnotes

Chapter One

[1] "Key Findings From a Nationwide Survey Among Parents of Zero- to Three-Year-Olds," conducted by Peter D. Hart Research Associates for Zero to Three, the National Center for Infants, Toddlers and Families, April 17, 1997

[2] Francine M. Deutsch, J. Brooks-Gunn, Alison Fleming, Diane N. Ruble, Charles Stangor, "Information-Seeking and Maternal Self-Definition During the Transition to Motherhood," in *Journal of Personality and Social Psychology,* 1988, Vol. 55, No. 3, pp. 420–431

[3] Ruth Marcus, "Pregnant Pause," in *The Washington Post,* February 5, 1995

[4] Penelope Leach, *Your Baby and Child,* New York: Alfred A. Knopf, 1987, p. 20

[5] Leach, p. 443

[6] Leach, p. 440

[7] Leach, from the dedication

[8] "Parents of Babies and Toddlers Face 'Information Deficit' on Healthy Child Development," a news release on the poll conducted for Zero to Three, National Center for Infants, Toddlers and Families, April 17, 1997

[9] Quoted in Christopher Lasch, *Haven in a Heartless World: The Family Besieged,* New York: W. W. Norton and Company, 1995, p. 108

[10] Lasch, pp. 108–109

Chapter Two

[1] C. John Sommerville, *The Rise and Fall of Childhood,* Beverly Hills: Sage Publications, 1982, pp. 21 and 27

[2] Christina Hardyment, *Perfect Parents: Baby-Care Advice Past and Present,* Oxford: Oxford University Press, 1995, p. 7

[3] Viviana Zelizer, *Pricing the Priceless Child: The Changing Social Value of Children,* New York: Basic Books, 1985, p. 25

[4] Hardyment, p. 10

[5] Sommerville, p. 121

[6] Hardyment, pp. 15–19

[7] A. S. Neill, *Summerhill,* New York: Hart, 1964, p. 114

[8] Sommerville, pp. 108–119

[9] Mary Cable, *The Little Darlings: A History of Child Rearing in America,* New York: Charles Scribner's Sons, 1975

[10] Daniel Beekman, *The Mechanical Baby,* Brooklyn, New York: Lawrence Hill, 1977, p. 67

[11] Cable, pp. 93–94

[12] Cable, p. 99

[13] Ibid.

[14] Barbara Ehrenreich and Deirdre English, *For Her Own Good: 150 Years of the Experts' Advice to Women,* New York: Doubleday, 1978, p. 195

[15] Ibid.

[16] Ehrenreich and English, p. 196

[17] Hardyment, p. 100

[18] Cable, p. 165

[19] Cable, pp. 171–173

[20] Ehrenreich and English, pp. 198–200

[21] Ehrenreich and English, pp. 207–209

[22] Cable, p. 176

[23] Ann Hulbert, "Dr. Spock's Baby," in *The New Yorker,* May 20, 1996, p. 87

[24] Steven Mintz and Susan Kellogg, *Domestic Revolutions: A Social History of American Family Life,* New York: Macmillan, The Free Press, p. 179

[25] Todd Gitlin, *The Sixties: Years of Hope, Days of Rage,* New York: Bantam, 1987, p. 14

[26] Mintz and Kellogg, p. 178

[27] Susan Littwin, *The Postponed Generation: Why America's Grown-up Kids Are Growing Up Later,* New York: William Morrow and Company, 1986

[28] Mintz and Kellogg, p. 178

[29] Ehrenreich and English, p. 226

[30] Robert N. Bellah, Richard Madsen, William M. Sullivan, Ann Swidler and Steven M. Tipton, *Habits of the Heart: Individualism and Commitment in American Life,* New York: Harper and Row, 1985, p. 82

[31] Sommerville, pp. 12 and 16

Chapter Three

[1] T. Achenbach and C. Howell, "Are American Children's Problems Getting Worse? A 13-year Comparison," in *Journal of the American Academy of Child and Adolescent Psychiatry,* 32: 1145–1154

[2] Natalie Angier, "Ultrasound and Fury: One Mother's Ordeal," in *The New York Times,* November 26, 1996

[3] Marylou Tousignant, "Keeping Up With Baby," in *The Washington Post,* November 12, 1996

[4] DeNeen L. Brown, "Virginia Students Feel the Pressure," in *The Washington Post,* April 13, 1993

[5] Hulbert, *The New Yorker,* May 20, 1996, p. 86

[6] Neill, p. 114

[7] Adele Faber and Elaine Mazlish, *Liberated Parents, Liberated Children,* New York: Avon Books, 1974, pp. 19 and 34

[8] Stella Chess, MD, and Alexander Thomas, MD, *Know Your Child: An Authoritative Guide for Today's Parents,* New York: Basic Books, 1987, p. 115

[9] Martha Wolfenstein, "Fun Morality: An Analysis of Recent American Child-training Literature," in Margaret Mead and Martha Wolfenstein (eds.), *Childhood in Contemporary Culture,* Chicago: The University of Chicago Press, 1955, p. 169

[10] Robert Karen, *Becoming Attached,* New York: Warner Books, 1994

[11] Diane Eyer, *Motherguilt,* New York: Random House, Times Books, 1996, p. 88

[12] Leach, pp. 198–199

Chapter Four

[1] Vince's name and the names of all other parenting class teachers and participants described in this book have been changed to protect privacy.

[2] The National Center on Addiction and Substance Abuse (CASA) 1996 "Survey of Teens and Their Parents"

[3] Don Oldenburg, "Kids and the Law, the Positive Side of Questioning Authority," in *The Washington Post,* September 2, 1993

[4] Aletha Solter, "The Disadvantages of Time-Out," in *Mothering Magazine,* Fall, 1992, pp. 38–43

[5] Marguerite Kelly, "Family Almanac: Minding Manners," in *The Washington Post,* January 15, 1997

[6] Karen, p. 275

[7] Chess and Thomas, pp. 28–34

[8] Ibid., pp. 71–91

[9] "How We Become What We Are," by Winifred Gallagher, in *The Atlantic Monthly,* September 1994, p. 52

[10] The Swedish statistics were described in Diana Baumrind's "The Discipline Controversy Revisited," *The Journal of Family Relations,* October 1996, p. 412

[11] Louis Harris Poll conducted February 6 and 9, 1995

[12] The Short- and Long-Term Consequences of Corporal Punishment, Supplement to *Pediatrics,* October 1996, Volume 98, No. 4

[13] Baumrind, p. 405

[14] Baumrind, p. 409

[15] Julie V. Iovine, "When Parents Take Charge," in *The New York Times,* November 7, 1996

[16] Robert Coles, *The Moral Intelligence of Children,* New York, Random House, 1997

Chapter Five

[1] Laurie Denton, "Real Life Wobegon No Joke," in *Psychological Monitor,* August 1988, pp. 8–9

[2] Victoria Benning, "Virginia Schools Scramble to Speed Learning," *The Washington Post,* February 24, 1997

[3] Jane Healy, *Your Child's Growing Mind,* New York: Doubleday, 1987, p. 37

[4] Jean Grasso Fitzpatrick, *The Superbaby Syndrome,* New York: Harcourt, Brace, Jovanovich, 1988, p. 66

[5] The National Institute of Child Health and Human Development (NICHHD) Study of Early Child Care, 1997

[6] Fitzpatrick, p. 31

[7] Elkind, *The Hurried Child,* Revised Edition, Reading, Massachusetts: Addison-Wesley, 1988, p. 56

[8] Sandra G. Boodman, "Attention Deficit Disorder: Do Millions of Americans Really Have It?" in *The Washington Post,* March 5, 1996

[9] Jane M. Healy, Ph.D., *Your Child's Growing Mind,* Revised Edition, New York: Doubleday, 1994, p. 85

[10] Healy, p. 190

[11] James Atlas, "Making the Grade," in *The New Yorker,* April 14, 1997

[12] Sandra Evans, "Play's the Thing," in *The Washington Post,* June 24, 1997

[13] Elkind, pp. xii and xiv

Chapter Six

[1] *Newsweek* Special Edition, "Your Child," Spring-Summer, 1997, pp. 8–9; *Reader's Digest*/Roper poll in the April 1997 issue of *Reader's Digest*

[2] David Van Biema, "Parents Who Kill," in *Time,* November 14, 1994, pp. 50–52

[3] Frederick P. Rivara, MD, MPH and David C. Grossmann, MD, MPH, "Prevention of Traumatic Deaths to Children in the United States: How Far Have We Come and Where Do We Need to Go?" in *Pediatrics,* Vol. 97, No. 6, June 1996

[4] National Studies of the Incidence of Missing Children, from the Juvenile Justice Bulletin, January 1989

[5] Statistics from the National Safe Kids Campaign

[6] "Baaad News: Local TV News in America 2/26/97," compiled by Dr. Paul Kilte, Dr. Robert A. Bardwell, and Jason Salzman

[7] Patricia Leigh Brown, "His Credo: Be Afraid. Be Very Afraid," in *The New York Times,* July 14, 1997

[8] Marcia Angell, "Overdosing on Health Risks?" in *The New York Times Sunday Magazine,* May 4, 1997, p. 44

[9] *Mothering Magazine,* Summer, 1996, p. 50

[10] Zelizer, pp. 3–55

[11] Jack Gillis and Mary Ellen R. Fise, *The Childwise Catalog,* New York: Pocket Books, 1986, p. 263

[12] *Parents Magazine,* April 1997

[13] John M. Broder, "Warning: A Batman Cape Won't Help You Fly," in *The New York Times,* March 5, 1997

[14] Warren Brown and David B. Ottaway, "Small Victims of a Flawed Safety Device," in *The Washington Post,* June 2, 1997

[15] "Playgrounds of the Future: They Ain't Got Swing," in *Newsweek,* May 12, 1997

[16] Gary Paul Nabhan and Stephen Trimble, *The Geography of Childhood: Why Children Need Wild Places,* Boston: Beacon Press, pp. 8–9

[17] Bob Levey, "When You Notice a Child Who Obviously Has Missed the School Bus . . . ," in *The Washington Post,* March 24, 1995

[18] Bruce Feiler, "Bedtime for Bozo," in *The New York Times Sunday Magazine,* October 27, 1996

[19] Lisa Leff, "A Zone of Their Own," in *The Washington Post,* June 8, 1994

[20] Jessica Mitford, *The American Way of Birth,* London: Victor Gollancz, Ltd., 1992, p. 129

[21] Jacqueline L. Salmon, "Home Alone with a Baby, a Hidden Agenda," in *The Washington Post,* July 8, 1996

[22] Cynthia Merrill, "The Final Summer Fling," in *The Christian Science Monitor,* September 2, 1992

[23] John Knowles, *A Separate Peace,* New York: Dell, 1959, pp. 239–256

Chapter Seven

[1] Stephen Kline, *Out of the Garden: Toys, TV, and Children's Culture in the Age of Marketing,* London: Verso Books, p. 161

[2] Kelly Shermach, "Reassure Parents the Product's Good for Baby," *Marketing News,* October 10, 1994, Vol. 28, No. 21, p. 1

[3] "Expenditures on Children by Families," 1995 Annual Report, U.S. Department of Agriculture, Misc. Publication No. 1528-1995

[4] Marcia Mogelonsky, "The Butterfly Barbie Effect," *American Demographics,* May 1996

[5] Robert Berner, "Now Even Toddlers Are Dressing to the Nines," in *The Wall Street Journal,* May 27, 1997

[6] *Washington Families,* May 1997

[7] Ralph Gardner Jr., "Babes in the Woods," in *New York Magazine,* April 28, 1997

[8] Jennifer Kingson Bloom, "To Make Grade With Parents, Banks Push Kids Stuff," *American Banker,* April 24, 1997, Vol. 162, No. 78

[9] "Demographic Trends Promising for Responsive Marketers," in *Selling to Kids,* May 14, 1997

[10] Ibid.

[11] Diane Crispell, "Hawking the Hunchback," in *American Demographics,* November 1996

[12] Pat Wechsler, "Hey Kid, Buy This," in *Business Week,* June 20, 1997

[13] Neil Postman, *The Disappearance of Childhood,* New York: Dell, 1982, pp. 36 and 80

[14] Geraldine Fabrikant, "The Young and Restless Audience: Computers, Cable and Videos Cut Into Children's TV Watching Time," in *The New York Times,* April 8, 1996

[15] Kline, p. 175

[16] Mogelonsky, *American Demographics*

[17] Wechsler, *Business Week,* p. 62

[18] Ibid.

[19] Laura Shapiro, "The Myth of Quality Time," in *Newsweek,* May 12, 1997

[20] Betsy Sharkey, "Beyond Tepees and Totem Poles," in *The New York Times,* June 11, 1995

[21] David Denby, "Buried Alive," in *The New Yorker,* July 15, 1996

Chapter Eight

[1] Sylvia Ann Hewlett, *When the Bough Breaks: The Cost of Neglecting Our Children,* New York: Basic Books, 1991, p. 73

[2] Trip Gabriel, "A Night on the Town (Bring the Stroller)," in *The New York Times,* June 19, 1997

[3] Jane Seaberry, "For Suburban Youths, Recreation Is No Longer Just Child's Play," in *The Washington Post,* May 31, 1993

[4] Eric L. Wee, "Good Night! Children Staying Up Even Later," in *The Washington Post,* March 4, 1995

[5] Postman, p. 124

[6] Brian Major, "Cruise Lines Cater to Kids," in *Travel Agent Magazine,* June 1997

[7] Robert Pear, "Washington Kidnaps Dick and Jane," in *The New York Times,* June 15, 1997

[8] Cheryl Russell, "Birth Order and the Baby Boom," in *American Demographics,* March 1997

[9] DeNeen L. Brown, "Children and Sexual Behavior: Youths Are Starting Earlier, Specialists Say," in *The Washington Post,* April 27, 1997

[10] David Elkind, p. xiii

[11] Barbara Strauch, "Use of Antidepressant Medicine for Young Patients Has Soared," in *The New York Times,* August 10, 1997

[12] Fox Butterfield, "With Juvenile Courts in Chaos, Some Propose Scrapping Them," in *The New York Times,* July 21, 1997

[13] Testimony of the American Academy of Child and Adolescent Psychiatry, February 13, 1991

[14] Sam Howe Verhovek, "It's the Season of Ghosts, Goblins and Green," in *The New York Times,* October 23, 1996

Chapter Nine

[1] Mary Pipher, *In The Shelter of Each Other,* New York: G.P. Putnam's Sons, 1996, p. 116

[2] Deirdre is not her real name.

Chapter Ten

[1] George Eliot, *The Mill on the Floss,* London: The Zodiac Press, 1978, p. 45

Index

Care and Feeding of Children, 51
Centers for Disease Control and
Prevention survey, 263
Century of the child, 51
*Change Your Child's Behavior by
Changing Yours,* 42
Chess, Stella, 87; 119–120
Child abuse, 244–245
reporting of, 233–236
statistics on, 123; 263
Child Care Information Exchange,
151
Child-centeredness, 3; 5; 23; 69;
247–250; 315
advantages of, 247–248
institutionalization of, 245
time for each child, 260
Child development
adolescents, 6
babies, 2; 131
cognitive development, 131; 142;
153
conference on, 142
environmental influences, 121
excuse for misbehavior, 112; 292
informational books on, 24; 112
"just a stage," 109–111; 122
monitoring stages of, 111
personality differences, 119
research on, 3; 112
school-age children, 6
superbaby syndrome, 133–173
temperament's role in, 117–122
toddlers, 2; 115
A Child Is Born, 18
Child mortality, 45–46; 188–189
Childhood
adulthood, blurred line with,
245
commercialization of, 230; 268
disappearance of, 226; 261
fleetingness of, 169–170
history of, 46–55
old-fashioned, 314–332
recent invention of, 226
Childrearing, work and, 58; 150–
153; 320
Childrearing experts. *See* Experts
Childrearing methods, 2

advice on. *See* Expert opinions;
Parenting information and
advice
as art not science, 65
attachment parenting, 91–92;
301
backlash against modern
parenting, 301–304
based on friendship, not
authority, 268
behavioral psychology, effect on,
52; 112–113
the big picture, 326–328
by-the-book, 11; 23–29
Christian parenting movement,
303
common sense, 16; 109; 177;
209; 288; 309–310
conservative practices, 303
different aptitudes for different
ages, 283
effect on child development,
151
grandparents' view of, 63–65;
287–290
history of, 46–55; 188–189
inspiration of children, 142;
311–312
instinct, 55; 233; 274–313
New Age parenting, 298–300
PC parenting, 214–243
praise vs. encouragement, 31–
32; 236–237
yo-yo parenting, 122–125
Children
acting like adults, 261–264; 267–
268
adults acting like, 55; 71; 266–
269
and adults as equals, 56; 104–
106; 253
changing role of, 188–189; 244–
273
as consumers, 223–226
controlling parents, 4; 109–111;
295
feelings of, 87–89; 234; 238; 262
inseparable from parents, 248–
249

If you are a "parent who thinks too much," and have stories of your own to share, write Anne Cassidy, c/o Dell Publishing, 1540 Broadway, New York, NY 10036.